"At a time when antifascist activity [is an] often misunderstood focus, this ri[ch history of] tions and documents constitutes a [... and beautiful resource.] These stories of powerful multiracial, queer struggle in the streets against violent fascist groups must not be forgotten: they offer vital lessons in the necessity of both community care and confrontational intolerance for fascist constellations that gain traction in our midst."
    —Natasha Lennard, *Being Numerous: Essays on Non-Fascist Life*

"*It Did Happen Here* is the engaging, true story of how a community stood up to fascism and racism. Not with sensitivity trainings run by professional consultants, but through on-the-ground actions of antiracist skinheads and street punks, commies and college students, doing the raw, messy and sometimes dangerous work of community and cultural organizing. This is how change happens!"
    —Stephen Duncombe, coeditor of *White Riot: Punk Rock and the Politics of Race* and cofounder of the Center for Artistic Activism

"*It Did Happen Here* is a cross between a thorough oral history and a well-crafted narrative. We can all benefit from such an amazing project, not just because the threat of an organized white suprem-acist movement is real, but even more importantly, to show that we have the ability to create and maintain effective resistance!"
    —Claude Marks, cofounder of the Freedom Archives

"The need for effective antifascist organizing is as urgent as it has been in decades, yet far too many of us don't know the history of groups who pushed back against neonazis in cities like Portland in the '90s. *It Did Happen Here* highlights the rich history of Portland antiracist organi-zations and explores how they navigated many of the same struggles, both external and internal, that we're dealing with in real time today."
    —Bruce Poinsette, author of *The Blacktastic Adventure*

"By understanding the detailed context and the successes and failures of past antifascist struggles, readers will find themselves far bet-ter equipped to resist a new generation of fascists fighting to 'make America great again.'"
    —Mark Bray, author of *Antifa: The Anti-Fascist Handbook*

"One of the most vibrant and essential histories of antifascism ever put together, and draws together a range of voices speaking to what it takes to keep us safe and transform our communities. This is es-sential reading."
    —Shane Burley, author of *Why We Fight: Essays on Fascism, Resistance, and Surviving the Apocalypse*

"Weaving together riveting war stories and hard-won lessons from urgent campaigns, *It Did Happen Here* provides a gripping oral history of Portland's antifascist scene. At once scrappy and introspective, the book should be required reading for everyone who recognizes that the fight's not yet over—and that coalitions and courage might yet win the day."

—AK Thompson, author of *Black Bloc, White Riot: Anti-Globalization and the Genealogy of Dissent*

"I literally couldn't stop myself from raving about *It Did Happen Here* to anyone who would listen. It's not merely that an inspirational moment in antiracist/antifascist history comes alive through the brave, self-reflective voices of the people who made it. Or that the lessons gleaned—such as the imperative to concurrently battle anti-Blackness, anti-Semitism, xenophobia, and homophobia—can aid in us not letting history repeat itself today, including us not making the same mistakes. Crucially, *It Did Happen Here* offers a detailed playbook of success premised on inventive strategies and tactics, and most compellingly, social relations of solidarity that cut beautifully across identities, making accomplices of punks, community organizers, queers, people of color, Jews, immigrants, working-class folks, and indeed anyone down for community self-defense."

—Cindy Barukh Milstein, author of *There Is Nothing So Whole as a Broken Heart*

"Offers a front-row seat to what really happened on the streets of the Pacific Northwest, when working-class people confronted fascism, white supremacy, and the far Right—head on. At a time when calls for combating 'violent extremism' often are synonymous with draconian surveillance and State repression, this book shines a light on the ability and courage of everyday people to defend their streets and communities. We would be wise to learn from this history."

—*It's Going Down* podcast

"By the time I moved my queer little family to Portland at the turn of the millennium, the city had a reputation as a homo-friendly bastion of progressive politics, so we were somewhat taken aback when my daughter's racially diverse sports team was met with a burning cross at a suburban game. So much progress had been made and yet, at times, it felt like the past hadn't gone anywhere.

If only we'd had *It Did Happen Here*. This documentary project tells the forgotten history of Portland's roots as a haven for white supremacists and recounts the ways antiracists formed coalitions across subcultures to protect the vulnerable and fight the good fight against nazi boneheads and the bigoted right."

—Ariel Gore, author of *Hexing the Patriarchy*

IT DID HAPPEN HERE

AN ANTIFASCIST PEOPLE'S HISTORY

Moe Bowstern, Mic Crenshaw, Alec Dunn,
Celina Flores, Julie Perini, and Erin Yanke

PM Press and Working Class History 2023

ISBN: 978-1-62963-351-0 (paperback)

ISBN: 978-1-62963-675-7 (ebook)

Library of Congress Control Number: 2022942543

PM Press, PO Box 23912, Oakland, CA 94623
www.pmpress.org
www.itdidhappenherepodcast.com

Cover image: Counterprotest to white supremacist rally at Portland City Hall, May 4, 1991. Photo by Dean Guernsey.
Frontispiece: Symbols for the Minneapolis Baldies, the Coalition for Human Dignity, Skinheads Against Racial Prejudice, and Anti Racist Action
Design: Alec Dunn
Image archivist: Julie Perini

10 9 8 7 6 5 4 3 2 1

Printed in the USA.

Well, if one really wishes to know how justice is administered in a country, one does not question the policemen, the lawyers, the judges, or the protected members of the middle class. One goes to the unprotected—those, precisely, who need the law's protection most!—and listens to their testimony. Ask any Mexican, any Puerto Rican, any Black man, any poor person—ask the wretched how they fare in the halls of justice, and then you will know, not whether or not the country is just, but whether or not it has any love for justice, or any concept of it. It is certain, in any case, that ignorance, allied with power, is the most ferocious enemy justice can have.

James Baldwin, *No Name in the Street* (1972)

Almost no one's entry point into violence is committing it.
Danielle Sered, *Until We Reckon: Violence, Mass Incarceration, and a Road to Repair* (2019)

FOREWORD
Eric K. Ward

If we've learned anything from these last five years, it is this: there is a danger in forgetting the past. There is also the risk of overromanticizing it.

The stories told in this volume, documenting a critical moment in antiracist organizing, have much to offer the present moment. These are the stories of how everyday people, the homeless, cultural misfits, working-class kids, and their allies defended themselves when hate groups sought to turn Portland, Oregon, into a horror story of bigoted violence and physical intimidation. Absent any adequate response from local and state government, an inevitable leadership vacuum formed, forcing those most often the targets of violent neonazi attacks to formulate their own defense for Portland at great personal cost and loss.

Self-defense was something I learned early as a young Black kid in Southern California. Community self-defense came a little later. I found my identity in the punk scene of the 1980s. Going to shows was where you found your community, and those spaces were under attack. At a Dead Kennedys show in Los Angeles in 1985, a white power punk walked up to me unexpectedly and said the next time he saw me, there would be blows. At a show in Reseda, he kept his promise. He swung on me and I swung back. Moments later, I realized I was not the only one. I found myself surrounded by other people, white and Asian kids from the San Fernando Valley. Kids I did not even know. They knew something that I was about to learn. It was not my fight; it was all of ours. No one else was coming to protect us.

In 1986, I fled the big city mayhem for a better life. I followed my bandmates north to Eugene, Oregon. I started out installing insulation in crawl spaces under houses for a white conservative Republican who was the only one who would hire me in that liberal college town, despite my long resume. That's where I was when I learned neonazi racist skinheads had stomped Ethiopian immigrant Mulugeta Seraw to death. I knew that fight wasn't just for the antiracist punks in Portland to fight. It was my fight, too. It was all of ours.

As someone who was there when "it did happen here" and is still here as the twenty-first-century struggle for civil rights and human dignity plays out, here's what must be said before I continue any further: the story you are about to hear isn't a playbook, but an honest and earnest warning.

If you are reading this introduction seeking to reinforce your notion of heroes, champions, or whatever serves as the latest cultural claim to the false god of masculinity and dominance, you will not find it here. If you are looking for self-reflection, contradiction, and nuance, you have opened the right book.

The people named in these stories are not looking for your praise, sympathy, or adoration. We understand that this story is not about us and it's not about anyone's warrior fantasies. This is a story about Portland, and community, and what happened when the most vulnerable were left to defend their own lives while police and elected officials looked on or chose to look the other way.

It's humbling to have played a small role in this story, and it's both humbling and embarrassing to admit that we did not necessarily know what we were doing. Let's be clear: when we were in the midst of defending ourselves from the racist skinheads and neonazis who made Portland their stomping ground in the late 1980s, we didn't know how the story would end. As longtime civil rights leader Scot Nakagawa put it, a lot of mistakes were made, along with some happy accidents.

Remembering that we didn't have a plan is an important antidote to the current wave of self-righteousness masking itself as politics in American society today. The violence came looking for us. We were not looking for revolution or some promise of a better society. We were mostly people wanting to be left alone so we could get through the mostly shitty days of poverty and alienation we had been plunged into because of our class, skin color, religion, gender identity, and sexual orientation. Our friends were our family and our family was under physical attack. For most of us, we were not trying to save the world, we were trying to survive it. The violence came to us.

Why and how so many stood up to racist and homophobic bullies, in one of the whitest cities in America, offers critical lessons. We are privileged that so many were willing to come forward to share stories that could not be told for over three decades. Yet you, the reader, have to understand one thing as you enter these pages. These are vastly contrasting times today. Back then, street brawls were just that. Yes, there was a dangerous racist ideology in the air, but today's white nationalists and authoritarian formations instigate and thrive on larger-scaled political theater that makes the national news and escalates state repression. When antifascists are baited into violent confrontations today, it often serves to prove the dystopian narrative of failed government that fuels the acceptance of far-right populism by the broader community.

Back then, racist skinheads had some level of organization and some connections to other white supremacist and white nationalist groups. But they didn't have the Internet. The efforts you'll read about here, combined with broader community mobilization, succeeded in suppressing the racist and bigoted violence of that time. It did not make the movement go away. It was driven underground and has since flourished on the Internet, where it has gotten far more sophisticated, better trained, and armed with far more than baseball bats and steel-toed boots.

This isn't a story based in nostalgia, which is generally an exercise in reduction. One dishonors the past by simplifying it. The historical moment this book revisits was anything but simple. This book seeks to honor the complexity of those times and to reflect on the time we are in now. It's your job to approach these stories not as marching orders from a glorious past, but as a collection of lessons to tease out and explore in lived relationship with our present-day, even more complex reality. Yeah. We are still punk rock like that.

The magic of this project, and of historical memory more broadly, is that it helps us look in the mirror.

Looking back into that mirror, I can see that we had our greatest impact when we were expansive, generous, outward facing. The times it didn't go so well were when we turned inward, got paranoid, cut ourselves off from the broader community.

With our multiracial democracy now in mortal danger, I can see that we were strongest when we helped close the distance between local government employees and the people they serve. I regret any times that explicitly or inadvertently helped to widen that gap.

Our most powerful weapon in those days wasn't our fists or our research or our analysis. It was—and remains—our ability to build a consensus around an alternative vision of what America can be.

When I look around at those primed for street fights, I can say this: I understand why gangs exist. I grew up around all different kinds of gang culture—street gangs, punk gangs. My main message to friends who were considering joining a gang of any kind was: You're going to do what you want, but I can tell you as someone who's walked that path, you don't want to. I can't stop you, but that's my best advice.

White supremacy and white nationalism were built off five hundred years of violence. These are the master's tools and the master's house, as noted by the great Audre Lorde. We know what that looks like and we know where that leads. It is time for a different vision that is more compelling than violence.

The stories in this collection are stories of bravery. It takes courage to stand up for yourself, to stand up for your community, and to say, we're not going to take it anymore.

Standing on the shoulders of my particular ancestors, though, and all who worked with them to build the multiracial democracy that still holds such promise, I can see another kind of bravery. The kind of bravery that we need to call up for today's struggle is the courage to be politically and culturally intimate with people who don't look or sound like us.

Segregation across the political spectrum is killing democracy. Racism needs to be understood most fundamentally as a powerful antidemocratic ideology. Same for anti-Semitism, Islamophobia and xenophobia, misogyny, and homophobia—all the forms of intolerance and demonization of "the other" based on differences of skin color, nationality, religion, gender, and so on. But so, too, is the intolerance of difference, the drive for ideological and community purity that can be found among those who call themselves antiracist.

I don't want this to turn into a lecture, so I'll end simply with this.

I'm glad you've picked up this book. I'm grateful to all who fought the good fight then and to all who have brought these stories into this present moment. This book, and the podcast it's based on, are critically important acts of remembering. Remembering the bravery, the complexity, and what we built and achieved, alongside where we fell short. Let us be sure also to remember and to honor all those who didn't survive those times, physically or emotionally—everyone, regardless of where they were politically. I hope everyone who participated in this project at every level knows how much their voice and their work matters to the dangerous times we are in today.

If you're looking for what that time might teach us about today, I'm just one voice. You'll draw your own conclusions about what's needed today. For me, that's honoring the multiracial democracy our ancestors built by doing the hard but expansive work of bringing more people into democratic participation—politically, organizationally, culturally, and on the personal level.

Here's the story I hope the next generation gets to tell about what happens here, today. I hope they say of today's antiauthoritarian, antibigotry movement: We built something up, instead of just tearing something down. We brought more people in. We practiced love, not hate. We used the people's tools of democratic governance and radical inclusion to build the people's house.

Eric Ward is a nationally recognized expert on the relationship between authoritarian movements, hate violence, and preserving inclusive democracy. He was the first American to win the Civil Courage Prize. He is a senior advisor at Western States Center and a senior fellow with the Southern Poverty Law Center and Race Forward. He helped found Northwest Communities Against Hate in Eugene, was a volunteer with the Coalition for Human Dignity in Portland, and was director of the Northwest Coalition for Human Dignity in Seattle.

March for Dignity and Diversity, October 7, 1990.
Photo by Kraig Scattarella, courtesy of *The Oregonian*.

INTRODUCTION
Alec Dunn

History, the cliché says, is written by the victors. In the struggle to drive nazi skinheads out of Portland, who were the victors? What is victory?

After the boneheads were driven out or driven underground, Portland enjoyed a two-decade respite from overt nazi terror, and that's some kind of win. But we certainly didn't come out of all that blood and pain as an antifascist state. Gentrification has continued unabated. Poor Black Portlanders survived nazi skinheads mostly intact but continue to be slowly and viciously pushed out of the city by punitive criminal charges, police profiling, gentrification, and multigenerational disenfranchisement.

Developers and the propertied class have, with economic support from local politicians, transformed this city and upheld these changes with unstinting violence by the police. In the US, land is power, and the people who control real estate don't bother rewriting history; they simply erase it. In the place of old neighborhoods they have created bright, politely designed ahistorical places. Time moves on and cities change, yes, but for those of us who grew up here, the rapid and ceaseless transformation of this city continues to be disorienting.

If you compare maps of the city of Portland from 1989 to today, the cartography isn't all that different. There are some new streets in Northwest, and there's a new stadium on the east side. Though it feels like a completely different place, the basic map of the city remains essentially the same.

This map could look very different if one changes the key—one map could show the immense change in housing prices, while another might show census tracts identified by race. We could look at crime, traffic, pollution, asthma distribution, the location of homeless encampments, the most popular names and breeds of dog by neighborhood. All of these would add dimension to the story of this city. We want this book to function as another key to looking at the city, at the way this city has tolerated racism and at the way that some people chose to fight back.

We recorded this people's history as a way to document a collective movement against local racism and fascism. We continue, all of us, to live with the consequences of those times, and we believe it is important to learn from the successes and blunders of this struggle.

In Portland, a coalition of people came together to confront the overt violent fascism of the late '80s and early '90s. As individual activists—punks, skinheads, citizens, queers—laboring within separate factions or cliques, this was not an exceptional group. Together, in moments of solidarity, they created a model for civic defense that fought everyday fascism both clumsily and brilliantly. We stand on that ground whether we know it or not.

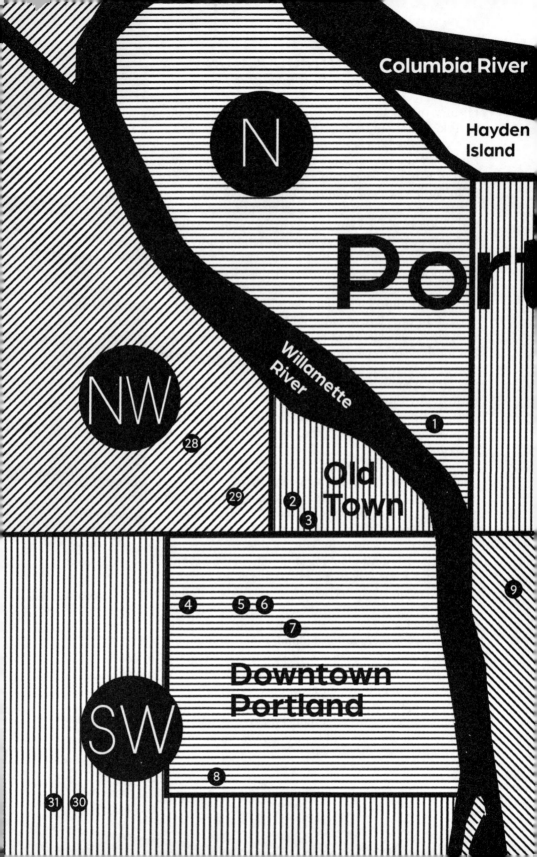

Vancouver, WA

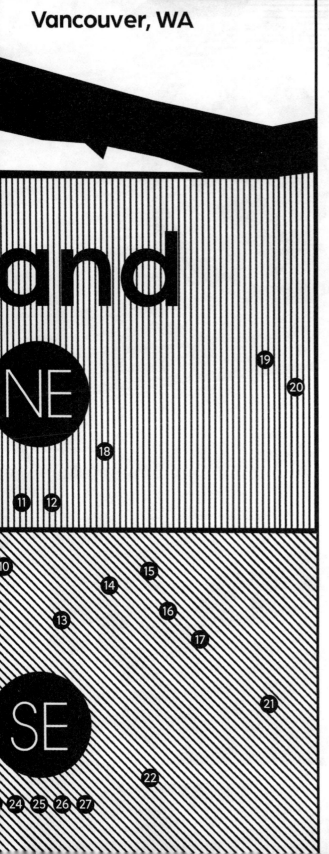

1. CHD's the Shop
2. Club Satyricon
3. Starry Night/Roseland Theater
4. Site of 1988 attack on Hock-Seng "Sam" Chin
5. Pioneer Courthouse Square
6. The Wall
7. The bus mall
8. Portland State University
9. The Matrix
10. Pine Street Theatre
11. Hollywood Fred Meyer
12. Metropolitan Community Church
13. First ARA meeting
14. *The Portland Alliance* office
15. SE 31st and Pine
16. Laurelhurst Park
17. Sunnyside neighborhood
18. Grant High School
19. Madison High School
20. Mount Hood Community College
21. SE 82nd
22. Jon Bair's rental house
23. Reed College
24. Kellogg Bowl
25. Milwaukie Bowl
26. Clackamas
27. Bob Heick's apartment
28. Metropolitan Learning Center (MLC)
29. Blue Gallery
30. Lewis & Clark College
31. Beaverton

NO HATE CRIME

Pioneer Courthouse Square, May 1992. Photo by Coyote Amrich.

Participants

Abby Layton – *Coalition for Human Dignity (CHD)*
Becky – *Portland Anti Racist Action (ARA)*
Cecil Prescod – *CHD*
China – *Portland ARA, Skinheads Against Racial Prejudice (SHARP) affiliate*
Cristien Storm – *Northwest Coalition for Human Dignity*
David Jeffries – *Minneapolis Baldies, the Syndicate, ARA*
Devin Burghart – *CHD*
Engedaw Berhanu – *Uncle of Mulugeta Seraw*
Eric Ward – *CHD*
Gillian – *CHD*
Iran Johnson – *SHARP affiliate*
Jabari – *Skinheads of Chicago (SHOC), the Syndicate, ARA*
Jackson – *Portland Baldies*
Jason– *Portland ARA*
Jay Nevilles – *Minneapolis Baldies, the Syndicate, ARA*
Jonathan Mozzochi – *CHD*
Jon Bair – *Portland Baldies*
Jorin – *Portland ARA*
Kate Boyd – *Northwest Coalition for Human Dignity*
Kelly Halliburton – *Portland ARA*
Krista Olson – *CHD*
Leonard Zeskind – *Center for Democratic Renewal*
Lorraine – *Minneapolis Baldies, the Syndicate, ARA*
M. Trelor – *CHD*
Malki – *SHOC, the Syndicate, ARA*
Martin Sprouse – *Maximum Rocknroll*
Marty – *SHOC, the Syndicate, ARA*
Mic Crenshaw – *Minneapolis Baldies, the Syndicate, ARA*
Michael Clark – *SHARP*
Mobonix – *Minneapolis Baldies*
Nissa – *Minneapolis Baldies, the Syndicate, ARA*
Pan Nesbitt– *Portland ARA, SHARP*
Patrick Mazza – *Portland Alliance*
Peter Little – *Antiracist skinhead*
Ron Herndon – *Portland Black United Front*
Scot Nakagawa – *CHD*
Steven Gardiner – *CHD*
Steven Wasserstrom – *CHD*
Tom T. – *SHARP, ARA, Portland Baldies*

Hotel Lenox, 1980 (now the site of the Multnomah County Justice Center).
Historic American Buildings Survey, Library of Congress Archives.

Chapter 1

Setting the Scene
From Broken Treaties to Brewpubs

O
ur story begins in the midsized city of Portland, Oregon. Nowadays, the city is home to about a million people in the metro area who occupy the ancestral home of the Clackamas band of Chinook, the Multnomahs, the Tualatin Kalapuya, the Wasco-Wishram, the Willamette Tumwater, and many other tribes who lived and traveled along the waterways, and who still live here.

The city's nicknames vary according to political and historical context: Stumptown. Slabtown. Little Beirut. The Rose City. Doomtown. Everyday life here is complicated by geography, history, politics, economics, and migration. To begin this story, we need to understand Oregon's explicit racist origins and the impact its founders' ideology have had, and continue to have, on its largest city and commercial capital.

The founders of the Oregon territory and then the state of Oregon dreamed of an explicit white Protestant homeland. Missionaries like Marcus Whitman, intent on bringing (Protestant) Christianity to the West, led thousands of white settlers along the Oregon Trail. The subsequent treaty–breaking Donation Land Claim Act of 1850 allowed for a huge influx of white people to "claim" millions of acres of land in Oregon for the purpose of building industry, most notably

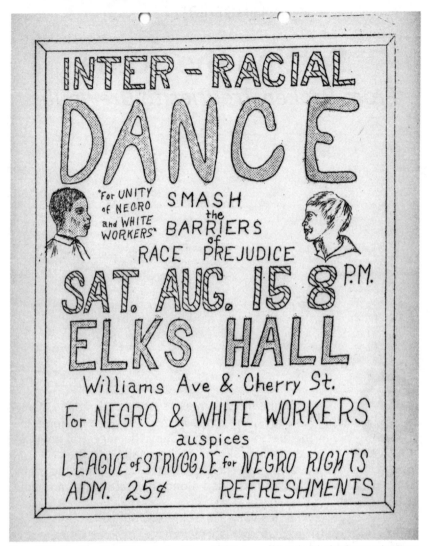

Flyer, 1931. The League of Struggle for Negro Rights was affiliated with the Communist Party USA. City of Portland Archives AD/10476.

the timber industry. In 1849, there were nine thousand white people in present-day Oregon; by 1860, one year after Oregon statehood, there were fifty thousand. By 1855, settlers had stolen over 2.8 million acres of Indigenous people's land.

Starting in 1844, these white emigrants put in place several "exclusion" laws discriminating against Black people. The ratification of the Fourteenth Amendment in 1868 invalidated most of these, but references to racist laws remained within the state's constitution until 2002.

Civil rights marchers in downtown Portland, 1965. City of Portland Archives A2004-005.38.

Throughout the 1920s, the Ku Klux Klan was a mainstream force in Portland politics; Oregon governor Walter M. Pierce worked closely enough with the Klan that modern historians count him as a member. George Baker, Portland's mayor from 1917 to 1933, had deep ties with the city's chapter of the Klan.

Such leadership often led the city to be at cross-purposes with minority residents; as a result, Black and Asian neighborhoods in the Rose City were under almost continuous pressure of displacement and dispossession. Portland's first Black neighborhood arose when Black railroad workers were permitted to reside in what is now Old Town. Segregation was made explicit in 1919, and the city government initially barred Black and Asian people from owning property. In later years, movements of Black and Asian populations were confined through redlining practices.

Between 1910 and 1940, more than half of Portland's Black population, around 1,900 residents, was pushed across the river into the Lower Albina neighborhood by the real estate industry, local government, and private landlords, who restricted housing choice to an area two miles long and one mile wide, an area that is now the Rose Quarter and Eliot neighborhoods. In the 1940s, roughly 23,000 Black workers migrated to Portland for wartime work in the Kaiser shipyards. City regulations restricted workers to segregated sections of defense housing developments in Vanport (in North Portland), Guild's Lake (in Northwest Portland), and the Albina District (in lower North and Northeast Portland). When the Columbia River flooded in 1948, the dikes around the Vanport housing development failed,

A section of the former Albina neighborhood, now the Rose Quarter, consisting of the Memorial Coliseum and the Moda Center (Trailblazers arena). Destroyed in 1956. City of Portland Archives A2005-001.92.

and that entire housing development was washed away, displacing over 18,000 people. Racist real estate policies funneled Black residents of Vanport into the geographically small Albina District, where over the next decade community members built a thriving alternative economy outside the Jim Crow–style segregation of the rest of the city.

Prior to the Vanport flood, the Albina District was a neighborhood defined by its location, on the east side of the Willamette River, across from downtown Portland. Following the Vanport disaster, "Albina" became a catch-all designation for multiple neighborhoods in which Portland's Black citizens were allowed to settle and own property. The specific location of Albina shifted, pushed north and east by urban renewal schemes.

Forced displacement continued with urban renewal and the construction of the Memorial Coliseum in 1960, the I-5 freeway in 1962, and the Emanuel Hospital expansion in 1973. This is a mere outline of the continuous assault on Black people—and other historically underrepresented groups—living in Portland over the last hundred years. The roots are deep.

Buildings on N Williams Avenue prior to their 1973 demolition, condemned by the city to make space for the failed expansion of Emanuel Hospital. City of Portland Archives A2010-003.

* * *

Gentrification began in the late 1980s, starting the process of dramatically displacing working-class residents from the inner city. At the time, Portland was a midsized city not unlike many other small metropolises across America. Its population was around 400,000 people, with about 85 percent of that listed as white—as compared to 2022 numbers of 77 percent. The average cost of a single-family home was $76,000, though that would soon rise astronomically. Oregon's minimum wage in 1988 was $3.35 an hour. The average rent for a room in a group house was around $100 a month.

By the late 1980s, Portland had earned the moniker "Skin City"—a haven for racist skinheads, many of whom were homegrown. These skinheads regularly roamed downtown, Northwest, and Southeast Portland unhindered, searching for targets. Gay men and women, men who did not fit masculine standards, interracial couples, lone punks, immigrants, Indigenous people, and Black Portlanders all fit the bill. Anyone who attended a local punk or rock show in the '80s knew they might encounter a beating at the hands of these bullies; the risk of violence was the price to pay for music fans in order to access the scene that kept their souls alive in the dingy city that the punks in those days called Doomtown.

Cultural life in Portland was insular, partly because of its geographical isolation. San Francisco is a twelve-hour drive away, Seattle four hours. Boise and Spokane are the closest cities heading east. At the time, plane tickets were expensive, not everyone had a car, and long-distance bus travel was uncomfortable. As a result, Portland developed a vibrant and unique alternative culture. In the late '70s and early '80s, the first wave of punk swept through Portland, giving rise to bands like the Wipers, who rose to national prominence fronted by lead singer, guitar player, and lyricist Greg Sage, a gay man. A pair of teenage sisters led the band the Neo Boys. Fred and Toody Cole from the Rats (and later Dead Moon) grew out of the 1960s hippie and antiwar countercultures. Portland's original punk scene, like a lot of early punk scenes in the US, was experimental, home to openly queer people and women who offset heteronormative clichés of mainstream society.

This did not last. Years of the Reagan administration's vicious policies against the poor, the mentally ill, and single moms, among others—along with the nascent rise of the Christian right—sharpened local tensions. The teenage punks of 1987 were angrier and more alienated than their artsy predecessors. The music was faster, more aggressive. Poison Idea—a local band who formed in 1980—specialized in nihilism and self-destruction. They played with blistering speed and rabid intensity, a perfect example of the shift in the subculture. By the mid-1980s, they were the only local band that mattered, the self-dubbed kings of punk. They played a fitting soundtrack to the often harrowing experience of leaving a show at, say, the Pine Street Theatre, where skinheads habitually jumped individuals exiting the club.

And for a long time, people just lived with it. Until a fateful night in November of 1988, nazi skinheads regularly avoided consequences and waged a campaign of fear against anyone they didn't like the look of. So what changed? And who changed it?

This is a people's history. Interviews in this book bring you stories of people—punks, antiracist skinheads, queer activists, grassroots social justice organizers—who, thirty years ago in Portland, Oregon, found themselves awake to a fascist reality about the damp little city on the Willamette River and forged a determination to stop it. Here are people who joined together and took action—with mixed results—when the alarms they sounded were ignored by the city and exacerbated by the cops. Their accounts don't always exactly align with each other. Memories are occasionally clouded, but facts are not our focus. We believe that the people who lived through this time hold expertise over their own histories. Here are some things we do know:

It did happen here. These people survived to share their personal histories. It begins in an atmosphere of cheap beers and cigarettes, at parties and shows and in the dark corners of Doomtown.

Above: Old Town, 1964. The building on the right would become the Starry Night nightclub. City of Portland Archives A2011-013. Below: Poison Idea, 1983. Photo by Janice Morlan.

CHINA
Portland Anti Racist Action (ARA) and Skinheads Against Racial Prejudice (SHARP) affiliate

I was born and raised in Portland. I grew up first in North and Northeast Portland, and that was actually a Black neighborhood. People think Portland didn't have much of a Black community, but we did have it. There was Unthank Park, and a lot of the area that's developed right now, that was the Black neighborhood. But my mom moved us downtown to go to school. I'd already experienced being disenfranchised at the time. I'd experienced being excluded. I started to come into a position of questioning society and questioning what was acceptable. I started to formulate ideas and started questioning the system.

I liked punk rock. The music appealed to me and the style appealed to me. Because we didn't have money, punk rock style was something that I could access. I could shred my shirt. Everyone at my school was wearing, like, Guess jeans and expensive stuff. So it was a real natural transition to become a punk rocker, I suppose. The more that I learned about it, the more it just meshed with me.

Portland was smaller back then. I remember when they were building Pioneer Square. Before Pioneer Square, there was a place called the Wall that people used to hang out on. There were street kids—rockers, punk rockers, skins. Different kinds of people, but people hung out together. . . . I was probably one of the only Black kids downtown in this scene. It was a tense environment, kind of volatile. Probably a little bit exciting as a kid, you know? And definitely you had to watch your back.

I remember groups of kids talking about how they're going to go beat up certain groups of people around town. I was young, but I always had a sense of what's right or wrong. I was like, why are we going to go beat up these people, because they were talking about going to the gay bars? Why would we do that? So there was this tension. There was a lot of talk, white kids saying the N-word a lot, and then I remember them saying, "Well, not you!" I always felt, you know, unsafe. I didn't know if I understood that it was directly racist. There was the beginning of awareness that, hey, something's not right here.

I remember when I was like thirteen or fourteen, this must have been '86 or '87. I just didn't know anything, and these three girls, all older than me, said that I stole their bus pass to buy dope. I didn't even know what dope was, that's how naive I was. All these people had gathered at Paranoia Park [aka O'Bryant Square] to watch these girls jump me! I was scared at first, but I just got in. I fought back. I remember kicking one girl in the head on the ground, you know? Then one girl hit me a few times. Then it was over. People were shaking my hand like, "Oh, you did good." I just remember shaking and feeling like, what the hell happened? Why didn't people come in? People that I thought were my friends, why didn't nobody break it up? They were like, "Oh, you can stand it."

Burning an effigy of George H.W. Bush during a presidential visit, 1991. Photo by Bette Lee.

I grew up in Northeast Portland, and you know, fighting was how we did things. The way I had grown up, somebody hits me, I'm not gonna stand there and be hit. So I gained respect, but that always hurt my heart. I didn't want to fight anybody, you know? That's what it was like in the beginning, being part of this scene. It was kind of cold. I realized that people wanted to see this. They wanted to see me attacked, and I was so naive. I didn't know anything.

I never shaved my head. I had a mohawk, but I wasn't a skin. But you know, skins and punks would kind of listen to some similar music. I remember actually hanging out with some of the skinheads when I was younger and them saying, like, the N-word and stuff, and I was kinda like, [laughs ironically]. I didn't know what to say, I was, like, fourteen, and they would be like, "Oh, not you. Your nose isn't like that." And then I remember thinking to myself, "Who are they talking about, my dad?" That anger started to build up and be to the point where I was like, "No, you're not going to talk like this." It was like a righteous rage, though. I don't feel bad about it. I'm like, "Hey, this was ridiculous."

In the scene that I was involved in in the late '80s, early '90s, there was a prevalence of white supremacist attitudes. This group, East Side White Pride (ESWP), and a lot of the people that were affiliated with them, weren't shaved bald. They would have long hair, they're kind of remnants from the rockers or carps, and I want to say they were working-class, but not everybody was working-class. But they were white people, from Southeast Portland mostly. That's, I think, where the nazi skinhead movement evolved from in Portland, this ESWP thing.

So I was in the streets and didn't have a lot of support from family or anybody. I'm getting jumped by skinheads. And other people were, too. It was like a group of school bullies. So we started fighting them, literally fighting back. I remember walking downtown with a friend of mine and these three men called me the N-word. My friend was like, "Hold on, I need the skateboard," and hit one of them upside the head. It was right across from Nordstrom's downtown. They hit me with a bottle. We were really fighting these men. So this kind of stuff was happening.

And I'm going to punk rock shows, really liking the music but then seeing these skinheads and just really feeling that fear. There was a show at Pine Street. It was, I think, Ken Mieskie and Kyle Brewster, their band called Machine. The big thing back then was to wear Doc Martens, and I had a nice pair of lady Docs that I bought. I was sixteen. I remember these girls, they're probably twenty-two, and they were like, "Why are you wearing white boots?" Mind you, these are black leather boots. I was like, "They look black to me." I remember sitting up on the stage because I was scared. There was a lot of them. They kicked a bunch of skinheads out because they were fighting. They were outside chanting, "Kill the ..." I'm gonna say it: "Kill the nigger." They were talking about me. I was this little Black girl. There was a group of people there that I knew, and they put a trench coat over me and snuck me out to this car. But the guy's car wouldn't start! He got out. The driver was Asian. He went out, but they didn't want him. I was in the back seat, and I had two people on either side of me. There were skinhead bodies all over the car! They got a bat, broke the windows. Seriously, everybody in that car got punched or hit, except for me. Finally, the car started, thank god, and we drove across Burnside back downtown. Those people really saved my life. The couple in the back, a white guy and his girlfriend, Rob and Gretchen, they had come up from San Francisco. The guy that drove, I forget his name, but there were, like, five people, and the bouncers, that helped save my life. This was a week before they killed Mulugeta Seraw, okay? So this stuff was already brewing.

Portland ARA activists Jason and Becky in burnable US flag costumes at a protest in downtown Portland, 1989. Photo by Alec Dunn.

JASON
Portland ARA

I grew up in the Portland area. I spent a lot of my youth tearing around downtown skateboarding and was involved in the punk rock scene, especially from '85, '86, on. So I was at shows and part of the community prior to '87, '88, when East Side White Pride took hold. I remember when they first showed up. There was very minimal structure that predated them.

There was a small group called East Side Fists, and some of them got recruited. The people from East Side Fists were part of the initial group that started ESWP. That was probably '87. So there would be a fair amount of scuffles and shit that would start. There were quite a few traditional or Oi skins that were not racialized.

There was a specific moment where everything changed. Some of them went white power; some of them on the fringes still hung out but didn't get quite as involved. Other people were more to the other side, wearing crossed-out swastikas, but they all still knew each other; they were part of this loose fabric. I was still just a punk kid going to shows and didn't know a whole lot of those people personally. I'd met a few through going to treatment and aftercare programs as a teenager. So there would be confrontations between skinheads that had become white power and those that were not. Some posturing, but nothing had really, really moved too rapidly until the rise of ESWP.

BECKY
Portland ARA

I was a punk rocker, living with my step-grandmother in a one-bedroom apartment by PSU on Hall Street. She had cancer and I was just too much to deal with. So she sent me back to the East Coast to live with my mom. And I immediately got into a fight with my mom and then lived with a stepfather for like two weeks. I was kind of violent. He dropped me off at a thirty-day runaway shelter in Bethlehem, Pennsylvania. I stayed there a year.

My boyfriend, Rob, was a skinhead. He ended up moving to Chicago, and he is the person that introduced me to SCAR, Skinheads Committed Against Racism. So I was a skinhead back in Pennsylvania. I moved back to Portland, and I was not white power, that was for sure. There weren't a lot of other skins. There were punks and then there were the boneheads.

Mic Crenshaw: Somebody said you were the first antiracist skinhead in Portland. Can you say more about that?
Well, if that's true, then it's happenstance. There's no badge of honor. I was antiracist, and it just happened to be that I was identifying as a skinhead.

I moved back in 1988, before Mulugeta Seraw was murdered. So I had a fringe. This is a picture that was taken at the Trinity Arms apartments. That's Fred Meyer in the background.

When I first moved here, I lived in Southeast for a little while and I met some skinhead—I think his name was Steve. I ended up partying with him. But he was East Side White Pride. Then it became pretty apparent to me, like, "Oh, these guys are white power." I don't remember dealing with that back east. I was fifteen, and I was used to having to take care of myself in difficult situations and be on my own, so I got out of there. I had one more incident I can remember from that period of time.

These two women that showed up at my work all the time, I think they were from POWAR [Preservation of the White American Race]. One night they stayed behind, they waited for me to get off my shift. I knew I was gonna have to deal with them. They're like, oh, we're gonna go to a party. They were definitely older than me. I knew it wasn't going to be a good situation. I got into their stupid car. They drove me deep out into Forest Park. They got me out of the car. I was scared shitless. I think they pushed me. I pushed back. I might have gotten punched. In the end, I ended up giving up my boots, those oxblood boots. I never bought another pair of Docs after that. They ended up bringing me back. They dropped me on Burnside, in my socks. Pretty humiliating, not anything I really wanted to talk to anybody about. I feel like there's many situations

---

On the fire escape, 1988. Photo courtesy of Becky.

like that, so humiliating and just fucked up. Portland, when I came here at fifteen, was not a good place for me. Those nazis were not going to be good for me. And the punks were jerks, they were assholes, like, I was never going to be punk enough.

Steve Vickers and I made a flyer about SCAR. There wasn't a number or anything to join. I think it was more just a call to fight against racism. I'm sure a lot of it was copied from whatever information we had from Chicago, which was my link. I remember I kept one copy, and I threw it out later because I was so embarrassed by all the misspellings.

MICHAEL CLARK
SHARP

I'm gonna own right here that I was actually born and raised pretty racist. But I didn't know any better, and I didn't have anyone around. As I was getting a little older, my aunt took in foster kids. I had a lot of foster cousins, some Hispanic, from different Blood sets, a couple of young men from India. It just became obvious that there was nothing to race. We were all together. We were all family. We were all dealing with the same stuff. So it really lost its power for me.

Late '80s, early '90s, I was already clean and sober. I quit drinking for the first time at age thirteen. So I was pretty much a straight edge little punk rock kid. Downtown, the Wall, which was on the back side of the courthouse, you could buy any drug known to mankind there. They had a camp where all the homeless, straight, and gay hookers cruised. Everybody was intermixed, and it was really interesting. At the time, '86, '87, the only skinheads that I knew of were white power skinheads. I hadn't seen or heard of any antiracist skinheads. I knew skinheads from being out at shows and from being in the punk rock skate scene. You would go to a show and the pit would be all the nazi guys. Pretty much you were gonna get hammered if you got in the pit, so . . . we would group up and go and get hammered, you know? [Laughs.]

Back then, it didn't matter if you had a mohawk. It didn't matter if you had a shaved head. It didn't matter if you had long hair, only if you were wearing boots . . . that was the big thing. Schools were trying to ban Doc Martens because of gang skinhead culture and things like that. So if you were in boots, you took a chance of people just assuming that you were a nazi. When I was thirteen or fourteen, I had a new pair of Docs, walking down Woodstock Boulevard. Two carloads of guys pull up: "Hey, little . . ."—you know, yelling at me—"give up the boots!" And then getting chased through Southeast Portland, trying to hang on to my brand-new pair of Docs. It definitely wasn't—I mean, it wasn't about not getting beat up. It was about not losing my shiny new oxbloods.

The guys who ended up killing Mulugeta Seraw are the same guys who used to try to steal my boots, from the same crew. It reinforced the danger that you were in. And—as having been a gang member—looking back in the '80s and '90s, Portland was not a safe place. You might have words with somebody, and out came knives, or people were pulling guns. So it really gave power to my sense of powerlessness. As a thirteen-, fourteen-year-old kid, being threatened by people—I didn't feel safe.

My willingness to get brotherhood was based on that. To be in a group where I wasn't afraid to say that I didn't like what you were saying and that I wasn't afraid anymore—it empowered a lot of people to stand up and make a little change.

JORIN
Portland ARA

I moved around a lot when I was a kid. I lived in Portland a few different times and came back in 1982. It was a very different place back then. It was definitely not a place that people moved to; it seemed like more of a place to move away from.

When I first started going to punk shows in the '80s, the presence of what I'll refer to as boneheads was pretty significant and strong. Pine Street Theatre was one of the main venues that we would go see either local or touring bands. My recollection was that it was always kind of scary. And initially felt like something that there was nothing we could do about it. At the time, we didn't really think of them as boneheads or nazi skinheads. They were just skinheads. They were typically bigger, they were often older, and they were bullies. Were we going to get messed with? Were they going to ask us what size our shoes were? I remember being probably fourteen or fifteen years old and being outside Satyricon in Old Town and seeing a kid get curbed for his boots. From that point on, I was always, always terrified that something like that could happen to anyone.

PATRICK MAZZA
Activist and journalist

In Portland in the '80s, you could be an artist and you could live on a few hundred dollars a month. You could get by here. And that was a lot of the reason for the vibrancy of the scene. There was some space and latitude.

But Portland had gotten a national reputation for being a place where skinheads could come. You know, there was this weird tolerance for intolerance. Even among the punk community, it was like, "Oh, we're all weird. We're all down." The skins came from typically poor and lower-class backgrounds. They were not prosperous people. They banded together, like gangs do, for mutual safety.

We know the history of Oregon and the history of Portland. The Klan history of the '20s. The ban on Black people living in Oregon for many decades. Portland got a reputation around the country as a place where nazi skinheads could come. For a city of our size, we had the most skinheads per capita; it was the skinhead capital. That drew people like Tom Metzger and other major, national skinhead organizers. The Aryan Nations people came in and said, "Well, you know why you're all screwed up? It's all those Blacks and Jews taking your jobs. It's not your fault." So you have an increasing ideological element to it, long before Mulugeta Seraw was killed.

They were beating up on Black people, beating up on gays. They hated the gays. This was going on for a number of years. And they were coming to shows and being violent. The nazis would be in control of the pit. People didn't want to confront them that much. In 1985, in 1986, Poison Idea did stop playing shows out of protest for the violence that was going on. So there was starting to be some pushback. What happened after Seraw was, the community got organized.

Ken Death, then known as Ken Mieske, he just was a visceral guy who was violent. That's what got him to be security chief at Monqui Productions at the Pine Street Theatre. The first I saw Ken Mieske was in this short film that Gus Van Sant had done, that he showed at an event at Northwest Service Center with William Burroughs.[1] And when I became a music columnist for *Portland Alliance*, Monqui put me on the permanent guest list. So I hung around Pine Street.

In 1986, we decided to stage this benefit at Pine Street to benefit the work against Hanford [nuclear production facility on the Columbia River]. The people at Monqui Productions, who were running Pine Street at the time, said, "You better get good security." Originally it was supposed to be MDC, Millions of Dead Cops, who were then from San Francisco, BGK from the Netherlands, and Cheetah Chrome Motherfuckers from Italy. They're all lefty, radical punk bands. We started getting hassled when we were putting up posters, and there was starting to be some bad vibes around the show. As the rumblings about the show got into the air, MDC said, "No, we're not going to come."

benefit against HANFORD

From San Francisco

MDC

From Amsterdam

BGK

THURS.
AUG. 21
9:00 P.M.

From Italy
Cheetah Chrome

$5.50 advance
$6.50 door

ALL AGES

PINE STREET

SE 9TH & PINE

Tickets: Django Records, Second Avenue Records, The Ooze, Music Millenium, Rockport Records

The night of the Pine Street show, skinheads turned up in large numbers. Sixty of them, or something like that. Ken Mieske/Ken Death, who was security chief for Monqui, had access to everything at Pine Street. He let some of his friends in. Our person working the door let some of them in. That was a mistake. When Cheetah Chrome Motherfuckers opened, the skinheads started sieg-heiling. The lead singer said, "We're not going to play. Our fathers died fighting your kind of scum. We're not going to play for you." All of a sudden, the entire floor disintegrates into little clustering, arguing groups of people. People arguing with the skinheads. This was 1986. We got the bands out. We got BGK over to our house in Sunnyside. Unfortunately, somebody had leaked where our house was, and we came home to find a whole house of skinheads. Fortunately, my partner had collected their baseball bats at the door.

So, it's this hugely uncomfortable scene: everybody kind of sitting around the band, nervous as hell, what's going to happen? I'm standing beside my stove in my kitchen, and a boot girl is preaching National Socialism to me. At a certain point, somebody called the cops. All the skins just go over the back fence. So we had one of the finest collections of baseball bats in Portland. We spent the next few days hanging out with the bands, with Cheetah Chrome Motherfuckers. . . . And the lead singer said, "Even though we didn't get to play, standing up and confronting these people was the best."

This is from my *Portland Alliance* column:

> The next day I was told that a number of local bands are going to do the same as Cheetah Chrome Motherfuckers, and refuse to play when people are pulling nazi crap in the audience. We spent the next couple of days with band members. Antonio of Cheetah Chrome told me that even though the group didn't get to play, it was the best show they ever had. Cheetah Chrome wants something beyond music. He said they want communication with the audience, and something that will change people's lives.

They gave people some inspiration to stand up. Obviously not enough, because of what happened two years later. You know, the skinheads were still around. That did not set off the wave against the nazis. It took the killing of Mulugeta Seraw to do that.

SCOT NAKAGAWA
Coalition for Human Dignity and AIDS Coalition to Unleash Power (ACT UP) Portland

I moved to Oregon in 1986, from Hawaii. It was kind of a big shock to come here, to go from a multiracial setting like Hawaii to a place like Portland, the whitest major city in the United States.

In Hawaii, I grew up in a very small, rural community on a still-active sugar plantation that was at the end of a discontinued agricultural road. So we were very isolated. I assumed that I would work in agriculture. And I did, you know, in my younger years, in my teens, and occasionally my early twenties. There wasn't a lot of mobility. Community was still relatively intact, and sugar, though on its last legs, was still a dominant force in the Hawaiian economy. The future didn't exactly look bright, but it looked predictable.

But I am a gay person. I recognized early on that it would be very difficult in this small, culturally conservative community, to make a life for myself that would be fulfilling to me. I was a person who had ideas and wanted to do things, wanted to try and experiment and learn and grow. While there's certainly a rich life to be had in rural Oahu, I set my sights elsewhere.

After a number of years of working as a service provider in Hawaii, working with low-income families and youth in crisis, I decided to leave Hawaii and move to Oregon.

I came here in 1986. First to Corvallis, where I worked at something called the Community Outreach Sunflower House, in a migrant shelter, food bank, free medical clinic, suicide crisis line, a variety of different kinds of capacities. Then, right around the end of that year, I moved to Portland.

When I first got here, I was a homeless service provider. I went to college for a year and basically failed three terms, you know, never got past my college algebra and wasn't sure what I would do.

My immediate experience here was basically being shocked by the dominance of a white perspective in this community. I literally came here and thought, when I listened to progressive white leaders in the community talking about issues, that they were intentionally trying to exclude people of color. It took me a while to figure out that it was completely unintentional and that it wasn't just, like, hurt-your-feelings racism that has been thrown around by the kind of ignorant spread of the hegemony of whiteness in this community. So it was a big shock.

Postcard of the Vanport public housing development following the 1948 flood.
City of Portland Archives 2004-002.7251.

Chapter 2

He Lived as a Peacemaker
The Murder of Mulugeta Seraw

In 1974, a military faction of low-ranking officers and enlisted men overthrew eighty-two-year-old Ethiopian emperor Haile Selassie, ushering in one of the bloodiest civil wars in modern history. For seventeen years, Ethiopians fled the country in search of a life without the terror that had become commonplace.

Mulugeta Seraw came from a family of rural farmers who had, in a previous generation, joined the Protestant faith through the Adventist church. Education, the family determined, was the way forward into modern life; they sent young Mulugeta to Addis Ababa to attend high school after he had advanced as far in his schooling as was possible in the rural highlands of Gondar Province.

After graduation, Mulugeta reached out to his uncle Engedaw Berhanu and asked to join him in the United States, where Berhanu was studying at Portland State University (PSU). In 1980, nineteen-year-old Mulugeta Seraw arrived in Oregon, leaving behind his war-torn homeland.

By 1988, Mulugeta was a cherished member of Portland's small but close-knit Ethiopian community. He kept in close contact with Berhanu, who had some years earlier moved to California. Mulugeta lived in the Parklane, an apartment building at Southeast 31st and Pine. Living around the corner at the Pine Terrace apartments were members of East Side White Pride.

The afternoon of Saturday, November 12, 1988, several ESWP skinheads got together at the apartment at Southeast 31st and Pine. In the apartment that day was Dave Mazzella, who had in February

Mulugeta Seraw.

of that same year appeared on the Oprah Winfrey show in an episode about racist skinheads, which gave the young man some cachet.[2]

Mazzella was a protégé of White Aryan Resistance founder Tom Metzger, a former Grand Wizard of the Ku Klux Klan and a suspected member of a neonazi group called the Order. While racist skinheads were dismissed by most of the white nationalist establishment, Metzger saw an opportunity to create a warrior class. He groomed young men like Mazzella as lieutenants. It was Mazzella's job to recruit and find other skinheads to serve as working-class foot soldiers and enforcers. He would then dispense hate literature and attract other disaffected youth to the racist cause.

Mazzella pumped the ESWP members up with self-importance and pressured them to distribute white nationalist flyers, despite Saturday being date night for many of them. After their "meeting," which consisted of Mazzella urging them to hype for Metzger, the racist skinheads went out partying with their girlfriends.

Mulugeta Seraw, on that same evening, went out to dinner with a friend and then to a going-away party for a member of the Ethiopian émigré community. Seraw had to work early the next morning; a couple of friends drove him home in a rolling party—Seraw had a beer in the back seat, and the other passenger had a cup of gin. When they got to 31st and Pine, they stayed in the car, talking.

Both sides of the street were lined with cars, leaving a narrow middle lane. When the white nationalist skinheads came home from their party and encountered the car full of Ethiopian men, the woman skinhead at the wheel was impatient, honking and yelling. The Ethiopians' car engine stuttered. The moment needed to start the car became a keystone of Portland history; the skinheads escalated to name-calling. Seraw got out of the car and headed to his apartment, only to turn back when he saw his friends in the middle of the street fighting two skinheads: Steven Strasser and Kyle Brewster.

Still in the car was Ken Mieske, aka Ken Death. When Patty Copp, the driver, egged him on, saying, "Well, aren't you going to do something about it, Ken?" Mieske grabbed a bat, entered the fray, and, after smashing up the other driver's car, ran to Kyle Brewster. Brewster was in the street with Mulugeta Seraw, who was urging everyone to calm down when Mieske brought the bat down hard on the side of Seraw's head, and then kept going while Seraw lay on the ground. Seraw was pronounced dead at a hospital a few hours later on November 13, 1988.

The murderers of Mulugeta Seraw are Ken Mieske, aka Ken Death, age twenty-three in 1988; Kyle Brewster, nineteen; and Steve Strasser, twenty. All three were members of East Side White Pride.[3]

Mulugeta Seraw and friend outside of Seraw's workplace, date unknown. From the Elinor Langer Archives, University of Oregon.

Operation PUSH protest, 1989.
Photo by Bette Lee.

Scot Nakagawa, 1992. Courtesy of the Oregon Historical Society.

SCOT NAKAGAWA
Coalition for Human Dignity and ACT UP Portland

Mulugeta Seraw, an Ethiopian student at Portland State University, was beaten to death by neonazi skinheads on the streets of Southeast Portland. Those neonazi activists were affiliated with a group called East Side White Pride. A couple of their members surprised people in the community.

Ken Death was a cultural figure in the alternative music scene here. He actually was the star of a short film by the filmmaker Gus Van Sant called *Ken Death Gets Out of Jail*. So, I had some familiarity with Ken and the circle that he moved in. That was a bit of a surprise, though not as much as the surprise that Kyle Brewster presented us.

Kyle Brewster came from an upper-middle-class family. He had been his high school homecoming king, and his mother was a progressive social activist in the city. These things defied stereotypes, these young men who brutally, really brutally beat Mulugeta Seraw to death with baseball bats and by kicking him, and for nothing. For some dispute over parking or something. It shocked the city that these were not your stereotypical street thugs, that they were highly sophisticated political thinkers, that they had national affiliations. East Side White Pride were affiliated with a national organization called White Aryan Resistance, which was led by a man named Tom Metzger.

Following the Seraw murder, hate crime statistics here started to go up. Where, typically, something like that happens in a community, hate crime statistics go down. Here, they went way up and up and up. It was an indication of a problem, something more than just a one-off.

Portland had a disproportionate number of anti-LGBTQ violent attacks. If you were African American in the city of Portland at the time, you were ten times more likely to be visited by a hate crime than a white person. If you're an African American, often the attacks were organized. There was a very big problem with anti-Asian violence here, and it was growing rapidly.

Then the Jewish community started to be attacked. We recognize this was more trouble than we even imagined, right? Because when white nationalist groups rise and attack Jewish communities, display that kind of anti-Semitism, it reveals the sort of political sophistication and connection to movements internationally that we didn't anticipate sleepy old Portland back in those days would have.

We now know of the long history of many of the white nationalist groups that were active here in Oregon. We've learned about the influence of groups like the Posse Comitatus, whose ideology was basically a blueprint for the Bundy uprising and occupation of the bird sanctuary in Malheur County.[4] These kinds of groups and ideas have always been a part of the political mix, have always been limiting our democratic potential here, have always targeted communities of color, women, religious minorities, and have always been able to play a really significant role in determining what political outcomes we will have here in Oregon.

In studying that history, we also see, for example, that the Ku Klux Klan was very active here in the 1920s. At one point, I believe it's true, that about one in three white men in the city of Portland belonged to the Ku Klux Klan. Their influence is something we still feel here. You know, one of the reasons why we have such a robust public school system here in Oregon, relative to many other places, is because of the activity of the Klan in trying to close down Catholic parochial schools. The reason why we have such a powerful free speech clause in our Constitution is, in part, the influence of the Ku Klux Klan. They are part and parcel of the story of Oregon; they are part of the history here. So we should never behave as if, because they become less visible, they've gone away. In fact, they've always been here.

We need to get away from thinking of white nationalism in terms of disease pathology, right? This is not a disease of white people. It is not a set of ideas confined entirely to white people, right? When white people act in racist ways, their whiteness gives that racism, those acts, particular dynamism and force. A particular kind of power and influence, but those ideologies can be adopted by anyone. We see now with the Proud Boys, for example, here in Portland, that there are people of color who participate, even at the leadership level of that organization, who have adopted these ideas. We shouldn't be essentialists, we shouldn't allow these racial categories, that were created in order to justify a white supremacy and exploitation, to appear natural or the cultural or biological propensities of any given individual.

White nationalism is something that is very, very old in the United States. The racist right in the United States is a permanent feature of American politics, and it requires constant vigilance. The United States was, after all, founded as a set of colonies originally, right? And then as a slave state. In its original form, the United States of America was a racial state, one in which only white, propertied males were able to participate directly in the franchise. You know, when I say white, propertied males, I am referring to almost all white males in the United States at the time; people often make the mistake of thinking there was a working class at the beginning of all of this, but there wasn't. For the most part, there was no such thing as a white working class at the beginning of the American story.

Nationalism is a relatively new thing. It hasn't been around forever. It comes in a variety of forms. There is civic nationalism, one in which, you know, democratic principles attempt to be the prevailing ones. And then there's ethnic nationalism, an arbitrary kind of nationalism, organized around ethnic identity. Those two kinds of nationalism have always been competing, because nation-states are rooted originally in colonialism, which is justified by a racist ideology, by a white supremacist ideology. And so, the liberal democracies are for the most part deeply influenced by ethnic nationalism and often began as ethnic states. So it's just a tendency that's always there and is part of the struggle that we must always be waging in our politics. We have to remember that racism and sexism are both antidemocratic ideologies. Beyond the harm they do to the people who are targeted, beyond the degree of exploitation those ideologies justify, they are ultimately antidemocratic ideologies. There are authoritarian ideologies that are meant to justify hierarchies that are unjust. And so, of course, authoritarian movements always go down avenues of race and gender when they try to build their case and build their base. That's what they're doing now. It's just a part of the story.

Movements like white nationalism rise as a result of cultural anxiety. White people, as a percentage of the population of the United States, are shrinking, right? Not just because of immigration and high birth rates in communities of color, but because of particularly low birth rates in white communities. So, the white population is basically aging out. You know, that is a thing that's going to cause anxiety in a state that has always lived up to a white supremacist standard. It's a reactionary thing that is about culture, not economics.

City of Unity Rainbow Rally, a city-organized memorial for Mulugeta Seraw, Pioneer Courthouse Square, January 17, 1989. Above: Pictured at the podium is Portland City Council Commissioner Dick Bogle. At far left is County Chair Gladys McCoy, who in 1970 became the first Black woman and first person of color elected to public office in the state of Oregon. Photo courtesy of the Oregon Historical Society, photographer unknown, originally published in *The Skanner*. Below: Gospel singer James Johnson. Photo uncredited, courtesy of *The Oregonian*.

RON HERNDON
Portland Black United Front

In the Black United Front, there were members from the church community, members from the activist community, members from NAACP, Urban League. We put together what we thought was a platform that could bring about change more quickly in the Black community. There were several of us who had been active in the Black community for years. We thought that even though we had worked hard in our separate efforts, we could bring about change a lot more quickly if we worked together.

The first issue that we took on was education. We organized very carefully, looked at all of the disparities that were occurring: this horrendous busing program that took a generation of Black children away from the community, separated them from the community, and sent them into sometimes very hostile environments. That happened only to Black children; not one white child was ever forcibly bused in Portland. That was left for Black children to suffer that indignity, and the Black community is still, I believe, trying to recover from that.

In terms of historical perspective, I think in the history of this country, there have only been two groups of children who have been forcibly taken away from their community, supposedly for educational purposes. American Indian children were taken away from their communities and sent to boarding schools that were four hundred or five hundred miles away. And Black children were forcibly taken away from their community, supposedly for educational purposes. So it is a very racist construct. Through that organizing, we were able to stop it, and we were able to ensure that Black children could go to school in their own community. That was a successful community effort. We went on to address other issues: police misconduct, economic disparities. So that was the beginning of the Black United Front. That would have been the late '70s, early '80s.

During the late '60s, all through the '70s, every year there was a big march and rally here in Portland called African Liberation Day.[5] It was to support African countries who at that time were still suffering from colonialism and apartheid. That event, every year, was meant to give support to the liberation movements in those countries.

Black people here in Portland sent supplies and clothes back to those countries. Communities who were intertwined and worked with each other invited people to their various events and holiday celebrations. There were efforts made between members of both communities to learn from each other, to support each other. So I think that's why it made it very easy when—I know you're gonna ask about, unfortunately, the death of Mulugeta Seraw—for the Ethiopian community to reach out to us as soon as they became aware of what happened.

Ron Herndon (standing on desk) at a Portland Public School Board protest. Photo by Steve Nehl, published in the *Oregon Journal*, March 30, 1982.

I remember getting a phone call the day after he had been murdered. Someone from the Ethiopian community that I knew said, "We need help. We don't know what to do. Can you come meet his uncle and members of the community?" So we said yes, and there were about four of us who went to this apartment in Southeast Portland.

I remember walking in the room, all these women who were just crying, crying, crying, and we met his uncle. He asked us what we could do. We said, well, one of the things we can do is have a press event to draw attention to this. We'll have a rally, a demonstration. So we did that, we had a press event, and we got him in touch with an attorney so that he would know what he could safely say, and what he probably shouldn't say, in terms of what was going to happen with the police investigation.

We had the rally on the steps of City Hall, and a couple hundred people came out from the white community, the Black community, and the Hispanic community to bring attention to what happened and to demand that justice be served. And then the rest is history.

The larger question was how Portland's power base—political, economic, educational—did not respond well or quickly enough to skinheads. It's almost as if you see that you got a cut on your hand and it's not healing well, and you ignore it. Then you wonder why you got poison streaming throughout your arm, and then now it's spreading throughout your body. Something should have been done when you first saw the cut.

And when this organization of those who espouse that racist dogma, when they first came to town, putting out their little flyers and hate statements, there should have been a far more assertive response to that then.

Historically, we've seen the harm that's caused all around the world when people begin to espouse that doctrine. And unfortunately, when we take the position that, "Well, it's just freedom of speech, they have a right to say what they want," and don't look behind that and what it can lead to, then we're being very myopic and, in my opinion, very foolish. I think that's the danger, that when this pops up—and it's quite cyclical—when it pops up, that there has to be an immediate, strong response from every possible segment of society to it. If we ignore that, we ignore it at our own peril.

Flyer courtesy of the Rutherford Collection at the Portland State University Archive.

AFRICAN LIBERATION DAY

Theme
"SOUTH AFRICA WILL BE FREE"

SATURDAY, MAY 24, 1986

March begins at 12:30 p.m.
from the KING Facility (N.E. 7th & Wygant)

RALLY 1-5 p.m.
IRVING. PARK
(N.E. 7th & Fremont)

Speakers:
RONNIE HERMION, Co-Chair, Portland Black United Front
MARHAMU ELTAYEB, Director, Church Council of Greater Seattle South Africa Program; Co-Chair, Seattle Coalition Against Apartheid
DEBRA COOK, Coordinator, Clergy and Laity Concerned, Human Rights and Racial Justice, Eugene, Or.
KHPAU SADIKI, POSAF (Portlanders Organized for Southern African Freedom)
AVEL GORDLY, AFSC Southern Africa Program
JOYCE HARRIS, Director, Black Educational Center
LAKITA DUKE, News Director, Grassroots News NW
MARGARET CARTER, District 18 Representative

- FOOD
- MUSIC
- BOOTHS
- ENTERTAINMENT
- CHILDREN'S ACTIVITIES

FOR MORE INFORMATION CONTACT: ALD PLANNING COMMITTEE **284-9552**

Black Educational Center, POSAF, AFSC Southern Africa Program   BETTER ENTERTAINMENT ATTRACTIONS NETWORK

Engedaw Berhanu and family mourning, 1988. Photo by Douglas Perry, courtesy of *The Oregonian*.

ENGEDAW BERHANU
Mulugeta Seraw's uncle

On November 13, 2018, thirty years after the murder, the Urban League of Portland held the Mulugeta Seraw Commemoration Conference to remember and honor Seraw. Participants spotlighted the history of anti–Black violence in Oregon and sought to identify ways to combat hate in Portland's communities. Guest speaker Engedaw Berhanu gave a moving tribute to his beloved nephew. On the day after the conference, organizers unveiled street sign toppers to permanently memorialize Mulugeta Seraw where the young man made his last, fatal bid for peace on that cold November night.

Any time I speak about Mulugeta, I get emotional. I like to be emotional, because he means a lot to me. Here we go.

When I arrived in the US from Ethiopia on a student visa in March 1973, I had no plan to remain in the US. My plan was to return home immediately after I completed my education. In fact, I was so eager to return home that I received my degree in journalism from Walla Walla College—now Walla Walla University—in three years, in 1976.

After I graduated, I was offered a position as director of the Seventh Day Adventist Publishing House in Addis Ababa, Ethiopia, where I worked as a translator and editor before I left for the US. When I wrote my father to tell him the good news that I was returning home, as a big shot, I did not expect his reaction. He told me not to return home at that time. He said it was not safe for me to do so.

You see, in 1976, Ethiopia was in the middle of a raging civil war. People were being killed in the streets randomly, especially young men. Instead, my father told me to send for my brothers and my nephew to bring them to the US, where he thought they would be safer. After a few moments of indecision, not knowing when I would be able to return home, it dawned on me that chances for my returning to Ethiopia were getting slimmer and slimmer. I decided to go to graduate school in the US.

In 1979, I enrolled in the Department of Sociology at Portland State University. It was at that time I received letters from my nephew Mulugeta Seraw and from one of my brothers, letting me know that they had graduated from high school and wanted to come to the US to further their education. By then, I had met and befriended a very kind couple, Clarence and Elsie Tupper, who lived in Goldendale, Washington. They were willing to sponsor Mulugeta and my brother.

I sent Mulugeta and my brother I-20s, that's international college acceptance letters. Mulugeta completed the process and arrived in Portland in December 1980. I cannot explain the happiness that we both felt when I picked him up at the airport. We had not seen each other since Mulugeta was a small boy. I marveled at how he had grown up into a handsome young man.

You see, Mulugeta and I always had a special bond. He was the second child and the first son of my beloved older sister, Fetenech. She was the person I loved more than anyone else, because she cared for my younger siblings and me when our young mother died. Unfortunately, she died at a young age, too. I felt it was my turn to help her children now. I was happy to have the opportunity to help Mulugeta.

Mulugeta moved in with me in my apartment in Beaverton, and he proved to be a very responsible young man. He quickly found a job, at first at a fast-food restaurant, later at a small Catholic school in Beaverton. He became a favorite of both the students and the staff, the teachers. He was hardworking, caring, kind, and respectful.

He also made a circle of friends from the small community of Ethiopians and Americans alike. He quickly was acknowledged as a leader and a peacemaker. He was also an avid soccer player. When I decided to move to California in January 1982, I suggested that he join me in my move. He politely declined. He said he liked living in Portland. He has his friends, his job, his school. He assured me that he could take care of himself.

During the following years, Mulugeta and I and my family kept in close contact. We would attend relatives' weddings and other major events together. He would visit my family in California frequently during the holidays, and I would visit him in Portland occasionally. In the process, he and my young daughter established a very special bond during his frequent visits. She just loved his beautiful smile and sweet personality. The last time I saw Mulugeta was during Labor Day weekend in 1988, a couple months before he was murdered, when we attended a relative's wedding in Walla Walla, Washington. He was very happy and still going to school.

Then, I received a phone call on that fateful Sunday morning at five o'clock on November 13, 1988. The voice on the other end of the line said that Mulugeta was hurt in a fight early that morning. But intuitively, I knew that something had gone terribly wrong, because Mulugeta was never a fighter. He always tried to stop fights. Even when he was murdered, he was not fighting, but he was trying to stop the fight between his friends and the skinheads.

This selfless act demonstrates the true nature of Mulugeta's heart even in the face of danger. My beloved Mulugeta Seraw lived as a peacemaker and died as a peacemaker.

Thank you.

Memorial street signs where Mulugeta Seraw lived and was murdered, commemorated in November 2018. Signs in both Amharic and English, with Amharic signs using the Ethiopian calendar dating system. Photo by Celina Flores.

ኑኔታ ስራዉ (1953-1981)

Pine   300
St

SE 31st AV

FIGHT

RACISM

Coalition for
Human Dignity

Chapter 3

Building Community Defense
The Rise of the
Coalition for Human Dignity

I n the months after Mulugeta Seraw's murder, Portland activists turned out in force to demand a response. People attended rallies, marched, wrote articles, and made other civic efforts to address their feelings of injustice and powerlessness. Finally, the violence was egregious enough that the city itself got involved and convened a meeting of a broad coalition in city chambers, where those in attendance agreed on an expansive and inclusive name: Coalition for Human Dignity.

It did not take long, however, for city officials to balk at the risk. When the new group proposed a trip to confront a white supremacist compound in neighboring Idaho, the city bowed out, and the broader group winnowed to a committee of youngish activists joined by a few seasoned advocates with deep local roots in social justice.

Susan Wheeler, a veteran of the Communist Party and other far-left-wing political groups, Donna Red Wing of the Lesbian Community Project, and Stew Albert, a Yippie veteran,[6] were some who helped mentor and support this small group of radicals. Through volunteer support, connections, and sheer tirelessness, by spring of 1989 Coalition for Human Dignity (CHD) activists began to make an impact in fighting racist violence and providing direct support to vulnerable Portlanders. Many developed into lifelong champions of human dignity, and they continue to organize

---

CHD's ubiquitous 1990 poster, designed by Steven Birch and Jonathan Mozzochi. Based on a 1931 poster by German communist John Heartfield.

locally and nationally, in networks and think tanks for individual and community empowerment, especially within and on behalf of historically oppressed groups.

It is important to note that protection against hate crimes in 1988 was limited to the 1968 Civil Rights Act, twenty-year-old legislation that granted protection to people who were attacked while engaging in one of six federally protected activities that did not, for example, include hanging out at the Pine Street Theatre. The subsequent 1994 Violent Crime Control and Law Enforcement Act granted hate crime status to federal crimes only, which, again, does not include most racist skinhead activity. It was not until the 2009 Matthew Shepard and James Byrd Jr. Hate Crimes Prevention Act expanded the Civil Rights Act to include actual or perceived gender, sexual orientation, gender identity, or disability and dropped the prerequisite that the victim be engaging in a federally protected activity that the level of protection would have extended to situations the Coalition for Human Dignity had regularly addressed twenty years earlier.

SCOT NAKAGAWA
Coalition for Human Dignity and ACT UP Portland

My parents always knew that I was gay, or at least had some inkling about it, and hated me for it. They also loved me as their son, but I felt that hatred. It was a difficult situation to be in. I was one of those kids who ran away from home a lot and occasionally would be pushed out. I occasionally had to resort to sex work when I was a homeless teen, because of being rejected for being gay. It's a deep history. When you're a gay, homeless teen, particularly in the '70s, the vulnerability you experience is so extraordinary. There is no place to turn. So if I were trying to get by by befriending tourists at the gay bars, if somebody decided to beat me up, they could do it with impunity. In fact, gay bashers could do so with impunity because the cops would just look the other way. In some instances, the cops were part of the problem. There's just no more helpless feeling than being a fifteen-year-old gay kid, standing alone in a dark alley, hiding from cops who are about to descend on you. There's nowhere to turn. There's no one to complain to. There's no report to file. There's nothing. That's what it was like in the beginning. But you know, as I got involved in politics here, what I can tell you is that for, I would say, the first fifteen or so years or longer of my political career, I just had to swallow the fact of anti-gay jokes. It just was everywhere.

So you know, you live with these fears, and you shape your life

Hate crimes reported to the police in 1987-88, assembled by the Metropolitan Human Relations Commission, from the November 24, 1988, issue of the *Portland Observer*, one of Portland's two Black newspapers.

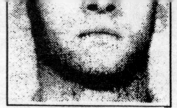

Brewster   Mieske   Strasser

mmary Of Reported Racially-Motivated Incidents 87-88
Metropolitan   Human   Relations   Commission

Vietnamese Seventh Day
ntist Church in Portland was
-painted with racist graffiti
a disparaged Asians and
s.

/87
up of youths believed to be
eads terrorized a black
an near the Lloyd Cinemas
lex, shouting racial epithets
r, spitting on her car and
tually throwing a chain
gh her car window. Pieces of
ying glass lodged in her cor-
nd she required treatment at
pital emergency room. No
ts were made for that inci-

/88
ents in Gresham, Oregon
d a publication denouncing
ro-White Marriages" in their
paper boxes. The publica-
printed by the Lord's Cove-
Church of Phoenix, Arizona,
found in the distribution of a
food magazine.

/88
als spray painted anti-Israeli
ti on the exterior to two syna-
es.   The slogans were:
OGNIZE THE PLO; YOU
E BLOOD ON YOUR
DS; JEW TRIUMPH = ARAB
TH.

0/88
e Skinheads were arrested
attacking an Asian-American
e coming out of a downtown
aurant with his family. The
heads were reported as say-
"GO BACK TO HONG KONG"
"GET OUT OF OUR COUN-
". They called his caucasian
a TRAITOR and called their
year-old daughter a "FUCK-
SLANT". During the assault,
American-Asian male was
ck in the face and kicked in the
head and stomach with heavy
bat boots.

7/88
ve Skinhead recruitment re-
ted at Fernwood Middle
ool and Grant High School.
heads promise that they will
ect white recruitees from the
rities.

school bus in the morning when
she confronted a white female,
who was reported to have hit her
children. The white female started
yelling, "I DIDN'T HIT YOUR
CHILDREN .....ONLY SHOVED
THEM". "YOU CAN CALL THE
POLICE ALL YOU WANT TO;

04/27/88
A large rock that had a swastika
and "DIE JEW" painted on it was
thrown through a window of Jewish
man's home.

05/02/88
Racist literature was found in a
phone booth located in downtown
Portland. The anonymous author
claims to spread the truth by inter-
preting biblical scripture to support race separation, white race
preservation, and to decry interracial marriage.

05/27/88
Hate mail was received by Commissioner Lindberg. The writer
expressed his anger against Lindberg's contribution to the Black
United Front Saturday School.

05/29/88
Two Skinheads were ap-
proached by two black males who
stated they were "Bloods". The
black males asked if they were
"Skins" and then assaulted them.
One victim was examined at Kaiser. Suspects gone on police arri-
val.

06/17/88
A white male and white female, who identified themselves
as Skinheads, assaulted two
nineteen year old females: a female of Filipino, Mexican and European descent and her compan-
ion, a white female.

06/21/88
Approximately twenty white youths
blocked the entrances and exits of
an apartment complex in North
Portland which is occupied by
several SE Asians families. The
youths began to go door to door,
kicking the doors and yelling racial epithets. One resident called
911. It took the Portland Police
approximately thirty minutes to
respond. One police car arrived
with one officer, who stayed in the
car, observed the activity for five
minutes, then left. The harassment
continued. One resident asked
the youths to leave. Upon refusal

06/01/88
An Asian man pulled up next to a
car containing two white males
who shouted racial epithets. The
passenger in the suspect car
pulled out a baton and started
beating the victim's car. A Police
officer went after the assailants.
No arrest was made. Later on, the
victim called 911 and the police
officer/operator asked about
damages. The victim said there
was no damage to the car. The
police officer responded, "IF
THEY DIDN'T DAMAGE YOUR
CAR, THERE'S NO LAW
AGAINST BEING RUDE".

06/09/88
A white female was arrested for
writing Skinhead graffiti on brick
enclosure.

06/17/88
While standing at a bus stop in
North Portland, two black seventeen (17) year-old males were
approached by three white males
wearing Skinhead-like attire (army
boots, shaved heads). The three
white males chanted racial epithets and assaulted the two black
males. The black males fought
back and were able to get away.
Upon notifying their parents about
the incident, one victim's parent

06/25/88
A white male was approached by
several black males. They asked
if he was "messing with the Home-
boys". They then pushed him and
subsequently assaulted him.

07/04/88
A black male was punched in the
face by a white male in Waterfront
Park. The black male states the
assault was unprovoked. The
suspect was chased by a group of
blacks and the incidents were subsequently controlled by the police.

07/07/88
Officer responded to a strong arm
robbery call. An elderly Chinese
male was assaulted and robbed
of $5.00 by two unarmed white
male suspects described as
"Skinheads".

07/30/88
Altercation between two white
males and two black males sub-
jects. The two white males were

07/17/88
Officers were dispatched to a
turbance involving a large cr
of Skinheads shouting racial s
at black male. It appeared tha
whites (two specifically) were i
gating a racial incident with
black male.

07/23/88
A fight ensued at One Main P
involving Vietnamese and wh
One white received a gash to
forehead necessitating stitche

07/27/88
Officer reported information fr
part-time park employee. A
namese gang is trying to take
the park. One of the gang m
bers brandished a handgun i
waistbands of his trousers.

07/17/88
Officers were dispatched to a
turbance involving a large cr
of Skinheads shouting racial s
at black male. It appeared tha
whites (two specifically) were i
gating a racial incident with
black male.

07/23/88
A fight ensued at One Main P
involving Vietnamese and wh
One white received a gash to
forehead necessitating stitche

07/27/88
Officer reported information fr
part-time park employee. A
namese gang is trying to take
the park. One of the gang m
bers brandished a handgun i
waistbands of his trousers.

07/30/88
Altercation between two w
males and two black males s
jects. The two white males
stabbed by two black males.

08/13/88
Shots exchanged between a
male and black male afte
white male yelled some
about "BLOODS" at the
male on the bicycle.

08/16/88
Assault and vandalism to veh
Two white males and two w

around them. But here in Oregon, starting at around '86, all the way up into the mid-'90s even, it wasn't always okay to be gay, even in progressive political spaces. People would often tell me, "I would never have guessed you were gay," as if it were a compliment.

I made the decision to do this work, in part, because right around the same time that the Seraw murder happened, I was attacked by a group of neonazi skinheads. They didn't harm me in any way, but they did terrify me. I was riding my bike home from work, and they tried to run me off the road. It was very clear to me who they were. If you know the Hollywood Fred Meyer, it wasn't there at the time. What was there was a construction site, so on a bicycle I was able to get away. I reported it to the police, because friends of mine encouraged me to do it. Then a friend who had access to the law enforcement data system asked me about my report and whether I'd filed it, and when I said yes, she told me that it was never actually filed by the police. It made me feel like there's some kind of problem here that's bigger than just a bunch of angry white youth going around and expressing racism.

A group called the Coalition for Human Dignity was formed. It was a coalition between the city of Portland and a variety of different community organizations here, groups that were concerned about hate crimes, groups like the Fellowship of Reconciliation, the American Friends Service Committee, the Lesbian Community Project, et cetera. That coalition attempted to address the problem in the community but fell apart over the desire, on the part of people who are in the community in that coalition, to go to Idaho to protest an Aryan Nations compound. So the city pulled out of the coalition at that point, because they were concerned about insurance liability. So the coalition collapsed into a committee, and at that point they hired me to staff the committee and try to rebuild it.

When the city's concern about insurance liability was preventing it from being able to take coordinated action with members of the community, there just seemed to be a really big problem. The other big issue with the police was that they were also reporting, through their gang enforcement team, that there were no neonazi skinhead groups in Portland. That there was no organized racist activity, and that people were exaggerating. So the Coalition for Human Dignity formed in order to respond to this problem and specifically created a research operation to monitor, document, and report on the activities of neonazi skinheads and professional neonazis.

I also worked at the national level in the LGBTQ movement. I was the field director for a while of the National Gay and Lesbian Task Force, what's now known as the National LGBTQ Task Force, in Washington, DC. The group that's now the Human Rights Campaign, in 1992, recommended that trans people and drag queens not appear in the March on Washington, because of the polarizing effect that they could have.

Punk rocker at protest of the acquittal of the LAPD officers who beat Rodney King, Pioneer Court-house Square, May 2, 1992. Photo by Coyote Amrich.

Whether or not trans people could be in the movement was a debate. The homophobia that we experienced, the heterosexism, the transphobia, was just, like, normative. That's just the way it was. And you just kind of lived with it.

The CHD did have a lot of contact with a lot of different groups. I was a staff person at the CHD; I was also a member of ACT UP in Portland; I had a very strong relationship with leadership at the Lesbi-an Community Project and in a variety of other places in the city. My connections became the organization's connections, and the organiza-tional leadership at the board level also brought many relationships to the organization. The Lesbian Community Project, at the time at which the CHD was working actively with them, was led by a woman named Donna Red Wing, who has since passed away. Donna and I basically conceived of this Homophobic Violence Documentation Project and did a little speaking tour around the city to talk to different groups

A Publication of the Coalition for Human Dignity Research Department

Masthead graphic from 1993's *The Dignity Report* (Vol. 1:2), the public newsletter of the CHD.

about it. I assembled a small volunteer base, and then the project got developed at the Lesbian Community Project, with a corps of volunteer leaders at the head of it.

The CHD also helped to create a bridge between ACT UP Portland and groups like Anti Racist Action (ARA) and Skinheads Against Racial Prejudice (SHARP). We introduced those people. We were the bridge organization. It was a very different time in the city of Portland. There was very little young leadership, and we were all people in our twenties when we first started out with the CHD, and we were a racially diverse group of people in the leadership of that organization. All those things made us interesting and different to people and allowed us to be able to exploit all the different connections that we had in order to be able to make these relationships happen. It's always the case, in my experience, that LGBTQ people can, if allowed, serve as bridges, because LGBTQ communities are a cross-class, multiracial community made up of people from every walk of life. So your relationships, of course, are going to be cross-cutting.

There was also longtime leadership in the organization who made a really big difference to us in grounding our politics and helping us to understand what we were doing and who we should be relating to. Among those people was Susan Wheeler, who passed away a number of years ago. She was the treasurer of the CHD. She did all of our bookkeeping for us for years for free, out of her living room. She showed up for every board meeting. She was, at one point, partner to Don Hammerquist, who is a historically significant actor in politics in the United States. He

Donna Red Wing and Scot Nakagawa with a Portland SHARP at a news conference on May 17, 1990. Photo by Bob Ellis, courtesy of *The Oregonian*.

is a person who's one of the fathers of the radical antifascist movement. He also was the leader of the Communist Party USA in Portland. Susan helped him to organize the chapter, and it was a particularly large and, I guess, active chapter; I don't know that much about that part of that history.

After they separated, Susan met Ronnie Williams and helped him to escape extradition back to Alabama from Oregon.[7] That effort, having been successful, then brought her to the attention of the American Indian Movement. She was involved in the Loud Hawk/Redner Offense/Defense Committee and the Justice for Dennis Banks Committee. That historic work of hers, and then work she did in the peace movement, was really useful to us, because it helped us to understand police repression and it helped us to understand political organizing strategy in general. People don't give her very much credit, because she was a very quiet person who behind the scenes would make contributions to the organization. But without her, I'm not sure the CHD would have been able to survive its early years. The twentysomethings who were the most visible people involved didn't have the strongest basis in organization building. So people like her who were involved made a really, really big difference. It was an intergenerational thing. And I would highly recommend to people now to think about that, that there are people of the older generation whose deep experience in community can be very, very informative.

ABBY LAYTON
Coalition for Human Dignity

I'm a fourth-generation Portlander. My great-grandparents settled in Portland in the late 1800s. They were a poor, Jewish family, peddlers. My family's always been dedicated to the Jewish community. I'm very grounded here.

In Judaism, we have a concept called free-floating hatred. That human beings are prone to project outwards with blame. When they've grown up in societies where "the other" is somehow bad and at fault for your suffering, they will go down that lane, because it is a natural human fault. And that's, I think, why it's so important to really understand oneself.

The beating death of Mulugeta Seraw was a real wake-up call. The Coalition for Human Dignity was born there with a dedication to monitor and research right-wing and neonazi activity in the Pacific Northwest. We had a parent group, the Center for Democratic Action, with Leonard Zeskind, who is a genius in terms of this work. He personally trained the people in the Coalition for Human Dignity to do this type of research. At that time, at the end of the '80s, what we saw was brown-jacketed, neonazi soldiers living in Southeast Portland. The idea, which was really scary, was they chose Portland. The reason they chose Portland was because it was the whitest place that they found. So it's purposely chosen with the idea of creating a movement and then annexing this part of the United States into a separate white supremacist country.

I'm not antiviolent. It's something I learned from organizing against nazis, that I'm not dedicated to nonviolence. My hat goes off to these young antiracist skinheads. I mean, they were in there with their whole being, and that's what it takes. We had each other's backs with love and support. We cared for each other. I brought in the Jewish community. The Jewish community had me speak to the Jewish Federation, which is the largest mainstream Jewish community in the United States. They had me speak about the Coalition for Human Dignity and the work we did. People started stepping up from all walks of life. We did these great benefits. One of them we did was a jazz breakfast, a pancake breakfast. Hundreds of people came. This became very important to the people in Portland. It was the first time in my life that I was with a group of people, and we were standing for caring for each other, for caring about what happened to other people. And that may seem odd, but in my generation, because I'm seventy, we didn't talk about the Holocaust. We didn't talk, none of it. So it was a real turning point for me to understand that I could be this caring, dedicated person that I am and have kindred people doing it with me, to teach me, to guide me. I just loved that moment.

Abby Layton with her therapy dog Simchah, 1999. Courtesy of Abby Layton.

STEVE WASSERSTROM
Coalition for Human Dignity

I was fairly new to town, had a new job, I had some small kids when a lot of this activity blew up and I found myself in the middle of it. I was, at the time, the only full-time, permanent Jewish Studies professor in the state of Oregon. My activities in the community at large were partly Jewish-connected and partly just connected to politics. But fairly quickly I met people who were activists and were drawn into the activist scene as things heated. I came in 1987. Those years from the mid-'80s to the mid-'90s were especially intense.

There were a number of very high-profile acts of violence, both regionally and nationally, including Waco and Ruby Ridge and Timothy McVeigh and the bombing of the Federal Building. There were a plethora of different kinds of groups, hardcore terroristic groups like the Order, who led a reign of terror in the early 1980s. They did bank robberies, murders, and a variety of things. They were a hardcore, neo-pagan terror cell. They also call themselves the Silent Brothers, in German. They eventually murdered the Colorado talk show host Alan Berg. The movie and play *Talk Radio* dramatizes that, his story, and it's worth seeing. We had the murder of Mulugeta Seraw. There was the militia movement. And then you had religiously tinged groups, like Christian Identity;[8] these were a little harder to describe what their worldview was. It was deeply anti-Semitic and anti-Black, and they had a whole scenario which goes back to the garden of Eden. There were neo-pagan groups. And then there's the KKK and there were international intruders, like David Irving from London. In 1992, Bo Gritz ran for president on the Populist Party ticket. So there was a growing sense of organized disruption. There was a lot of agitation that included things that were indirectly related, but that added to a sense of anxiety about the world, like the Rodney King riots in April and May of 1992 in LA. These things all sort of fed into each other.

A number of local violent activities [were perpetrated], including in-the-street skinhead intimidation, which got to be quite a problem in the late '80s and culminated in the kicking to death of Mulugeta Seraw, here in Southeast Portland. The murder catalyzed a number of us to start looking more seriously [into the murderers' connections], and that led to Tom Metzger, who was the guy who was running White Aryan Resistance, WAR, out of California. Metzger was successfully prosecuted, and so that continued the high-profile state of affairs. And there's a wonderful book about the event called *A Hundred Little Hitlers* by local writer Elinor Langer.

We're still unpacking the complexity because there was a confluence of kinds of movements targeting the Pacific Northwest more generally, and Portland specifically. Portland, of course, is the whitest large city in North America. It has a long background with, originally, ex-Confederates moving here after the Civil War, and then a serious problem with the KKK in the first part of this century. Housing issues, discrimination of all kinds exist here. So, these folks—targets of our interest—knew and saw Portland as a special kind of opportunity.

There's been a fair amount of press focused on two Portlands: Portlandia on the one hand, and the Proud Boys on the other. That split was particularly stark in the '90s because there was an influx of folks. Housing was still a lot cheaper than other parts of the country. So Portland was this growing green and diverse place with liberal representation on the one hand, and then you had this activity on the other. They were two separate worlds. That remains true today. Unless the group chooses to go out and have a rally down by the river, you might never know that they're out there. There was implicit segregation to the way people lived, where they didn't see each other.

Networking at that time was very different. They were still publicizing by printing their own newspapers or putting pamphlets under windshield wipers on cars, and stuff like that. The digital revolution meant that all [right-wing] folks could suddenly have reach that was national, international, instantaneous, more or less overnight in a very short period of time. In the early '90s and mid-'90s, they suddenly had communications that were incalculably more powerful than they had before. And when that happened, these groups became more and more internationalized.

Our local groups denied their connections to European movements, and other movements, and other parts of the world, but they were definitely communicating. Incidentally, all of that fell off after 9/11 because they passed the Patriot Act, which was very repressive and part of this new surveillance state. So a lot of these groups returned to where they had been before the '90s, which was underground until the last few years, when everybody's come back to the surface.

There is a variety, a range of so-called white power, white supremacy, ethno-nationalist groups. Ethno-nationalism is a term that has become more popular in Europe, and some academics use it. Folks use "fascist" less frequently than they used to, but it somewhat replaces the kind of dynamics that we see in historical fascism and ultra-nationalism based on ethnic identity. These groups had in common not just hate, but violence.

As these kinds of activities started to happen, I felt a little more responsibility. And I got hooked up with a few people who were starting to do this work. Somebody had to do this kind of work. Everything was accelerating at the time, and converging, and became more and more complex. There was more and more need for citizen activists to do this kind of work or to fill the gaps that the authorities were not. There was a feeling that our community was targeted and therefore threatened, and so we felt called upon to do what we could to draw attention to it and shed some light on most of these folks who are otherwise acting surreptitiously. There's a lot more work to be done.

STEVEN GARDINER
Coalition for Human Dignity

I'm a cultural anthropologist by training. These days, I work for Political Research Associates, based in Boston, as an assistant research director, working on issues of racial and immigrant justice.

The Coalition was founded in the immediate aftermath of the murder of Mulugeta Seraw, an Ethiopian student in Portland, by neonazi skinheads. A large number of groups in the racial and social justice space came together, along with people from the city, and had a march, held a number of meetings to try to figure out what to do about the fact that Portland seemed as if it were being invaded by skinheads, by neonazi boneheads. They were in the music scene. They were intimidating people. They were committing bias crimes. And then there was a murder. So what should we do?

In the original incarnation of the Coalition, there were folks, of course, from the religious community, particularly from the Metropolitan Community Churches. There were people from the Jewish community. There were people from the Black community, from the Urban League.

Abdi Hassan at a rally in front of City Hall following the murder of Mulugeta Seraw, 1988. Photo by Doug Beghtel, courtesy of *The Oregonian*.

There were people from Portland State, people who came out of Abdi Hassan's classes. Abdi Hassan was another immigrant professor, from Somaliland. He's now back there and has worked as one of the ministers of state in Somaliland. I haven't talked to him recently, so I don't know if he still is, but he was one of the founders.

So it was a really broad coalition, including folks from the mayor's office and the Metropolitan Human Rights Commission. But it was more of an uneasy alliance, if you want to think of it that way, because you had folks all the way from city government and very mainstream institutions, to some people who were pretty radical in their politics. The original Coalition, it's important to keep in mind, was kind of a one-off in the aftermath of the Seraw murder. And then after that, a core group of people stayed together and retained the name "Coalition," even though it became sort of a standalone organization that mostly worked through forming strategic partnerships with people in the Black community, the Jewish community, immigrant community, LGBTQ spaces, and so on, to try to bring folks together to recognize that they were fighting a common battle, whether it was against the neonazi skinheads or against the Oregon Citizens Alliance. Even though we were always clear, these weren't the same enemies, but they were the same kinds of threats to people's dignity and life, to the basic tenets of democracy.

I was a student at Lewis & Clark College. I'm a military veteran.

I got out of the army and almost immediately started doing anti-imperialist, antimilitarism, and peace work, particularly Central American solidarity work through student groups, supporting the Sandinistas and supporting more democratic systems in El Salvador, as well as anti-apartheid stuff. The same folks who were involved in helping to found the Coalition for Human Dignity—Jonathan Mozzochi, Scot Nakagawa, and others—were students there as well, and that's where I met them. And we'd been involved in activist things for several years already. At that point, I went off to New York to start a PhD in cultural anthropology, and basically ran out of money and came back. I came on in about 1990. They asked me, "Well, would you like to start working with us?" Which I did as a researcher at first, then as a writer, editor. I went from doing it in, I don't know, three-quarters of time, basically as a volunteer writer and editor and researcher, to living fight-the-right antifascism all the time, living in a really, kind of, oddly intimate relationship with the far-right world, who would routinely call me up and threaten my life. I did a lot of field work inside of neonazi organizations—not the skinhead type, but more Christian Identity, Christian Patriot sorts of groups—and then eventually became the research director and executive director at times when there was no one else to do it.

That was the kind of organization we were in. It was a seat-of-the-pants kind of organization. There were probably three or four of us, maybe five, who were constantly trying to do things. But then there were a whole bunch on the second tier, mostly volunteers, some of them who were board members and very close to us. Others were part of community organizations that became affiliates of ours, or close associates, anyway. So people over in eastern Washington who were looking at anti-Indian activity. And people who would go to events for us, people who had clean identities. This was a pre-Internet time, so if you had a PO box, and you're not an author or something like that, people could be pretty anonymous going to meetings and finding out what is going on directly from nazis, or from fascists, or from Christian Patriots. There were probably another twenty to thirty people who were closely involved with us doing that from time to time, plus a whole bunch of people in community organizations.

Pages 74-75: Counterprotest to a white nationalist demonstration in front of City Hall, May 4, 1991. Photo by Dean Guernsey.

CECIL PRESCOD
Coalition for Human Dignity

I was active with the Coalition for Human Dignity in the late '80s and early '90s. At that time, I was serving as pastor of a local church. It was a small African American church in Northeast Portland around the time that a lot of incidents of attacks and the rise of neonazi type groups were happening, and culminating, for me, at least, in terms of my awakening, was the murder of Mulugeta Seraw. I felt the need to do something more than wondering what's happening here in Portland. I think I saw some write-up about the Coalition for Human Dignity, and they were having a meeting at that time at another church. And I started attending meetings for the Coalition.

People had been gathering for some time before I became involved, as I recall—people gathering, some as representatives of organizations, a lot just individuals, you know, coming together for meeting and for information. And by that time, there were some individuals who were well familiar with the scene and the anti-Nazi organizing and youth organizing around those issues. And then they had people like myself who were more established, from being from a church in the community. So it was a rather eclectic mixture of people, some longtime activists, anti-war activists, peace activists, people who'd been active in movements, or for Black Power, so to a wide variety of people involved, in terms of the Coalition itself, in meetings.

M. TRELOR
Coalition for Human Dignity

I was an organizer with the Coalition for Human Dignity here in Portland from roughly 1989 to 1994. The political situation in Portland at the time was, if I may use this word, hegemonic—Democratic control of City Hall and, in a large sense, control of the state government. So there was this whole liberal, "everybody's cool" atmosphere. That had no appeal for me. I came out here to raise my kid. I was asked by a couple of members of what became the Coalition for Human Dignity to help them deal with what they saw as a rising neo-fascist skinhead subculture.

I'd had some experience in Chicago dealing with the neo-fascists, because they had started to pull together. The new neo-fascists allied—in Chicago—when a group that was composed of the Illinois Klan, the Illinois nazis, and a group called Romantic Violence, which was a young neo-fascist skinhead formation, came together. I was part of a coalition in Chicago that fought them for a couple of years and successfully, I believe, lessened their political impact. The John Brown Anti-Klan Committee

---

Communities Against Hate (Eugene, Oregon) flyer from 1992. Courtesy of the Rural Organizing Project.

No one is free

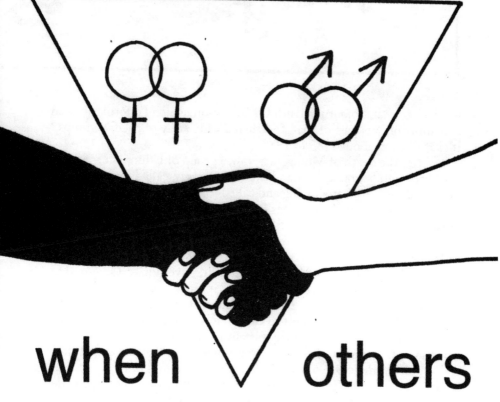

when   others

are oppressed

Please put this up in your window to show support for the lesbian,
gay, and bisexual community.

distributed by Communities Against Hate

was part of that, Sojourner Truth Organization, which I'd formerly been a member of, was part of that, and then a wide array of pacifist groups.[9] It existed from about 1985 to 1988.

After the death of Mulugeta Seraw, a group of Ethiopian students, mainly centered around Portland State University, called for a rally. Africans did the initial organizing and called for the initial rally. Hundreds of people showed up. It was clear from that organizing that there was a resistance. What also happened, and I think this is important because it continued throughout the organizing, is this white guy showed up and asked to speak. So they said, "Yeah, you can go ahead and speak." It turned out that it was Neil Goldschmidt, governor of Oregon. He realized that there's a movement here and it must be co-opted. I'm sure he recognized it as a Jewish man, that these are neonazis and we have to deal with it. So I don't want to completely dismiss his concerns, but just say that from the start, there was always an active effort to take this new movement and put it back in traditional Democratic Party stuff. I ended up coming to one of the first couple of meetings of the Coalition for Human Dignity. There was already an organization and, again, already attempts to draw it into the mainstream of Portland politics. By that I mean, they were meeting in the city council chambers. There were already a number of people within the group who wanted to make this part of the normal political process within Portland but, at the same time, be antifascist. And also, there wasn't a whole lot of clarity about how to deal with the nazis. What were we going to do? The real basis of the group had not been laid down.

There were seventy-five people in that meeting and a lot of enthusiasm, but I suspect everybody has been at a meeting like that: a lot of enthusiasm, but as to, "Okay, in one month from now we'll be doing this, two months from now we'll be doing this," that wasn't there. That wasn't there at all. There were good, experienced organizers in the group. Susan Wheeler, who unfortunately passed away several years ago, had been in Portland for decades. She knew what fascist groups were. There were

Journal of the

CHD

COALITION
FOR HUMAN
DIGNITY.

P.O Box 40344
Portland, OR 97240
(503) 335-0207

Big tent organizing, graphic from *Oregon Witness: Journal of the Coalition for Human Dignity*, 1991. Courtesy of the Rural Organizing Project.

also a bunch of punk kids, a bunch of "concerned housewives," and then a sprinkling of college kids as well, who had good hearts and didn't like nazis. So that was my first meeting.

I want to speak to the political context, because I think that's important, particularly relating to now. While the boneheads were there, the Oregon Citizens Alliance were always there as well. They had first put forward Measure 8 in 1988. They put forward Measure 9 in 1992. And then Lon Mabon, who was head of that theocratic group, ran for US Senate on the Republican ticket in 1996. So they were the major force in Oregon Republican politics. And a little bit batshit crazy, let's be clear, but they almost won on all of those measures. So while they were saying, "Let's attack queer people, let's get rid of abortions," that was the political background in which the neonazis were also organizing. And there was never a direct link, but that was the train on which they operated, so that when, in 1992, Measure 9 was to ban teachers who were gay, lesbian, or in some way nonconforming, that was going on when Hattie Cohens and Brian Mock were firebombed and killed in Salem, on September 26, 1992, by neonazis.[10] So, the two existed side by side.

Understanding that, and the change in the political-economic climate in Oregon, making this transition from the timber economy to the modern economy that you see around you now, such as it is, that was throwing all of these folks who otherwise would have had a secure job as adults into a real turmoil as to, "What am I going to do when I'm grown up? Because I can't do what my dad did," creating the basis where neonazis could do some real organizing, which is still the case.

KRISTA OLSON
Coalition for Human Dignity

I was a young college student from Colorado. I was a teenager in Denver when [radio talk show host] Alan Berg was murdered by neonazis, so I was already a little bit aware of the rise of the white supremacist movement. I gradually came into contact with the work of the Coalition for Human Dignity through other organizing work I was doing. For me, I was really just learning the terrain—bringing some skills in community organizing from anti-intervention work in Central America, and from feminist organizing—but really learning more about working in solidarity with communities of color who were threatened by neonazi violence in Portland. For me, that was integrated into the punk music scene at the time—both the rise of neonazi skinheads, but also the antiracist skinheads and antiracist punk movement.

I came into social justice work from the antinuclear movement. I always came with an equity lens—looking at how the ways that we're organizing in our process creates space, or doesn't create space, and brings solidarity with those folks who are inherently more in danger and more at risk in the work that we're doing. I was involved in bringing some speakers to the Northwest to talk about the role of pacifism versus the role of more active resistance. And so I think that probably connected me with folks who were looking at how to keep communities safe in the face of rising skinhead violence.

JONATHAN MOZZOCHI
Coalition for Human Dignity

I spent 1984 through 1998 living in Portland. I came out of a very left-wing activist background. I was involved in South African anti-apartheid work. I had traveled to Central America in the mid-1980s and did solidarity work with groups against American imperialism there, against the Contra war in Nicaragua. So my perspective on Portland was colored by my involvement in the left, and the left in Portland at that time was the *Portland Alliance*, it was work around farmworker campaigns, antiracist campaigns. There was the movement to change the name of Union Avenue to MLK Boulevard, which was very controversial. In some ways, it wasn't, but there was opposition and some of that opposition was racist. My activism in the early 1980s began to take a focus on what, at that time and what I continue to believe today, to be the two pillars of the American form of fascism. Those two pillars are the Christian right and the white nationalist movement. If American fascism is ever to totally take power and move into a regime phase, it will have to go through those two movements. So that's part of what the Coalition for Human Dignity was formed to focus on, was to have a, what we called then, a research-driven approach to fighting the right.

KGW television coverage of the March for Dignity and Diversity, October 7, 1990.

I was in a group before the Coalition for Human Dignity, tracking the racist right. In the aftermath of the Seraw murder, we began to work with street-level antiracist groups, in particular Anti Racist Action and Skinheads Against Racial Prejudice. Their work was primarily organized around protecting the alternative music scene and their neighborhoods from infiltration and organizing on the part of racist skinheads, and their more professional sponsors, like Tom Metzger, and the White Aryan Resistance, Aryan Nations—outfits like that. We worked pretty close with them, originally out of an office located at 333 Southeast 3rd. It was a radical left-wing collective called the Matrix, and the earliest CHD files were compiled there. There were radical environmentalists and antigentrification activists, a pretty broad collective there. It was a home to a printing press, where radical publications were published. Our work with Anti Racist Action and Skinheads Against Racial Prejudice started out of there. There were music venues, like the Pine Street Theatre and Satyricon, that routinely became sites of conflict between antiracist and racist skinheads. From the Matrix, we worked with ARA folks to protect those scenes.

We did a program of infiltration focused on the Oregon Citizens Alliance, which was at that time building the Ballot Measure 9. Measure 9 was a statewide ballot initiative that would have banned LGBTQ rights within public employment. The Oregon Citizens Alliance in the late '80s had already successfully overturned a governor's order banning

discrimination in public employment. They had already succeeded in doing that by the time that they made this ballot measure statewide. And
you got to understand that, on the left, among many liberals and progres-
sives, the Christian right was often treated as something that was from
the past, that we had already overcome. They were just dismissed as an
irrelevant political force. Back then we were like, "No, no, no, that's not .
. . that's not the case." These movements have always been with us. They
will always be with us. And they always must be fought. There has to be
an ongoing permanent effort to fight them. So with the Oregon Citizens
Alliance, which was becoming more politically powerful, we managed to
secure their whole donor lists, internal memos, and all kinds of information. Some of that was very, very important in getting a better picture of
who their donors were, what their social class backgrounds were, and the
demographics of their donors. Also, you get a sense of the culture within the political organization when you get to read their memos. There's
nothing quite as good as being "at the breakfast table" with them. That's
a part of the work that the Coalition for Human Dignity did. It's by far
the most work that I did.

So this work was carried out by myself and a few other people.
And the late Stew Albert, who was a somewhat famous Yippie from the
'60s, who was instrumental in the Coalition for Human Dignity, he was
on our board, and he trained and he trained and helped people like me
develop these skills with intelligence gathering. He died a few years ago,
we miss him, I miss him terribly! But he was a wonderful link also to the
1960s radicalism and what was then the contemporary left.

M. TRELOR
Coalition for Human Dignity

The first thing was to establish, yes, we're going to fight on this cultural
front. Let's look at what Rock Against Racism did in England.[11] Steal
from them, you know? So the Coalition for Human Dignity organized
a Rock Against Racism show that had hundreds of people show up. Poison Idea played, Sweaty Nipples played, groups like that. The bands took
open anti-bonehead positions from the stage. One of the groups changed
their name there. They had been called Wehrmacht, which was the name
of the German army in World War II.

The second thing that the Coalition for Human Dignity did that
was different was to openly state that we were going to drive the boneheads out of Portland. That was controversial. People up to that point had
not said, "Oh, that's our task, drive them out." The third thing was to say,
"We're not gonna meet at the city council chambers anymore." We had
to go out and find a place in the community. That ended up being the
Metropolitan Community Church, which was also a stronghold of queer
organizing for that decade. So we were meeting in the basement there,

Above: The site of the Matrix, 333 SE 3rd Avenue, in 2022. Photo by Celina Flores.
Below: Flyers courtesy of Kelly Halliburton.

Friday Night Anti-Authoritarian Coffeehouse:

Every Friday night Matrix plays host to a coffeehouse for anarchists, rabid greens, direct actionists, fighting feminists, anarcho-punks, queer nation citizens, animal liberationists, situationists, republicans of the Irish sort, class warriors, earth firstlers, anti-fascists, groucho-marxists and our friends. 8 pm to 11 pm, children, animals and adults welcome.

MATRIX RESOURCE CENTER
333 SE 3 AVE., PORTLAND, OR. 97214, USA
503-238-1927

MATRIX:N.;;;SOMETHING WITHIN WHICH SOMETHING ELSE ORIGINATES OR DEVELOPS.

MATRIX RESOURCE CENTER

333 SE 3 ave. Portland, Oregon, 97214, USA
503-238-1927

Sunday Videos

Aug. 4th- To be announced. call us.
Aug. 11th. Surrealist night.
Aug. 18th Portland Demonstration videos, postponed from last month, Bush, Quayle and more!
Aug. 25th Hemp for Victory. Two videos on the many uses of hemp and why the government continues to ban marijuana.

FRIDAY NIGHT ANTI-AUTHORITARIAN COFFEEHOUSE

anarchists anonymous hosts a friday night "anti-authoritarian" coffeehouse at matrix. some coffeehouses will have presentations for discussions, others will be open, for anarchists, rabid greens, direct actionists, fighting feminists, anarcho-punks, queer nation citizens, animal liberationists, situationists, republicans of the Irish sort, class warriors, earth firstlers, anti-fascists, libertarian marxists and our friends. 8pm-11pm children, animals and adults welcome.
Aug. 2nd- Central American Poetry reading.
Aug. 9th- Video and speaker on resistance in the military during the Gulf War.
Aug. 16th- Open
Aug. 23rd- Open Mike for political songs
Aug. 30th- Open

MATRIX MEETING

Plan what goes on a Matrix at our open meeting Monday, Aug. 12th Pot-luck dinner starts at 7pm.

Earth First!

meets at Matrix, Thursday, Aug. 8th at 7:30. For more info. call 231-0207.

DIRECT ACTION!

which was a good place. It was in the inner Southeast. We could pretty much invite people from every community in Portland there without them feeling intimidated.

I have to give immediate props to a crew of people from Lewis & Clark [College]: Krista, Gillian, Scott, Jonathan, several other folks—and they can kick me in the head next time they see me if I've forgotten their names. They were the basis for the research aspect that the Coalition for Human Dignity started almost immediately, which was good. Nobody really had a real handle on: how big is this problem? So one of the first things we did was just go out and photograph and count some of the racist, neonazi graffiti that was sprouting up all over Portland. And there was a lot of it. So that was one of the first things that that group did, was just document. They continued to document stuff like that throughout. They started counting. Here's ESWP. Here are the Boot Boys. Here are the various little gangs, which had been neighborhood gangs that were making the transition to becoming organized bonehead groupings. Nobody, other than the police, had a sense of these gangs, how big they are, and what they were doing. Coalition members began counting that, and documenting that, and then documenting stuff like how many attacks were actually occurring on individuals, neighborhoods, et cetera. The Coalition started documenting that stuff and started releasing it, and that was very important because it gave us a basis with which to speak to community groupings, with which to speak to the media, and amongst ourselves, to have some sense of: this is going on. Yes, there are hundreds of these people, and to get some idea of the interplay of the various groupings which did become important a little bit later on.

ERIC WARD
Coalition for Human Dignity

My travels that eventually led me to being a board member of the Coalition for Human Dignity and a supporter started in Eugene, Oregon. In the late '80s and early '90s, I was a racial justice organizer in Eugene. We were working to advance race equity and challenging a lot of the racism that was happening institutionally. Then in 1991, there was a punk band called Fugazi that was touring around the United States and getting threats from neonazi skinheads. Fugazi was scheduled to play a show in Eugene.

The story goes, a Portland Police Department officer stopped a neonazi on the streets of Portland and in his back pocket found a flyer that was calling on racist skinheads to disrupt the show in Eugene. That information created community panic. People were threatening to shut down the show. People weren't sure if they were safe. Under pressure, the local club was forced to cancel the show. Many of us saw that as a huge loss. We were fans of Fugazi, we knew Ian MacKaye, we knew their stance

Poster design by Mike X. King, 1989. Courtesy of Kelly Halliburton.

as antiracist musicians. The idea that neonazis could just shut down our show based off a threat seemed very dangerous to us. So a bunch of us got together. And eventually, over the next year, we built what became known as Communities Against Hate. As we were touching base with national organizations at the time, including the Center for Democratic Renewal, Political Research Associates, and the American Jewish Committee, we were made aware of a group in Portland called the Coalition for Human Dignity. We were a hundred miles away in Eugene; we didn't know much of what was happening in Portland, outside, of course, the murder of Mulugeta Seraw. Many of us were part of the punk scene, so we certainly had dealt with neonazi skinheads. But we weren't aware that this organization had formed around responding to the murder of Mulugeta Seraw and responding to neonazi threats.

When we got in touch with the Coalition for Human Dignity, our entire world changed. We were in awe of this organization. We met leaders who had done both deep research and organizing against what we would come to know as the white nationalist movement. They were so open to sharing their knowledge, research they had gathered, that in many ways, Communities Against Hate was an extension of the Coalition for Human Dignity. And the Coalition for Human Dignity is where many of us, who are still grounded in the work of human rights and marginalizing the white nationalist movement, came to find one another.

Leaders like Pat McGuire, Scot Nakagawa, Jonathan Mozzochi, Steve Gardiner, and many others who were so committed to taking on racism and really believed that communities themselves could make a difference. It was empowering. They taught us that we really did have the power to shape our communities and that those could be communities that could successfully challenge organized bigotry.

In the days of the CHD, we interacted with everyone. We were less interested in fighting over tactics than aligning around values. I'm not saying there weren't debates over tactics. I'm not saying there weren't huge disagreements. What I would say is that we realized that our values were more aligned than maybe we wanted to admit. That value alignment was essential to keeping our community safe. In many ways, what the Coalition for Human Dignity played a big role in was helping us redefine—what did we mean when we said community defense? What did community defense feel like? What did it look like? This was through education, through research, through advocacy, through engaging everyone from conservative Republicans to punk rockers, who may not have agreed on anything except that overt bigotry shouldn't have space in their community. It was a very powerful alliance, and for many years that resulted in white nationalists not feeling like they had a home in Portland, and they were exactly right.

Above: Eric Ward (on right), 1989. Below: CHD informational meeting. Behind table: Jonathan Mozzochi, Elinor Langer, Jeannette Pai-Espinosa, and Scot Nakagawa. Date unknown, courtesy of Jonathan Mozzochi.

ANTI-RACIST
SKINHEADS
LET'S KICK SOME ASS !

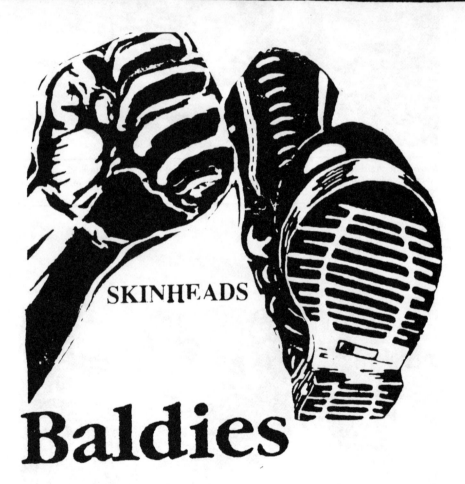

SKINHEADS

Baldies

Baldies in care of Rabl
P.o Box 10854
MINNEAPOLIS, MN
55458

Chapter 4

From Uptown to the World
The Minneapolis Baldies, the Syndicate, and Anti Racist Action

Almost every time we interviewed a Portland SHARP or ARA veteran, and even some CHD members, we heard stories of the Minneapolis Baldies and their influence and support in organizing against racist skinhead activity in the Pacific Northwest. So who were the Baldies?

In the mid-'80s, in Minneapolis, a small street crew was born out of a group of close friends. These youth adopted a skinhead identity and took on their new subculture seriously and conscientiously. They learned of the origins of the subculture—that skinheads had their roots in the styles and music of young Jamaican emigrants to England in the 1960s, who intermingled there with white working-class youth. These Minneapolis youngsters were also a mixture of different ethnic and racial backgrounds and therefore felt kinship in their representation of the skinhead.

In taking on the name the Baldies, the crew differentiated themselves from racist connotations associated with the term skinhead and also paid homage to the infamous multiracial Minneapolis Baldies gang that ran the streets of the Twin Cities in the '50s and '60s.

As the bonds of the group grew tighter, nazi skinheads were becoming ubiquitous in hardcore punk scenes across America—spreading like wildfire due to sensationalist media coverage and talk show

Baldies sticker, courtesy of Pan Nesbitt, date unknown.

appearances. A crew called the White Knights emerged in Minneapolis, organized by neonazi skinhead and Ku Klux Klan member Paul Hollis.

Immediately, the Baldies began confronting the White Knights, first through diplomacy, suggesting that they renounce their commitment to racism and violence. They warned those who refused to stray from their overtly racist beliefs that the Baldies would deliver violence. A street war erupted; bloody conflict between the two groups was ongoing.

While some consider the Baldies a gang, many Baldies were opposed to this label. They evolved from a group of friends into a fighting force committed to direct action as a form of community defense against organized racists, white supremacists, and neonazi boneheads. The Minneapolis Gang Task Force targeted the Baldies through surveillance, harassment, arrests, and brutality.

The Baldies belonged to a vibrant national hardcore scene and DIY networks of the '80s and '90s. Through these channels, they reached out to like-minded comrades in Midwestern cities who faced similar infestations of racist skinheads. Eventually, the Baldies, along with these other punks and antiracist skinheads, created a network of mutual aid and solidarity that reached all the way to Portland.

Mutual aid and solidarity—and the support of Skinheads Against Racial Prejudice in Portland and groups like Skinheads of Chicago—formed connections across the country.

Ultimately, the bond between Portland skinheads and the Baldies would become so strong that Portland alone became the only other city in the US to have its own chapter of the Baldies.

MARTY
Skinhead of Chicago (SHOC)

Here in America, gang culture is synonymous with unspeakable violence, drive-bys; no emphasis is really put on the fact that kids have always formed gangs or cliques or clubs. There's a whole social tradition of working-class kids coming together to protect the neighborhood, to help each other. You know, if you're an orphan, your mom ain't there, your dad's in jail, or whatever.

It's always been this mutual support system that working-class street kids extended to each other. I think we get tarnished with a negative brush, considering that American gang culture is especially notorious in the public imagination, you know, like the Crips and the Bloods and the Gangster Disciples. You hear all the horror stories. It's kind of interesting. I got this book on the early Chicago Vice Lords, on the West Side of Chicago, right? They started out in a political formation with the social impetus that they created to clean up the neighborhood. They had employment centers; they had little dance clubs for the kids. Motivated by real intentions to clean up the neighborhood, to be an asset to the community and not this stereotypical sort of a kid that's a loser.

Marty, 1987.

That's how America works. America has a history of shitting on its working class. America has never had this real appreciation for working-class street kids, especially those at the bottom, if you Black or Latino. I think it's an exception a lot of times for the white working-class kids, Irish kids, and how they came up and had gangs and got involved in bootlegging and got involved in gambling and took control of the neighborhood. They were able to parlay that little street power influence into legitimate political formations. That's how the Kennedys got started. I think that's how the Daleys, you know, in Chicago, the Daley political dynasty, got started.

I've always been attracted to history, and the experiences of the Chicago Black working class. I'm not some kid that's always been striving for an identity. I mean, I know who I am, I know where my ancestors are from. I understand the socio-political development of Chicago. I root myself and ground myself in that.

I was always a kid who liked rock and roll, coming out of high school. I was working a work study at the University of Illinois at the time. Some white kids were in there, and I had my head shaved since forever. And they were like, "Man, you look like one of those skinheads from the North Side, you should go to this punk rock show with us." At that point, I was basically exposed to heavy metal and hard rock and stuff you hear on the radio. I had no conception of punk rock as a subculture. So I decided to go to this concert with these kids. Suicidal Tendencies, I think, was headlining, a West Coast skate punk band. I saw the different energy and all these different young people. You had metalheads, you had skinheads, you had goth kids, you had punk rock kids. It's a really diverse crowd. I just immediately was drawn to it.

I made it my business to kind of come around more. I was like, twenty, twenty-one at the time, 1985–6. I started to identify with some of the kids I met. We'd come up to Belmont Avenue, hang out and meet kids. I was corny, you know, had little combat boots, no sense of skinhead fashion. I was new to the game. As Black men in particular, right, we've

Stencil graffiti. Photo from *Minnesota Experience: The Baldies*, Twin Cities PBS, date unknown.

always had to sort of define ourselves. Self-determination has been one of our key points in our history in this country—define ourselves before somebody defines yourself for you. It's important as Black men that we've been able to articulate our experiences in this country, through the lens of real working-class struggle, and I think that's how it's gone for me. But the biggest challenge I find is trying to reconcile who we are as Black men in a largely white, European subcode.

When I deconstruct that in my mind and what that really means, you know, I look at British working-class youth culture. They basically identified with the Jamaican working class, who also were identified with the American blues artists, soul R & B artists, whatever, of the late '50s, early '60s, right. So everything kind of points back here. American working-class kids are the origin of music, jazz, blues, hip-hop, R & B, gospel. We are rooted in authentic cultural expression, and that animates and expresses itself in the gangs and the cliques in the clubs and in the youth organizations that influenced the Jamaican kids, the rude boys that influenced the British mods, you know what I mean? The Beatles, Rolling Stones, and all those white rock stars, they love Black R & B American blues artists. So I think it all kind of points back here. We are the essence.

Mic Crenshaw in Minneapolis, 1988. Photo by Rhonda Schafer.

MIC CRENSHAW
Minneapolis Baldies

By the time I got to Minneapolis, I didn't really fit in, and I was tired of always going to new schools and trying to find new friends. That's when the hardcore punk scene started to appeal to me, because I started meeting people from that scene and I was like, "Well, these guys aren't trying to fit in." The music we were listening to spoke to me, 'cause it was hard and it had a lot of energy, and it had a message. My group of friends and I were straight edge, skateboarding together. It was me, this brother Jason Nevilles, who's a Native American kid, and a couple working-class white kids. There were about seven of us at first.

Early in the Baldies, our days of consolidating our image, look, and style, we discovered a book called *Skinhead* by Nick Knight. It was a history of the skinhead subculture starting in the late '60s in England, complete with pictures and information on ska and Oi, the two musical genres that defined a soundtrack for the skinhead lifestyles. It also talked about various stages of social and political development, as well as the wardrobe and uniform associated with the subculture. Many of us would mix our skinhead style with elements of hip-hop and gang culture—hoodies, Adidas Sambas, baggier khakis, flannel shirts—and then the skinhead style was bomber jackets, suspenders, buttoned-down oxfords, Fred Perry polo shirts, jeans, army fatigues, Doc Marten boots, creepers, brogues.

EDUCATION is the best way!!!
DIRECT ACTION is the only other alternative!!!

The Baldies' ethos illustrated. Graphic by Jason Nevilles, 1989.

Rude boys—which were basically Jamaican street cats that were cool—they were hip, they were with it, they had the style, and they were where it was when it was happening. Rude boys wore porkpie hats and fitted shirts, a look influenced by Black soul and R & B singers from the United States. When I first became a skinhead, I didn't realize that the first skinheads were Black rude boys. I almost felt like a metaphysical, cosmic, spiritual thing: I discovered this and I was drawn to it, but I didn't realize that it was my people who also brought it.

Around the time of our founding, national news stories and talk show segments began to bring publicity to the rise of neonazi skinheads. There were no popular media stories at that time of the real roots of the skinhead subculture. The news shows like *Sally Jessy Raphael* and *Donahue*—they started giving a platform to white power boneheads. These skinheads were often on talk shows with a panel of other guests, including members of the Ku Klux Klan, American Nazi Party, White Aryan Resistance, and American Front. The public image of skinheads was that we were all racist.

We started to see these kids who were just copying what they saw on TV, and we're like, "That shit is wack!" They started showing up where we were hanging out and coming to shows. We got wind that some of these guys were white power, so we confronted them. My friends and

I, we'd step to them and be like, "Hey, man, are you guys white power?" and they were like, "Yeah, man, we're the White Knights," and we're like, "Well, you know, that's not gonna fly around here. We're going to give you a chance to denounce that shit, and the next time we see you, if you're still claiming white power, then there's going to be a problem."

The White Knights had been organized by a racist skinhead named Paul Hollis. One of my early memories of Paul was him having a conversation with me and trying to explain that he totally supported Black pride but he didn't support Black power. He ultimately became the leader of the White Knights, and he went on the news to confirm not only that he was the leader of the White Knights, but that he was a lead organizer in the local chapter of the Ku Klux Klan.

And from that moment, he was our enemy.

Once the Baldies became aware of the White Knights and their affiliation with the Klan, confronting them became a priority. The Baldies were now on a mission. We were driven. Our main purpose was to confront, fight, and ultimately banish the White Knights from our scene.

We would see them and fuck them up, and sometimes they would see us and we'd be outnumbered and they'd jump us. We were carrying weapons everywhere. Shows were often violent. We started to build allegiances with people outside our immediate clique. We started to reach out to some of the gangs—the Black, Latino gangs, people in the Native American community, and their street organizations. In addition to that, we built alliances with other punks, skaters, radical feminists, and anarchists. An anarchist bookstore was the center for our organizing and meetings and cultural events.

Eventually, we reached out to people in other cities who were having the same problem. Madison, Milwaukee, Chicago—strong allies in Chicago—Lawrence, Kansas, a lot of cities in the Midwest. And I think it was in about '87 or '88, we had our first meeting, over a hundred antiracist skinheads and antifascist activists from different cities. We had a meeting at the [Walker] Uptown library in South Minneapolis. We formed what we called the Syndicate.

That meeting was one of the first times that as a young adult, I got up. People were like, "You should get up and say a speech," and then I got up to say the speech, and I looked at the room, and I was like, "Aw, shit." I felt tears coming. It was a very powerful, humbling thing to know that us as children had been able to pull that off.

You know, to think about it today, it does sound weird to talk about how central the library was a hangout for teenage skinheads. I don't know who the adults were that worked there, but they must have been supportive and sympathetic to our cause. They let us use the conference rooms for free. They let us use their biggest conference room for that first Syndicate meeting, and they didn't interfere. You know, I don't think I saw one adult. There must have been a point of contact in our crew, I think it was Kieran. And they just would let us do what we wanted. So we were always respectful. We never put graffiti on the library. Matter of fact, when people—when other people would, we would get upset because we felt like they were gonna damage our relationship.

The Syndicate was basically this network of antiracist skinhead crews and antifascist crews that were ready to hunt down nazis in their cities because we understood that in order to confront violent racists, we couldn't just do it ideologically with words and language. We were doing all those things, but we had to be willing to find them where they were and fight them. That was the beginning of that culture. Little did I know at that time that, simultaneously, there was an antifascist movement in Europe that mirrored what we was up to. I didn't find that out till later.

There was some of us in the punk scene who traveled a lot, or people who were in bands that were on tour, and they would meet people from different scenes and they would hear about what was happening in those cities and they'd get people's contacts. You go in your kitchen and you pick up your clunky telephone, dial the number, and you call somebody. Or you'd go to a phone booth. There were even chain letters.

There was a punk zine called *Maximum Rocknroll*, there was another one called *Your Flesh*, and in these zines, these black-and-white paper rags, there would be scene reports from different cities. Shinder's Books had these zines and you'd buy them and there would be reports from the West Coast, the Southwest, the East Coast, and you started to see all these people are fuckin' having nazi problems everywhere right now. You reach out to people in those scenes. We built the network that way, and that network came all the way out to Portland.

The emerging network of antifascist fighters needed a name. The Baldies decided to call this broader network Anti Racist Action, or ARA. We believed that we had to confront organized racial hate with direct action, not just words and ideas. In 1989 and 1990, a number of Minneapolis Baldies became aware of the white power skinhead problem that was happening in Portland. They traveled to Portland as a group and provided material support for Portland's antiracist skinheads.

LORRAINE
Minneapolis Baldies and ARA

I'd started running away to Uptown [Minneapolis] when I was eleven. I would run away from home, go hang out up there. I was bouncing around for a couple years, in and out of the Bridge [a homeless youth shelter]. In junior high, I met Megan Cook, so we started tagging along with her big sister, Colleen, and checking out what was going on. Megan Cook brought me to Loring-Nicollet [alternative public school] to visit. I ended up going there. I thought it was cool to meet actual smart kids who knew what was going on, going to school with some of the faces I'd seen Uptown.

Lorraine, 1987.

I shaved my head in ninth grade. I remember driving home with Mic, with me and Stacy in the car one night. We went up to Paul Hollis's car. We'd parked at Ember's. And somehow we got a brick. I'm like, "Where are you going, Mic?" He's like, "I think I'll throw a brick through Paul Hollis's window." And I was like, "Well, why?" and he was like, "Why not?" I remember sitting in the back seat going, "Yeah! Why not!?!" [Laughter.]

I had this attitude like, "Educate first and then ass-kick second." So then I remember trying to do that. I remember being in a truck talking to some supposed nazi who was Yugoslavian. He wanted to smoke a joint with me, and I was trying to ask him, like, "Why are you hanging out with Paul Hollis? Don't you know?"

I remember after that summer I was into direct action, after our big ARA meeting in the library. We had a phone list and someone gave the phone list away and then someone bombed Brandon's house. The hearsay was that this girl gave the list away, a blonde punk girl named Linda. And this is the hard part: I kicked her ass out in the parking lot. It was the first time I'd ever hurt someone like that. I blacked out while I was doing it. I vaguely remember it. Mic told me to stop: "That's enough, Lorraine!" That's when I stopped. That has haunted me ever since. I felt so bad. That was all based on hearsay. Basically every rage moment in my life came out on the poor girl.

Afterward, a friend was like, "Linda joined the army and she's gonna kill your ass." And then I would be scared, I'd be like, "Shit! I'm gonna get killed by Linda!" I don't know if I need to go on *Oprah* and apologize to Linda. That bugs me that I did that to her.

When I started hanging out with Spencer Sim, I wanted to be more down and be part of the group. I liked that all the kids—we came from a similar background, we talked about being working-class, having these different ideas about society. I liked the music and the excitement of concerts and hanging out doing things as a group. Mine was not the super individual choice; it was definitely fueled by this thing with Spencer. But I didn't like that it had this, like, relationship connotation—like I was doing it because of this boyfriend. That bugs me in hindsight. But at the same time, I wanted to prove my own toughness, my own whatever.

NISSA
Minneapolis Baldies

I'm from Minneapolis, Minnesota. I started at South High in 1984. I met people hanging out Uptown and at school. The scene was a punk rock—a hardcore punk scene. There were subsections, there were skaters, you know, there were kids who looked like British punks. There were goth kids, and there were skinheads. I was also really interested in politics, and this was during the Contra wars and there was a lot going on with Take Back the Night and feminism and antipoverty work in the Twin Cities.[12] So at first I was more drawn to the politics. Like at the May Day bookstore and the Backroom Anarchist bookstore. I was drawn to the scene and activism in general.

When we were in the Baldies, skinhead culture and the music and the scene and the history of it wasn't as deeply important to me as it was to everybody else. To me, it was like: I need to put my money where my mouth is. If I was going to be a part of this movement and fight White Knights, I really thought it was important to shave my head and be a part of that and stand for what I believed in. I thought it was really important to seize that imagery.

One of the really important things we were doing was blurring that line and seizing that look back, because that look could be so intimidating. They were trying to turn it into something really scary, when really the origins were a musical culture, and looking fine, and listening to cool music, and being sharp, and standing for something. I didn't want them to have that.

Lorraine was the one to shave my head, and I remember having to work up to it for, like, weeks and weeks and weeks! I thought it was just so important that I participated in that and was brave enough to do that. I just felt like I really had to do it.

What I look back and love the most about those times is that it wasn't just, "Okay, we're Baldies. Now we're all going to listen to a certain band and we're all going to go to certain parties." We all kept talking and

Minneapolis ARA banner, date unknown, photographer unknown.

kept developing as people, and everyone was open to learning. It was community building. It was community building in a really fundamental sense, because we weren't homogenous at all, politically. We weren't homogenous musically. We weren't homogenous in the way we dressed, necessarily. We were listening to all kinds of music and going to all different kinds of shows. We were developing as people and developing as a community and developing as individuals.

You know, there were anarchists, there were socialists, there were just liberals, there probably were some Republicans. The men were willing to listen to the women about gender-based discrimination and sexual orientation discrimination—that became an important topic. There were arguments, but it still was about growth and community building, that 100 percent commitment, and knowing that growth takes time. That's stayed with me throughout my life, and that influences me today, too.

I think community defense can never be equated with terrorism. Defending civil rights, and defending people's right to exist, can never be equated with terrorism. Even if that defense needs to be physical. What we were doing—we weren't exerting power.

I recall this, clearly, there was always an opportunity given, like, "Cut it out. Join us, learn the true history. White supremacy is a lie—you're being tricked by it." The men, I remember, would actually try to talk to those guys sometimes, especially individuals. But if they were having a concert or trying to go jump people in the name of white supremacy, they had to be stopped.

We did a great service to the Twin Cities, that we stopped them. This would be a different city— Minneapolis, or the whole metro area, would be a radically different place if we hadn't stopped them. That could never be considered terrorism; that could only be considered defense, support of the community.

MARTIN SPROUSE
Maximum Rocknroll

My connection to this thing is through the punk rock scene, the early '80s punk rock scene. I grew up in Southern California. I was doing a fanzine with my friends Pat Weakland and Jason Trager called *Leading Edge*. We started that in 1982, '83, and did it until about 1985. Then in 1985, I moved to the Bay Area to join the staff at *Maximum Rocknroll*.

So pre-Internet, *Maximum Rocknroll* was one of the largest international punk fanzines. It was big, thick, and shitty, on newsprint. The idea was to keep it as inexpensive as possible and get it around as much as possible. We put a huge focus on communication—printing addresses, scene reports, letters, contacts, fanzine reviews, record reviews, record label reviews. There was always a lot of pen-pal writing and phone calls going on.

The scene reports would consist mainly of talking about bands, if they had a demo tape out or a record out. It always included addresses and talked about local fanzines or anybody else that were doing good— record stores, promoters. It could be from a big city like Chicago or a small town where there's only one or two bands. So we get—I don't know—a couple of them every day? And every issue would have ten to fifteen scene reports from all over the world, not just the United States.

Kieran [from the Minneapolis Baldies and ARA] came out to San Francisco in 1989 for the Without Borders Conference, a loosely based international anarchist gathering. Kieran gave a workshop there about Anti Racist Action and militant antiracism. It just was so different from all the other workshops. Coming from the punk scene, we've always confronted racist skinheads, but it's really interesting to find skinheads beating the shit out of racist skinheads. "This is the way we dealt with it. We think this works."

That workshop was crowded as hell, because in 1989 everyone was dealing with skinheads. There were people from all over the country. Kieran, he's a union president now for his local chapter, he had this really amazing ability to organize a meeting. He was just right there, really present. His politics were very hard, very militant, but very inclusive. He just caught my attention. I was just like, "Oh, this guy knows what the fuck he's doing."

I introduced myself, and I brought him to the *Maximum* house, and we did a long interview with him. We made it the center spread of

Kieran. Photo from *Minnesota Experience: The Baldies*, Twin Cities PBS, date unknown.

Maximum; I think this was issue 78. Kieran talks a lot about the Baldies and ARA and doing community organizing and their tactics for dealing with things and doing outreach with other cities. Kieran didn't shy away from the violence or beating the shit out of skinheads, but talked about working with the community and working with other groups and people outside the punk scene to really confront and stop these racist skinheads. It was very inspiring to people in other cities to do the same thing, and also probably start organizing other chapters in other cities.

Maximum also had a surplus of cash from ad revenue and stuff. Every end of the year, we'd give money away to different groups, different fanzines, different bands, different organizations; this could be like a hundred dollars, five hundred dollars, a thousand dollars.

Kieran reminded me of this story. He said that the second time me and him met that he had just come down from Portland with two other Baldies. They needed some money for some people in their group in Cincinnati to get out of jail. So *Maximum* gave them money and Kieran wired that money to Cincinnati.

Minneapolis Baldies (Kevin, Bob, Jay, and Jer) in front of the Walker branch of the Minneapolis Public Library, 1987. Photo by Rhonda Shafer.

Jay and Mic, 1986. Photo from *Minnesota Experience: The Baldies*, Twin Cities PBS.

JASON NEVILLES/JAY/GATOR
Minneapolis Baldies

All the best groups of friends I've ever had throughout my whole life have always been a mix of everybody. It's like Black kids, white kids, Native, Asian, whatever. All kicking it together. It's always different. If it's like all Black kids, all white kids, all Native, it's a different kind of vibe. But when it's everybody coming together, it's just like, everybody's just being a kid. I think with the Baldies, we didn't have nothing to lose. We just ran with it. It just took off. [Laughter.] I mean, I love that part of it, just it was like a natural progression of just kids being kids, and us trying to figure out what we were as people.

They're like, "ARA was the first Antifa," I was like, well . . . there's been a lot of people fighting racism and fascism for a long time before us. The Baldies started out of just a bunch of friends liking the skinhead culture. You know, the more we got into it and started understanding what it was about, it was even cooler than we thought. We just wanted to have a crew, and then it just blew up.

That's just how it was. We all know, nazis only understand and respect one thing, and that's a ass whoopin'. We used to talk to those clowns all day long, you know, it didn't change 'em. We knew that wasn't gonna change 'em, but we had to let them know, you ain't coming to our town, putting roots down, and think you're going to get a crew growing in here. So I think the violence kept a lot more of the serious ones away.

We all know they're fucking scared. They don't want to fight straight up; they want to jump people and do all their shady shit like they always do. They're not straight-up brawlers. I mean, look how many threatening letters we got. "Oh, we're gonna come kill you." I mean, dude, they had so much access to—they coulda gunned us down in a heartbeat. They used to threaten that shit all the time. They talk a lot of shit and they don't back it up.

DAVID JEFFRIES
Minneapolis Baldies

I have always been around violence, and it took me a long time to, like, understand how it's so immersed in our culture, as Americans, or living in America, or whatever you want to call yourself. If you grew up here, if you grew up in an inner city here, you've been around violence. You've been programmed.

Jay: Poverty is violence.
Hunger is violence. Being treated like shit is violence. I've always been around that. And then we perpetuate that on the people we love a lot. You know, because that's where you first learn it, unfortunately. Because that's where the system is, you know? Like, my dad taught me violence. "Don't ever let nobody do this to you. And if you do this, I'm gonna do this to you." I don't want to glorify violence at all, but I'm gonna be honest: I don't know if I got any remorse about who we ever beat up.

Jay: I know what you mean, being Black, being Native, knowing that the Klan represented racial terror. The only motherfuckers they want to be peaceful is everybody that they're afraid of. Because if you get violent towards them, then they gotta move farther away, out in the country or something. Because they don't really want that. I mean, how many nazis came up to us and squared up?
None.

Jay: None. They want to talk shit. They want to drive away and talk shit. They don't want to get caught. When they get caught, they're all like, "Uh, um, um, I didn't mean it."
I wish we would have got more of them fuckers, that's what I think.

Mic: Portland has been a hotbed for so-called Antifa organizing, demonstrations with the Proud Boys, Patriot Prayer, and lots of street fights, right?
I've seen it, and this ain't going to be PC: If it was a bunch of niggas or brown folks out there in the street doing that . . . man, they would have SWAT teams, machine guns, you know them armored vehicles with the

machine guns on top they used in Ferguson? But it's a bunch of middle-class white kids, who all kind of look the same to me. I'm not saying that the Antifa isn't righteous in their cause, you know, but it's all this white privilege spilling out. I don't even know if they realize that that's white privilege.

Mic: Some of the people are going to say that the reason they're in the streets is because they do have white privilege. That it's important for them to put their bodies on the line.

I think if you're white and you're doing that, you need to be putting in work in a different way if you really want to make some changes. You don't need to do it in the middle of the day with a bunch of ninja masks on and shit, and doing like shitty roundhouses, and all that other stuff. Do some direct action, go get them at night.

Shit, your mom and dad probably work with half of their moms and dads … get 'em! Figure it out, like work on intelligence, work on outin' 'em at work, doing those kinds of things, you know? I don't really care if nazis march down the street, because they've been doing that since we've been kids, since this country's been founded. Shit, the Klan is worse than nazis, and the Klan is part of this country, you know? They've been protected by the police, you ain't gonna stop that.

But what you can stop is at night when people are just living. If you want to do direct action then do it that way. Being out in the streets, in columns that can't brawl, you look just stupid, man. Proud—what'd you call them?

Mic: Proud Boys. Patriot Prayer.

Yeah, fuck that. Who cares? Let them motherfuckers pray. They need help. I mean, I just really don't give a fuck. What does it do for brown and Black people? Go fight against the police. That's our biggest threat. Shit, I ain't never seen a Proud Boy in North Minneapolis, right? [Laughter.] What the fuck? But I do see five-oh rolling around and beatin' the shit out of people and murdering people. Real talk. That's what we need help with, Antifa. Help get rid of the police.

JABARI
Skinhead of Chicago

Back then, people called me Corky. Born in Memphis, Tennessee, raised on the South Side of Chicago. My mother had family already in Chicago, part of the second great migration of Black folks from the South.

One day I'm just clicking around looking for different music on the radio. I find some rock music. I discovered Judas Priest, AC/DC, Iron Maiden, whoever was popping at the time, and I find myself being drawn towards heavy guitar styles. As I got into rock music, I started looking

Marty and Jabari from SHOC with unidentified person. Photo from *Minnesota Experience: The Baldies*, Twin Cities PBS, date unknown.

for more of that sound, more of that vibe, more of that feeling. I find this radio show called *Fast and Loud*. This dude named Rodney Anderson did the show. I found out years later that he was a Black kid; I didn't know that at the time. But I would just tune in, trying to get my radio in the right position to hear this music that he was playing. It was Battalion of Saints. It was DRI. It was Seven Seconds, Articles of Faith, whoever it was.

I found myself being drawn towards that style of music. I started reading about this music and about the subcultures that were associated with the music. And then I started connecting the dots. There was one kid who came from LA, a Black kid. I don't know how or why we started talking, but he started telling me about stuff that was going on in LA. He's teaching me about this stuff. I'm teaching him about our stuff. We started to exchange tapes. He starts passing me these tapes of these bands, really extreme hardcore punk rock from Los Angeles. That became my way in.

So I'm looking around. There were these kids who lived on the South Side like me. Jamie was the singer for this band called the Stitches. One of the members was white, but three-fourths of the band were Black dudes. They're on the South Side. They're a hardcore band. I knew Jamie in passing. I always thought he was into Prince because of the way he wore his hair. But I eventually learned that he was one of the progenitors of the Chicago hardcore scene. He was just a counterculture Black kid like any of us, but years later I realized how significant a person he was.

So all these pieces just started to fall into place: How do you craft a look? How do you associate it with a subculture and thereby express your identity? The music was the on-ramp, and then camaraderie, the friendship. Learning about other ways of thinking about life excited my brain. I'm like, wow, you know, there's so much more to the world than this bullshit that we experienced on the South Side of Chicago.

Mic: Who was the first Black skinhead you actually met?
Skinhead Vince Cromwell. He had been around for a minute. So there was a whole range of other, more established skins who, you know, they didn't have it all together. Vince was probably the first one that I met who claimed the name, who had an expression of the style, and who had a degree of coolness about him that I could respect. He surely influenced me.

So there was CASH (Chicago Area Skinheads), which eventually became white supremacist, but the CASH actually existed before Clark Martel came along. Clark Martel splintered CASH. All those originators of CASH decided that they were no longer in step with the right-wing stuff. So, you know, you get three choices: join them, fight them, or drop out of the scene. And those are the routes that people took.

The Bomber Boys, they're just down to brawl. Get drunk, brawl, and damage people. CASH was pretty much pushed out already by a coalition of punk rockers and leftist skinheads. When I came up with the idea of SHOC, I pulled together all my thoughts of something needing to have an ideology. We need a name that people can say, "Skinheads of Chicago." I went through a bunch of different permutations of it. And came up on SHOC. That works. That's good.

The first person I revealed the idea to was Sonny. We were hanging out with this young lady I was dating outside some club that we were trying to decide if we're going into or not. Sitting in the backseat of her car getting drunk, I said to him, "Sonny, I got this idea for this new skinhead group," and I laid it out for him. The name, the look, the idea. The mission, you know, what I was thinking.

And so this is Sonny. He grabs a marker. He's like, "You got a bigger marker, man?" Like, "Man, I'm trying to talk to you." He's like, "Nah, man, I need a marker. You got a magnum? See if she has a magnum." Everybody carried magnum markers at that time, 'cause we were all wannabe graffiti artists. So sure enough, there's a magnum in there. So he goes, "Come on." So we go over to this window, and he drops "SHOC" and puts crosshairs in the O. So while I thought he wasn't even listening to me, he's jumping on it. So I'm like, "Man, we can't use it. We can't use the crosshairs." He's like, "Why can't we?" I'm like, "Man, that's the British movement wheel." He's like, "Nah, man. This is gonna be our

IN THE SPIRIT OF MARTIN LUTHER KING DAY- Midwest Meeting of Anti-Racist Skinheads!

For the past few years white supremacists have been recruiting and training "skinheads" to fight their racist war. Because of the racist's success and media distortions of the skinhead culture and movement, we've had to pay the price. But now we are starting to fight back in the media and on the streets. The line has been clearly drawn, you are either a sucker for the racist scum or you are true to what being a skinhead is all about: the racial harmony of Ska, the working class solidarity of Oi!, and the scene unity of Hardcore.

To win the war against the Klan and their bald toys we must put away our differences and unite. On January 15th and 16th in Minneapolis we are holding the first meeting of midwest anti-racist skinheads, with the purpose of uniting all the midwest crews. The nazis have a head start, but we have the strength of our beliefs. We need to be organized and united if we are to turn back the tide of racist scum. We will share information on fighting racism in our hometowns. We will participate in some strong anti-racist actions (including any neccesary dealings with local nazi scum). There will be a concert with Minneapolis skinhead band **Blind Approach** and Omaha's **X-Factor** and a party afterwards to celebrate our beliefs and unity.

JAN 14-15 Minneapolis

As people come into town Friday night or Saturday morning they can meet people at the corner of Hennepin Av. S. and Lagoon (one block east of Lake St.) or call (612) 871-8221.

For Places to stay call and leave a mesage at (612) 228-0059 (leave name, phone#, and number of people coming). No one will be turned away. Bring sleeping bags and other provisions.

Organized by: Baldies/Anti-Racist Action (Mpls.)
Endorsed by: Brew City Skins (Milwaukee), Skins Committed Against Racism (Chicago), Anti-Racist Action (Indianapolis), Cincinatti Regiment of United Skin Heads, and skins from Des Moines IA and Omaha NE.

Keep writing to Anti-Racist Action at: PO Box 7471 Mpls. MN 55408.

thing." I'm like, "Nah, man. I don't feel good about crosshairs." He's like, "If you hate the crosshairs, then you have to break this window. Either the crosshair stays, or you break this window right now." So then we had our logo. That was the birth of SHOC.

There were people who brought ideology to the clique, and who brought muscle to the clique, and who really brought useful points of view. So, thought and muscle. Which was crucial. But it wasn't until summer of '88, when y'all came down, that we got the vocabulary that was missing. The idea of direct action.

Up to that point, we just liked to brawl. We just liked to fight in the streets. That was it. While we believed it had some philosophical underpinnings, when it came down to it, you know, we were just fighting. Fighting and drinking. But then, when y'all gave us the language of Anti Racist Action—direct action, confrontation, and principled antifascism—it's like, "Here we go!" That's what we were missing. That was the missing component. Now people are like, "Oh, shit, yeah. Direct action? Yeah. Let's go deliver some direct action!"

MALKI
Skinhead of Chicago

Jabari, we used to work together at a bookstore down on Michigan Avenue. We would be back there reading, bro. Reading books, sparring, and conversing. I was in school at Columbia College. We started talking about what we're going to do with the crew. So that's when ARA came up. That's when the Syndicate came up. And it was like: lead. So people started to look to us.

Really, what kind of jumped it off was one night we got into a fight with one of the Bomber Boys. His name was Chris. White guy, and, you know, he used to rock a swastika, and Dwayne used to stick up for him, all, "He cool," whatever, whatever. Like, "No, he not cool." He got in my face, and we got into it, man. It was an all-out brawl. I destroyed this kid.

He was one of the toughest skins in Chicago, right? And I whupped his ass in front of everybody. After that, we were like, "This shit is over. We takin' over the scene. This is it. Y'all done."

There was a point where there was a question mark about diversity for me. My parents were Panthers, and then my dad subsequently became a nationalist. So it was all about Pan-Africanism and pure Black nationalism. So he and I were at odds about my white girlfriend at the time, my white friends at the time, but I saw unity in the diversity. Our movement evolved, right? It evolved from just young kids hanging out, enjoying the musical type, punk and Oi music, hardcore . . . to actually seeking to make a difference in society, right? By joining the antifascist, antiracist movement, ARA.

However, once I started reading Garvey, and started reading Mal-

Photo from *Minnesota Experience: The Baldies*, Twin Cities PBS, date unknown.

colm, and started reading other things, I then found myself moving in a nationalist direction as well. But during my time as a skinhead, it was just pure love for my brothers.

And I began to see some things that I didn't like in the white skinheads who were antiracist, but they were not void of white privilege. They were not rejecting their white privilege. I saw that through examples of us being arrested. The Black skinhead Marty used to get arrested every weekend, bro. They would never take none of the white kids. And of course, eventually that kind of shit started clicking for me, and I was like, "Why? You know what, what's going on?" Me and Sonny, we all got arrested all the time! [Laughter.]

Mic: Me and Adam . . .
Yeah, Adam! Damn! [Laughter.] Will, Quinn . . .

Mic: Just for being in an alley, we got arrested.
Those things started to stand out to me. The white kids didn't understand it. And so eventually, that was what made me move away from the skinhead movement. I started to see even that trend within our own organization. And I was just like, "This ain't right, bro." And so with the music, with Public Enemy and Boogie Down Productions, it just started to speak to me differently, and I had to take my lead from that, and I grew dreads and started, you know, moving in a different direction.

MARTY
Skinhead of Chicago

COVID and the George Floyd murder has basically shown us what we've always known: you take a population of Americans, and you render them to the bottom, you give them shitty health care, you get them crowded living conditions. You give them a poor quality of life, minimum wage, poor access to health care, poor access to nutrition, and then when a COVID-19 type virus comes through the community, of course it's going to hit the most vulnerable people first. I mean, we've always been the most vulnerable people in America. We've always known this, though. Liberal white America is like, "Oh my god, how can this happen?" This has always been how America has treated us.

Right, so racial murder is still going on. Black folks still got dirty water. Flint, Michigan. There's hookworm in Alabama. There's certain parts of this country where we're living in third-world conditions, right? The richest nation on Earth, that your ancestors built, I think what's happening is that there's an awakening in liberal white America. "Oh my god, how could this thing still go on?" You know, there's all this shock and outrage, whatever, about phenomena, social phenomena we've known for years. So that's what we're seeing.

You look at the data about how Black life has been constructed and built in this country. You'll see that the average Black family is worth about $1,700 dollars. White fools got $117,000 average median wealth. There's a disconnect.

I think skinheads promoted this idea of a united, harmonious working-class unity between Black and white, which looks good on the face of it, right? It looks good, it makes people feel good, but I think a lot of it works to hide and mask the reality of how Black life has built this country. Skinheads don't wanna go there for a number of reasons. It tears off that sort of happy mask that Skinhead culture and punk rock culture creates for itself. It shows that despite all its sloganeering about having a united working class, a united front against racism, that Black life is still at the bottom in this country.

We need specific policies, specific ideas that reference that, which means tapping into whiteness. You got a lot of white folks coming out and making these grand sort of statements, symbolic gestures—whatever it is—to show that they are against police misconduct, but that's not what we need.

I don't need white tears. I don't need liberal whites telling me how much they hate racism. I need them to denounce whiteness. I need them to denounce the privilege, the accrued advantage, the generational wealth, the racial wealth gap, if you're going to be a real asset as a liberal

Detail from *Maximum Rocknroll* 78, November 1989. Adapted from the Agnostic Front record *Live at CBGB* (1989).

ARA

P.O. Box 7471

Minneapolis, MN 55407

white person, I need you to push for reparations for Black people in this country, not for immigrants, not for LGBT, not for persons of color, right? For the people, the ancestors who built this joint, you know what I mean?

That's when the conversation changes, because that means undoing whiteness. In my mind, whiteness is predicated on anti-Blackness. So for every white family that's able to get a home in the suburb, that's one less Black family that's able to get a home loan or whatever. Then you look at the data of how this wealth was built, how it was stolen, reappropriated, reinvested into itself at a time when America was blowing up, you know, the whole postwar boom, 1950s to the '70s. Right? White folks was on the rise as a particular demographic. At the same time, the federal government, in collaboration with civic society and average working-class whites, they locked Black folks out. So there's been a systematic building up of one group and a systematic denial of another group.

The core sort of principles of ARA were education and direct action. In a large sense. A lot of us as Americans—Black and white—we all need political education, as we're still kind of stuck in the opulence of the '80s, we still stuck in this Cosby-era sort of mentality of prosperity and projecting ourselves into some middle-class lifestyle. That basically ain't based on reality, on how we really living out here. So I think it just goes back to education. A lot of us need political education.

Who are you? Who are your ancestors? What did they contribute to the building of this country? I'm not looking to Africa. I'm not looking back to the Motherland, in terms of redress and reparations, that sort of thing. I'm looking to this country that my ancestors built to defend my citizenship here. We helped build this first-world economy, and we need to be compensated. That goes back to education, having that solid political foundation, intellectual framework where you can articulate yourself and who you are and the role your ancestors laid in building this bitch, right?

And also, direct action. I don't think nazis and fascists and right wingers need to be coddled or need to be debated. I think individuals like that only respond to violence. I don't think they have the right to speak. I mean, constitutionally you could say that they do, technically speaking, whatever, right? Actual practice, giving them the right to speak basically denies you the right as a human being, as a man, to participate in business, to own a home, to do stuff on the streets, whatever. So giving them the right to speak basically denies you the right to exist.

America has eaten its own lies, it's convinced itself that it's this benign, benevolent country—democracy and the rights of man or whatever. We know this country is built on murder, slavery, robbery, theft. And any attempt to kind of shift the conversation, right, onto the real nature of America always comes back to racism is just a few bad apples, the few misguided individuals, Klan members in the South, whatever, but no, it's baked in the cake. You know how this country operated.

Our so-called founding fathers, they all owned slaves, right? So one minute they preach, like Thomas Jefferson, democracy and liberty and all this shit, when you fucking your slave girls. You know you're holding people against they will. So I think America has a sort of a cultural schizophrenia in how it sees itself. It wants to portray itself as this benevolent sort of nation, right? But deep down, it won't confess, it won't admit to the fact that it's steeped in blood and murder.

Photo on pages 116–17: Minneapolis Baldies: Rox, Maggie, Krishna, Jay, Jon, and Mic, date unknown.

Chapter 5

The Action Part
The Portland ARA

I remember Jonathan Mozzochi was driving a van. There's all these skinheads downtown and we drove up to this gas station. I saw these dummies, like skinheads, standing there. And I was like, "Are you white pride?" And he was like, "Yeah."

I slapped him.

"Are you white pride?" "Yeah."

I slapped him.

"Are you white pride?" And I slapped him.

I slapped all three of them! Jumped back in the van and drove away. I mean, we were on such a high, like, coming into our own. That was a good feeling.

—China, Portland ARA

After the Minneapolis Baldies and other antiracists formed Anti Racist Action, with its vow of no tolerance for white nationalism, Portland was an obvious spot for a chapter to start. Like in Minneapolis—both in the '80s and in 2020—there were no meaningful, lasting attempts by any governmental bodies in Portland to address the escalating attacks by organized white racists. No committee convened to investigate or catalog hate crimes. No department implemented data based on direct reports from communities. The biggest, most visible governmental action was the incarceration and planned prosecution of the three young men who murdered Mulugeta Seraw (one of whom, at the time of this writing, continues to actively participate in Proud Boy events, proving once again that prison is not a place for rehabilitation). Nothing had, it seemed, changed.

When hate attacks did happen, it was not uncommon for the city to dismiss them as "random" rather than a targeted assault.

Group shot of Portland's first ARA meeting, SE Belmont St., 1990. Photo courtesy of Becky.

For example, on March 10, 1988, boneheads attacked Hock-Seng "Sam" Chin, a twenty-seven-year-old Chinese immigrant from Singapore, on the streets of downtown Portland in the early evening. News coverage of the attack quoted the city's refugee coordinator as saying he did not believe racist skinheads posed a threat to Portland's immigrant population.[13]

In some ways, the spring '88 attack on Chin mirrored the deadly attack on Mulugeta Seraw just nine months later. Chin had moved to Portland from Singapore to attend Portland State University in 1981, a year after Seraw. He was set on by three teenage skinheads who were revealed to be recruits of Aryan Youth Movement, a hate group out of California led by Tom Metzger's son John. But the racist youths were armed only with hands and heavy boots rather than bats, and Chin made it to his car with injuries that did not require hospitalization. It was only 8:15 p.m., and there were no racist girlfriends egging on the assault.

What if the refugee coordinator had taken the assault as a serious threat to the refugee population? What if city officials had listened to Chin's description of the hate crime and mounted an aggressive response inclusive of immigrant communities? Why are the police granted so much power in defining the character of street violence as opposed to the people experiencing the violence?

JORIN
Portland ARA

There were a lot of different people that were organizing at different times. So I don't even really have a clear recollection of who said, "Hey, let's do this. People in other parts of the country are doing this. We can do it." The first meeting Portland ARA ever had was at Karen's house on Belmont. A bunch of people showed up, some of whom became integral to organizing and some of whom may not have been that involved at all in the long term. Someone presented information about the organizing that was happening in Minneapolis and Chicago—and Europe, to some extent.

I think it might have been Karen, who had a lot to do with connecting the dots between what was happening in other places and what was happening in Portland. I think she proposed that we do something there. For many of us, the idea was initially just about the bullying that was happening at shows and let's take our scene back. There's more of us than there are of them. And the reason that they've been walking all over us is because we haven't stuck together, we haven't done anything when this is happening. Less about Mulugeta Seraw—but definitely influenced by his murder.

Another big impetus for our organizing was the Coalition for Human Dignity's Rock Against Racism show that they put on at Pine Street

1990 national SHARP/ARA convergence held in Portland during the trial of Tom Metzger. Photo courtesy of Pan Nesbitt.

Theatre. I remember talking to Jonathan Mozzochi and Scot Nakagawa a lot. They were older than me and more experienced. They were definitely folks that I looked up to. I think the Coalition for Human Dignity was an organization of people that we looked to a lot for, how do we make this a viable political movement rather than just gang fighting? We wanted to be a political movement, and one of the ways that the Portland police actively tried to work against us was painting us as nothing but a gang. Certainly that was not what we wanted to be.

I was a kid, I actually was in high school the whole time we were doing this work. I did go to school. I worked at night. After we started actively organizing, when we formed ARA, it was not safe to walk down the street by ourselves. You know, in the mid-'80s, some of the daytime talk shows that had portrayed racist skinheads on TV—a lot of people who are not involved in the punk scene saw no difference between punks and skinheads. So being by myself with spiky hair and a studded leather jacket could get me beat up by people who saw me as being a skinhead. Or I could get beat up by the boneheads for being ARA, connected with SHARP. So it meant that when I wasn't at school and work I, I always had to be on the lookout.

KELLY HALLIBURTON
Portland ARA

It was really personal for a lot of us because we were getting attacked and confronted. We started forming bands back in the late '80s that were totally outspoken politically. We didn't have any room to, like, "live and let live." You're either with us or you're against us. That was where it started and ended. That was one of the things that started setting our scene apart.

We really alienated a lot of people, because we were so outspoken. We were teenagers, our hearts were in the right place, but we were probably really, really obnoxious. And then things changed culturally. A lot of violence scared people off. Then the grunge thing hit and that just further splintered everything. So when we started out, there weren't that many people coming to our shows. We'd play to like twenty people or something like that at the Blue Gallery or the Audio Addict, places like that. The nazis weren't coming to our shows anymore, because they knew that was an unsafe environment for them. But they were still going to these bigger shows at the Starry Night and the Pine Street and some of these other venues. We were like, "How can you play in front of these people? How can you not call them out?" I think a lot of the bands were afraid to lose their crowd. Some of the other bands were physically afraid of these people. It was a weird atmosphere.

At that time, we had to deal with the Gulf War. There were these groups like the Oregon Citizens Alliance that were sponsoring all these anti-gay legislative measures. So racism and the street-level nazi skinhead racist stuff was just a part of the big picture. There's a real sense in the punk scene that if you were going to talk the talk, you had to walk the walk; you're a hypocrite if you just played music and yelled from the stage and then you went home and lived a normal life. A lot of us tried as hard as we could to be as active as possible. Various people from Deprived were really involved in the anti-apartheid movement, canvassing and stuff. Then when ARA started having their meetings, a lot of us were going and being a part of their activism, their marches and some of these other things, like playing benefits for the Coalition for Human Dignity.

Changing times—punk flyer with explicit anti-bonehead messaging, 1990. Courtesy of Kelly Halliburton.

NO FASCIST USA!

Deprived

RESIST

CORRUPTED

NAZI-SKINHEADS
GET OUT!

UNAMUSED

$5
ALL
AGES

SAT.
NOV.
10

PINE ST. THEATRE

M.N.A. PROD. 1990

CHINA
Portland ARA and SHARP affiliate

I remember we're all hanging out at this apartment on 21st Street, like twenty of us. Someone brought the news that they've killed somebody, those people that we've been fighting. And it was, like, silence. We were all like, oh my god, this is real shit. This is real. We knew that it was, but having someone killed like that . . . I mean, it was, like, a sadness, and we realized that what we'd actually been fighting was something that we totally needed to fight.

I was sixteen, I think, when we had the first Anti Racist Action and Skinheads Against Racial Prejudice meeting at a house on Belmont Street. There was the Coalition for Human Dignity, two guys and a woman, and they were like, "Do you guys want to meet?" They were joining us, even in some of our street fighting, it was a lot of showing up and fighting, like people jumping out of cars and throwing punches and stuff like that, gangland type of stuff. So we had that meeting on Belmont Street.

I want to say there was something righteous about the movement. I mean, the people that were fighting the nazis were very sincere and were moved by stuff that had happened. I think there was just a real raw need for change with youth and what was going on. It was real organic. As far as I'm concerned, it wasn't some highly organized process. It was a group of us that already knew each other and that were already together.

These people that came in reached out to us, and then because of our presence, other people would come to us, or fight us, or whatever. Even people that we'd fought, later would want to switch over. I think a lot of it came from people wanting to belong. People just wanted belonging and space to be accepted. I have kids in high school right now, so I'm learning about that. But there was an element of sincere desire for change. This was real, and this is about lifetime decisions and choosing who you're going to be, not just "we're hanging out and we're looking cool."

JASON
Portland ARA

I remember being at Pine Street, I wanna say it was '88. Some kid had gotten his braces kicked through his lips, and earlier in the night I was standing outside between bands. I was five-foot-five and 120 pounds, long hair, sitting up against the wall with a friend, and I was approached by this very large white supremacist and he wanted to recruit me, and I said, "I'm not interested." And he disappeared. Couple minutes later I look up and he's right back in front of me with his back to me. All of a sudden he swung around and sliced my face open. My friend ran off, I

Portland ARA flyer, 1990. Courtesy of Pan Nesbitt.

DESTROY RACISM **FIGHT THE** DESTROY SEXISM

POWER

WHITE POWER, WHITE SUPREMACY, RACIST GROUPS, HATE ORGANIZATIONS

ALL THESE FACTIONS OF OPPRESSION
FLY UNDER THE BANNER OF GENOCIDE.
GENOCIDE IS THE iRRADICATION OF AN
ENTIRE RACE. THEY WANT THE DEATHS OF
AFRICAN-AMERICANS, JEWS, HISPANICS, ASIANS, AND
ANY NON-WHITE RACE.

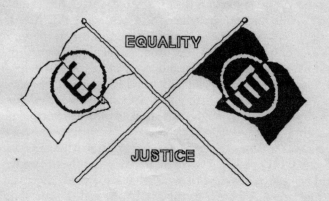

EQUALITY

JUSTICE

ANTI-RACIST ACTION

A.R.A. 1951 v. Burnside, Box 1928, Portland, OR. 97209

The Centenary Wilbur Building housed a midsized music venue from the 1970s to 2005. It was known as the Pine Street Theatre from 1980 to 1991. Photo by Celina Flores.

grabbed my skateboard, and all of a sudden I was surrounded by twelve decked-out, ready-to-go people.

I had gone to school with a woman that was in POWAR [Preservation of the White American Race]. She recognized me, came over, and got them to chill out, and she talked me down, 'cause I didn't wanna back down. She was like, "You need to stop, otherwise they're all gonna attack you and it's gonna be bad." A few other incidents happened that night. They beat up a few more people, and a few of us tried to help. A couple other strangers came to my aid and stood by my side. People I'd never met. It seemed like it was getting to that point where it's do or die. We have to figure something out, because people were just getting picked off left and right.

There was a show at the Starry Night after Mulugeta Seraw was killed. Some CHD people were there handing out flyers. A guy gave me one, and I was pretty psyched to get it. That same week, there was a show at the Pine Street. A bunch of the punks showed up, the spiky-haired crowd, and within a week we had gotten a meeting together and decided that we were gonna fight back.

At the first ARA meeting, the main topic of discussion was: are we going to try and stand our ground as a group, or are we actually going to fight. And that was a big, long argument for a long time. A lot of people did not feel comfortable with fighting or straight-up attacking them. A lot of people wanted to find alternate avenues for that. We said, "Okay, that's great. But we're going to be part of the Anti Racist Action network. The 'Action' part of that says that we had decided we're going to fight them. We're not going to wait for them to beat someone up again. We're going to attack them."

The group said, "This is the first show we're going to go to as ARA." We made a very serious presence. Everybody showed up with bats and stood out front. We got the Pine Street to agree to not let any boneheads in. And the boneheads could tell something was different when they showed up. There were a lot of people out front waiting. It wasn't just like a big line of people holding bats, people had stuff tucked away.

There was a couple scuffles, a couple of fights in the blocks around there. Mostly people pulled up in their cars and tried to jump out to attack. They would get beaten back down, and they'd jump back in their cars and tear off. That happened for three shows in a row.

And then they just quit coming. We were pretty shocked that it happened that quickly. We expected this to go on for months. I think the three shows probably happened within a month and a half. Then over the course of that year, it got more and more organized. The Minneapolis Baldies and Chicago ARA folks came out here and really helped us when we asked them to. They came out in '89 and in '90. And we decided that it wasn't enough to protect the shows, people at those shows. We wanted to push further.

We kept hearing that the boneheads would be out in Beaverton, beating people up at the mall or recruiting at the teen homeless shelter, or out in Milwaukie at Kellogg Bowl and Milwaukie Bowl, and starting shit at all these different places. So we would go to those places. And go to Beaverton, and go to Milwaukie. And actually, at this point in time, upper Hawthorne had a huge presence. There were several different apartment buildings that were heavily populated, so we would go to those places and go to Beaverton, and go to Milwaukie, go, you know, all the places where we had run into folks before.

So within that following year, they quit coming to the punk shows and they started going to metal shows. Some of the bands, one in particular, Dead Conspiracy, were very antiracist and did not like what they saw going on, and so they asked us, "Hey, would you guys come to the shows and set up a table?" We did that. Set up a table inside. It was a huge metal show. Most of the bands were with us. They agreed with us. But some of them still didn't care and had friends that were nazis, and a lot of nazis showed up to the show and came and confronted us. But a ton of people signed our mailing list and wanted to get involved. We made a lot of good connections. It really helped. This is probably '89, '90.

A Portland ARA activist on KATU's *AM Northwest*, a live-audience news show, calling out the leadership of the Oregon Citizens Alliance for their ties with nazi skinheads, 1992.

PATRICK MAZZA
Activist and journalist

I wrote for *The Skanner* from '88 to '91. This is from 1990:

> Within Portland's youth culture, a new resistance to racist skin-
> heads is growing. A multiracial network of young people known
> as Anti Racist Action. Outside apartments where neonazi skin-
> heads live, ARA can be seen demonstrating. At hardcore mu-
> sic shows where racist skins have done much of their recruiting,
> large groups from ARA now block their entry. When racists get
> in and sieg heil to the music, they are verbally confronted. When
> they still insist on preaching white power, ARA members es-
> cort them to the door. "It has never been that way before," ARA
> member Karen Keel [*sic*] said. While youth in the music scene
> have been trying to organize themselves against nazi skins since
> three skinheads murdered Ethiopian Mulugeta Seraw in No-
> vember 1988. "Only in recent months has there been a consistent
> resistance," Keel said. "It just finally took off," she commented.
> "People are so sick of nazi skins. ARA has even successfully
> blocked two performances of a band with a nazi following."
>
> But while ARA has been moving against racists, its activi-
> ties are being overshadowed by one of its ally groups, the Skin-
> heads Against Racial Prejudice, also known as the SHARPs. The
> national organization has had a local chapter here for about six
> months, but over recent months, SHARPs and racist skinheads
> have been involved in a number of fights.
>
> "Most weekends lately, relations between the two factions
> have been punctured by brawls and beer bottles tossed through
> windshields," says Loren Christensen, a Portland Police Gang
> Enforcement officer. "Just who is inciting violence is the sub-
> ject of conflicting stories," Christensen said. Spokesperson Mark
> Newman says the SHARPs are not a criminal gang. "We're an
> organization that has banded together to fight racism." You have
> Karen Keel, from ARA. Keel believes SHARP members should
> now step back from confrontation with racist skinheads and let
> other antiracists take care of the job.
>
> Jonathan Mozzochi of Coalition for Human Dignity be-
> lieves that the media has overemphasized the SHARPs com-
> ments, "They are part of a much larger antibigotry youth move-
> ment, a no-compromise antibigotry movement. So far, police
> and other forces in the city have defined their relation to that
> movement as adversarial."

They were certainly advocating an evil philosophy that had

implications of people getting hurt. I think some level of demonization is justified. You also have to understand where this whole thing comes from. People who were on the bottom end, who feel left behind, on the outside, no one cares for them. They strike out and they're easily manipulated.

It's easy for demagogue kind of people to say, "It's not your fault. Your problems come from this group. The abandonment of people, you know, of decent social benefits, decent advance in society. That's where this comes from." Obviously, we know, we have a society that's infused by racism and bigotry. So it's not hard to pull it out to the surface.

They learned you have to confront. You can't let it go by; you have to confront. You can't just let these people bully you. You have to stand up. I think that's what we learned. There has to be a community resistance, a strong community message that we just don't tolerate this kind of stuff.

JASON
Portland ARA

The ARA scenario lasted intensely for only two years. The national meeting was in Portland in '89 and in '90. And we tried to do more in '91 but it was just proving really, really difficult. It was hard to get people more involved. I think, one, because we had already made such strides that it wasn't life or death anymore. People felt like they could sit back a little bit. And they did. I did not.

I was totally willing to put myself out there. I was not an obvious target to them. So, one, I can sneak in and get pretty close before they notice. I've used that as much as I can. It's gotten me a lot of information. And it got me a lot of proximity to be able to spot folks and be like, "Okay, so this is what we're up against right now." It's been something I've always been willing and wanting to do.

I remember a couple people that got involved with them early on. And it was, "Hey, white guy that's alienated and part of this, don't you think this is cool?" It was manipulation. They play up anti-immigrant fears and unemployment. "Aren't you sick of those guys, and you should do this, and you should come out there with us."

Portland was really gritty then, and it didn't have an economic hub. A lot of people just worked in restaurants or worked construction, and that was their shit. They would go down to the homeless shelter and say, "Oh, man, you got it rough. We can help you out. We'll help you get a job." And you start hanging out. It was pretty classic.

And Portland, fuck, man, at times, it was so incredibly pale. I think I knew two Black guys in the punk scene. One of them got recruited onto the other side. I've talked to him since, and he was like, "Yeah, it was a really brief period in my life. And they took me in and were like, 'Well, you, you're half white. Do this with us.'"

ARA sticker, 1991.

JORIN
Portland ARA

We didn't see ourselves as being a local movement. We were pretty closely connected with the Baldies and ARA in Minneapolis, the Chicago branch of ARA, very closely connected with Bay Area Anti Racist Action.

It was probably 1990 that we had set up a conference to coincide with Tom Metzger's trial in Portland, where he was ultimately convicted of organizing the boneheads in Portland that led to Mulugeta Seraw's death. We were definitely hoping to get folks from these other places so we could all learn from what we were doing.

Again, we saw ourselves as being more than street fighters. So we were talking about ways that we could more broadly organize, using tactics that were, to some extent, influenced by the boneheads themselves: how could we go out and talk to young people, before they were recruited by boneheads.

I think so much of the racism in Portland, especially back then, existed without questioning. What were all of the angles that we could work to fight the spread of fascism in Portland and around the country? We had a very large contingent of Bay Area folks that came up for that, a few people from Chicago and Minneapolis, and folks from Minneapolis that had come out a few times. So we felt very connected, being part of something much larger.

One of the things at the time is, we were very upset by any suggestion that we were a gang in any way. We were a *political* movement. But some of the actions that we engaged in would be very difficult to tell the difference between that and being a gang.

A lot of it was very exhilarating at the time. Now that I look back at it, it was pretty terrifying for me. A lot of the fighting worked pretty well. I definitely think that some of the younger recruits of the boneheads saw it as a lot less appealing when they realized that there were physical consequences for associating with the fascists.

We weren't doing great data collection back then. I don't recall handing out flyers at schools against the fascists as being especially effective. I think, ultimately, the thing that was the most effective was unity. We started off being, essentially, a bunch of individuals that were letting ourselves get pushed around. And we organized together and as a larger group had a lot more strengths and also protection. The ability of the punks and those antiracist skinheads to organize with one another was pretty profound.

I imagine that the toll it took on the broader community was actually probably more on the people who were not as actively involved. There were times where it felt pretty dangerous to walk down the street. I imagined that there were some punk kids who had nothing to do with any of this that ended up getting their asses kicked because they were assumed to be part of ARA. Those of us that had really bought into it, on some level, we knew the consequences. We knew the risks we were taking. I think that changed a little bit when things got a lot more violent. When people started getting shot, I wanted nothing to do with that.

Anti-bonehead stickers, late 1980s/early 1990s. Courtesy of Pan Nesbitt.

NAZI-SKINHEADS GET OUT!

BECKY
Portland ARA

That photo [page 118] was taken at Karen's house, and she's probably the one taking the photo. I was not at that meeting, probably for a good reason. You know Eric Lamon raped me, and I wasn't going to be near that guy. I have more positive things to say about the men in this group than I do negative. But there was a reason why I wasn't there. A lot of these people were assholes.

In the summer of '89, the ARA meetings were happening at the Matrix. I remember the first ARA meeting that I went to, and it was exciting. I think hooking up with Jason, he's such a nice guy, and everybody liked him so much, that it probably gave me a little bit of protection. People probably didn't fuck with me as much.

I would also hang out with the dance crowd, like the people that would go to [gay teen dance club] the City. I did a lot of LSD and so many drugs during that brief little period. But by the time I got involved with ARA, I didn't do anything; I didn't drink at all. Jason was clean and sober, and we were really just dedicated.

We were really involved in going to a lot of different community meetings. At an ACT UP meeting, there were reports of several gay bashings that had happened downtown, and we decided that we were going to do a patrol. So we were looking for some basic self-defense. That's the way that I got involved in martial arts.

So that was our life. We trained in martial arts, and we did a lot of surveillance. I remember just hanging out, and watching houses, and getting license plate numbers, and then going down to the DMV. For a while there it was free, you could get up to five addresses at a time. We just were compiling them and trying to make connections and then putting candy into gas tanks so people couldn't get around.

All that stuff that Jason and I were compiling—we went to some house on Fremont, some punk house, and entered it into someone's computer. I have memories of us repeatedly trying to destroy that church sign on Sandy Boulevard, it was like a Lon Mabon church. I just remember doing menacing things like that.

I'm not quite sure when I stopped really identifying, but I will say that it was not my goal to be a SHARP. I remember being like, "What the fuck?" when Jason shaved his hair, and then Pan. I was probably trying to get away from that violence.

I feel like there was a period of time where we all came together, like this small group of people came together in Portland and worked across boundaries. It was punks, it was skins, it was queers.

The CHD was a lot of Lewis & Clark people, who weren't that much older than us, and I've heard people say, "Don't you feel like they used us a little bit?" No. I mean, they were straddling divides we couldn't. That was an amazing little period of time. I feel like a lot got done.

Attendants of the 1990 national SHARP/ARA convergence, at Pioneer Courthouse Square. Photo courtesy of Pan Nesbitt.

GILLIAN
Coalition for Human Dignity

In our groups, women were at the front of what was happening, with ARA particularly. I think that's crucial, in that it kept it from feeling like the way it was characterized by the police: two competing gangs. I think that kept it clear that there's a core political difference. There's the core belief system.

I don't think that always happened with SHARP. I think sometimes the SHARP responses to neonazis maybe felt a little more like macho, guy energy. I wonder if there may be a difference . . . The way that the ARA effort was focused around the music scene, which made it feel like claiming a stake in a piece of the community. This was a safe space for young people to come together. I think that the neonazis were intent on breaking that up.

There's definitely more of a feeling of ARA defending a little corner of the universe that was critical to this group of young people who had each other's backs and didn't have a whole lot else in many cases. It wasn't drawing only people who were interested in going to protests. It was drawing, also, people who wanted to create a space for young people of all races, who've really cared about each other, and about tearing down racism and sexism.

ARA flyer, 1992. Courtesy of Jon Bair.

M. TRELOR
Coalition for Human Dignity

I was never a member of the ARA. I was never a member of SHARP. I worked with them closely. The problem was that you can't organize a political grouping around "find 'em and attack 'em." But, if we retain that political attitude of "let's drive them out of Portland," then we could figure out what the next step was. Can we drive them out of the neighborhood? Can we drive them out of their apartment? Can we drive them out of their jobs? Is that ethical on our part? Is that what we want to do?

And I thought that the best thing we could do was, we could attack them politically. We could successfully say, "This person is a nazi bonehead, by virtue of, they participated in this attack, and therefore, they need to be driven out of civil society, political society, in Portland. They can't have an apartment, and they can't be part of the community."

We would go to the landlords and say, "These people are here. They're nazi boneheads. We're going to organize an action where we will show up and we will announce they live here so the neighbors all know. So the neighbors can protect themselves. And you, as an apartment owner, you notice all this new graffiti? They're the ones doing that. They're the ones putting up the swastikas."

We worked with established community groups. We would go to them and say, "The police aren't going to do this. You need to do this. We'd like you to come to these things. We're going to do it regardless."

We drove people out of their apartments. We drove people out of their communities, so that they could not hold weekend beer bashes that were one of the major ways then—and now—that they organized. That was one of the first things we did.

Then the other thing we did that was a little bit more controversial within the group, we said, "They can't hold a job. If we find out that they have a job anywhere within fifty miles, we'll show up and we'll tell their coworkers." We did that several times.

We found out where somebody was working. Again, this was because we had put out a public banner as, "We're here, we're going to drive these folks out." People started calling CHD up. We had a physical location; there was a place mail could be received. We had a phone that we would answer and call people back.

I can't stress how important that is. Call people back if you're politically organizing.

So folks would call it and say, "So-and-so is nazi and he's working here," and we'd investigate it. It was not always true. But it was true often enough that we would get together fifty, sixty people to show up at the Olive Garden and picket there. We put their name and, if possible, their photo on a flyer. We would say, "Here's what they did"—public information. We would leaflet the coworkers first. Then we would tell the manager, "We're going to be here. Everybody who eats here and works here deserves to know you got a nazi in the back room."

That drew people towards us, gave us credibility, and gave us a sense that what we were doing mattered, because it did. Every time we did it, they lost their job, and I'm proud of that. It drove them out of where they were and made their lives more difficult.

We would talk to them through secondary sources. We just put the word out. If you don't want this to happen, all you have to do is say, "I'm no longer part of this grouping." If you drop out of this grouping, we'll leave you alone. If you stay part of this grouping, we're going to make your life hell wherever we find you.

Some of them, it probably pushed them more so into the grouping, as in, "Everybody hates me, therefore I'm gonna stick with my nazi brothers." Many of them quit. There were two hundred, three hundred nazi boneheads in the area at one point, and the ones who did not go to prison drifted away. And they drifted away because their choices were either to form a new tightly knit grouping or cease to be part of this to get on with their lives.

CHINA
Portland ARA and SHARP affiliate

For probably four years, this was my life. It was a movement that I am really still committed to, actually. It was definitely a big part of my life.

At first it was just a few of us standing up against these nazis, and I think a lot of people were scared to speak up against them because they presented this force, like they were going to beat your ass if you said anything.

They were terrorizing all kinds of people; they were just a nuisance to everyone. They were harassing anybody that they felt was weaker. So we were literally in their face standing up against them, letting them know. The police certainly weren't checking them in any way. We probably all know why that is.

So when we got together and stood up as a force against them in their face, that was pretty powerful. I remember driving around and we would see nazi skinheads jump out of the car. We were like, "Are you white pride? Are you white pride?" And we would start swinging.

We were standing together and calling it out and knowing—and trusting that what we were doing was right. Back then, we stood up against something and we had no backing, just our own conviction. So I think what works is having other people stand with you and having strong voices in the community with power, and money, and clout that speak up against these alt-right forces.

Informational flyer for Community Defense Coalition protest at Olive Garden, 1991.

We are gathered together this evening to demonstrate our outrage at the hiring of a Neo-Nazi at The Olive Garden. At this time when racist, anti-Semitic, homophobic, and sexist violence is on the rise, we as members of the Portland community feel that it is time that we reclaim our neighborhoods and workplaces from Nazis. AARON HARLAND is a Neo-Nazi organizer. He has been implicated in beatings and stabbings. AARON HARLAND does not just preach white supremacist and violent homophobic ideas, he has placed these ideas into action. Hiring Neo-Nazis enables them to financially continue their programs of harassment and violence in Portland. Portland should be a a safe place for all its residents. Say No to Neo-Nazis in Portland or anywhere!

Community
Defense Coalition
P.O. Box 40344
Portland, Oregon 97211
(503) 232-2159

PROTEST OF NEO-NAZI WORK PLACE

THE EMPLOYEE WE ARE PROTESTING IS AARON HARLAND. HE IS AFFILIATED WITH YOUTH OF HITLER AND AMERICAN FRONT ORGANIZATIONS. BOTH OF THESE GROUPS HAVE BEEN INVOLVED IN SEVERAL ATTACKS IN THE PORTLAND METRO AREA, INCLUDING THE MILWAKIE AND CLACKAMAS AREAS IN WHICH OUR PROTEST IS BEING HELD. LAST YEAR THREE MEMBERS OF YOUTH OF HITLER WERE ARRESTED FOR ATTACKING A MAN OUTSIDE OF HIS WORK IN THIS AREA. THE AMERICAN FRONT HAS BEEN LINKED TO A NUMBER OF ATTACKS IN THE PORTLAND AREA, INCLUDING TWO STABBINGS DOWNTOWN. IT IS PAINFULLY OBVIOUS THAT THIS MAN, AND THE ORGANIZATIONS HE IS AN ACTIVE PART OF, ARE A DIRECT THREAT TO THE COMMUNITY AND THEIR PRESENCE MUST NOT BE TOLERATED.

It's like being a soldier. People nowadays are shocked if I ever tell them. But if I see somebody, or something kind of weird happens, I feel that tension. I'm ready. You know, and as a mother, I'm ready.

But I had to work so hard to step away. Being tone-policed and, like, action-policed, by people being self-righteous about their punk-rockness and their peace movement and all their ideologies. And me, having to put my ass on the line to defend myself and others, backing up their ideology. They were just sitting there feeling self-righteous.

I'm kind of bitter about it. I have the same spirit as I did years ago, but definitely in a different packaging. I guess I'm still kind of grappling with it, like, no, it was not a completely white thing.

I keep using that word righteous, but that's what it was! We were fighting out of what we saw in our heart, what we felt, what we'd experienced. We were reacting in a very visceral and intense, gut-reaction way to the violence that was happening.

Making the scene in the park blocks of Portland State University during the 1990 national SHARP/ARA convergence. Photo courtesy of Pan Nesbitt.

Chapter 6

Diversity of Tactics
The Big Tent of the CHD

Coalition work is not work done in your home. Coalition work has to be done in the streets. And it is some of the most dangerous work you can do. And you shouldn't look for comfort. Some people will come to a coalition and they rate the success of the coalition on whether or not they feel good when they get there. They're not looking for a coalition—they're looking for a home! They're looking for a bottle with some milk in it and a nipple, which does not happen in a coalition.

—Bernice Johnson Reagon
Coalition Politics, Turning the Century (1981)

A ll too often, people who are meant to be working together to create a better, more just society for all instead spend considerable time, energy, talent, and labor fighting each other over nuances of ideological stance. Rather than covering news or strategizing support for real individuals in crisis, mainstream media asks us to form opinions about whether or not smashing a window or setting fire to an empty police station is morally defensible, and it takes our measure based on our responses. We splinter into arguments about our ideologies when, time and time again, humans have shown that when we stand together in relationship to each other as humans rather than as representations of ideas, we can support each other and help to bring positive change.

A fundamental belief of the Coalition for Human Dignity was that fighting white nationalism required a diversity of tactics and a respect for political difference. Pacifist Quaker? Militant queer vandal? Iconoclastic rabble-rouser? Communist/socialist/anarchist? Nonprofit worker? All of the above? It did not matter; within the Coalition for Human Dignity, as long as people respected and accepted each other, the CHD welcomed and valued the experience, tools, and skills individuals brought. Using this method of organizing—

Protest of the verdict acquitting the police who beat Rodney King, Pioneer Courthouse Square, May 2, 1992. Photo by Coyote Amrich.

sometimes also referred to as "big tent" organizing—the CHD, along with its allies, shared a basic understanding that all people have a right to human dignity, that we are all in relationship together as humans, and that we have a responsibility to support and defend each other using the tools and skills we bring together. Applying a diversity of tactics values relationships over ideology.

The Coalition for Human Dignity had a small staff and two separate locations. The group maintained a public-facing office where activists could meet and gather as well as an office in a secret location, known as the Shop. In the pre-Internet world of the Shop, CHD members compiled extensive paper files on white supremacist activity in the region—eventually filling over thirty cabinets with news clippings, newsletters, posters, personal information, and other paper trails of the violent right wing.

Outside of the Shop, the work of the CHD resembled grassroots organizing at its broadest, asking the question, "When white supremacists attack, what do people need and how can we support them?"

SCOT NAKAGAWA
Coalition for Human Dignity and ACT UP Portland

Back in the day, with the rise of neonazi skinheads in Portland in particular, it became necessary to try to out-organize them at their projected base of support. So, specifically, what that meant was professional neonazis were deploying neonazi skinhead youth to organize and build base. One of the places they were doing that, the primary place, was the alternative music scene here in Portland.

There were nazi bands, they would flyer, they would terrorize people. They would polarize things in the scene—such that people who felt vulnerable often would join neonazi groups, because they were afraid. They were also very susceptible to the racist ideas that they represented. But, you know, the primary lever was fear.

So in order to be able to counter that influence, we needed to get into the scene and do the same thing. That meant doing things like walking around wearing "fight racism" t-shirts, and occasionally getting up onstage and making a speech, or throwing yourself into the mosh pit and trying to polarize things, too. So we did do that.

And that meant that there were times when neonazi skinheads would come after us, and violently. And in those instances, we did defend ourselves. There were significant amounts of violence happening here. Stabbings, assaults . . . There was an instance in which a small group of neonazi skinheads attempted to break down the door of the office of the Coalition for Human Dignity with pickaxes. There was another incident in which it is reported by neighbors that about fifteen neonazis organized themselves in paramilitary fashion in order to attack the home of activists with Anti Racist Action. This is the kind of thing that people were facing.

So of course there was violence. Of course there was. There was no choice.

GILLIAN
Coalition for Human Dignity

At the time, there was a lot going on in youth movements that were connected to the music scene: direct action that was related to racism, the environmental movement, the queer movement. There was an explosion of energy that was occurring, around changing the world that was progressive and left, and then also neonazi and right-wing organizing. It felt like there was a lot of energy, and it was polarized energy.

I was connected to Jonathan and Scot through Lewis & Clark College. That's how I got involved. I wasn't as core to the center of the work as, like, Scot, Jonathan, or Pat. I was showing up for specific needs. I did a little bit of intelligence support here and there. There was a part of it that seemed to me really crucial, which was supporting the youth movement that was in the direct line of fire—Anti Racist Action and SHARP. For me, I felt like that was part of CHD's work: supporting people who were most directly in the line of fire but also who had the most ability to influence other young people around how to respond. They were an alternative to young people who might have been otherwise recruited by the neonazis.

And so there were different ways of supporting people. One of them was intelligence gathering. We had informers who put together the pieces: who all the different players were, where they lived, knowing what cars they drove, following them, and figuring out what their plans were. Feeding that information back to the youth—who were in the ARA particularly—was helpful.

There was a show that was going to draw a lot of people within the ARA, and we expected a disruption. So a little group of people I worked with disabled cars to reduce the possibility of that disruption.

Another piece was being physically present—just showing up. As people in our early twenties who were not the direct targets of skinheads, we were able to be support. That physical presence was helpful.

Another way of being physically present was keeping close track of neonazi graffiti, which was exploding everywhere. And doing counter-graffiti. The idea was not taking the city's approach of covering it over with white paint, but leaving it there to be seen, so that people were aware this was occurring, and covering it with counter-messages. I wouldn't want neonazis to feel like they were a small, martyred group—but that their views were not welcome.

Jonathan Mozzochi and Abby Layton (second and third from left) with other CHD activists in NE Portland protesting Christian nationalist Bo Gritz and his Spike Training Workshops (small arms combat training) in 1993. Photo courtesy of Jonathan Mozzochi.

DEVIN BURGHART
Coalition for Human Dignity

I was a researcher at the Coalition for Human Dignity. I grew up in Spokane. Coming up in the punk and alternative scenes and seeing—every weekend—neonazi skinheads trying to either recruit or beat up my friends made me pretty aware of the issues and the ideas swirling around the Pacific Northwest. After the Mulugeta Seraw killing, I heard about the work that the Coalition was doing.

I became involved while I was going to school at Western Washington University. Jonathan Mozzochi and Steven Gardiner came to do a presentation, and they mentioned the fact that the organization had internships. I immediately signed up and got involved.

From the very beginning, they put me to work going to militia meetings and Klan rallies and other types of events around the region to try to gather the really important investigative research that the organization has become known for. I had the privilege of being one of the first interns of the organization as they moved from that exclusively grassroots organizing effort that took off after the Seraw killing to taking on more of that role in the investigative and research side of things.

CHD employed pretty much all of the investigative reporting techniques possible. That included the ability to infiltrate and go undercover at events to find out what far-right organizations do. We got beyond the public face these organizations put forward, found out their real intentions and their real agendas behind the scenes. We had the ability to go to public meetings and events, submit reports, and write about what was happening at those events. That gave a better sense—for our organization and other community organizations around the region—about what was happening; they could get prepared for the next wave of activity, rather than always having to worry about what had just happened. It was intense. You always had to be alert and concerned about your security and security of others.

Going undercover was enlightening, because it really helped dispel a lot of the mythology around neonazis and far-right activists. It introduced me to how they interact with one another, the factions and schisms, how they look at the opposition, how their paranoia impacts all of their activity—all of those kinds of things. You really saw how much race and racism and anti-Semitism were at the core driving a lot of this stuff, even though when they were talking to the public, they tried to often cover up or downplay that stuff. It was helpful to see the kind of bifurcation between the public and the private faces of these organizations.

What was really most informative was seeing the impact of exposing what was going on behind the scenes to the larger public and using that information to make a difference. The only thing that worked effectively was a diversity of tactics. At CHD, we never believed there was one tactic that would be a magic pill to eliminate racism in the Portland area. The research told us it was going to require a multiplicity of tactics; it required direct action organizing to expose and confront white supremacists when they were rallying and holding public events, because that sent a message that the community wasn't going to remain silent, that Portland was no longer going to be a fertile recruiting ground for folks. And it let other folks know that they could face the fear together, that in the wake of white supremacists' activity, that they weren't alone. That was really important. But it was really important also to expose their activities to other folks where white supremacists were targeting new recruits. So in essence, trying to inoculate communities that were vulnerable to white supremacist recruitment from their activities and get them to draw a line to exclude white supremacists from their subculture, or from their organizing, or from their other work. That was really key.

Back then, it was really hard. It was often dismissed as local street gang activity. It was dismissed as harmless graffiti or just street thuggery. But by doing effective and long-term research and organizing on it, you could show the larger community that this was, in fact, politically motivated. It was designed to harass and intimidate Jews and people of color; it was designed to bring about the kind of society that white supremacists have dreamed of. There was more to it than simple random acts of violence.

CECIL PRESCOD
Coalition for Human Dignity

I did work with local churches—Ecumenical Ministries of Oregon—and was many times a voice, or someone who was able to speak to grassroots activists and some more mainstream organizations, making the religious community aware and reporting how we should respond. So I was a go-between sharing information, maybe helping people to know more about one another. Who are these people, who are our possible allies? We have no interaction ordinarily, but because of this crisis, we have to sit around the table and get to know one another and find common cause and common ground.

It was a strange time. You had the rise of these racist fascists, and the oppositions like SHARP. Then you had this whole different religious right organizing, just beginning here in Oregon in the mid-'80s. And then in the late '80s, you had the first anti-queer ballot initiative. So that was a lot of things that were going on, and churches were among "mainstream organizations," and there was a need for understanding. Are these nazis similar to the OCA [Oregon Citizens Alliance], are they different, how do we respond to them? A lot of things were going on at the same time.

We all had our own lane to travel, in terms of organizing against the right. There were many different ways in which people needed to respond. My background was pacifist. I was active in peace organizations like the Fellowship of Reconciliation; we had a whole other different way of dealing with conflict and confronting hate.[14] But we also realize that other people come with a different perspective and different philosophy. We are united by the need to confront the right but respect that there are different paths to do it. That doesn't mean that there were not fundamental philosophical differences in terms of how to confront the radical right—especially with how you confront those who were willing to engage in political violence, which threatened all of us.

One of the strengths of the Coalition for Human Dignity was the research, which was very good, and at the time was rare in its accuracy. Rather than, "Those are nazis, we hate them," we had an understanding of their background, of who all the different players and individuals were, their individual histories, how they were connected, and also were there differences among those groups? Could you possibly find weak spots? If there were tensions between individuals, how do you work that, to defuse their power and their influence?

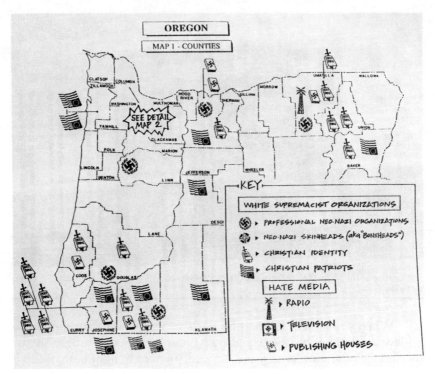

Map of hate groups, from CHD's 1990 report *Organized White Supremacists in Oregon.*

JONATHAN MOZZOCHI
Coalition for Human Dignity

My involvement was in research and intelligence. The Coalition for Human Dignity, in my view, had two unique contributions.

First, to recognize that the vigilante far right, that the threat of an American-born fascism would come through the Christian right and the white supremacist movement. And while that doesn't sound provocative or in any way controversial today, it actually was. Because most groups back then—like the Southern Poverty Law Center and the Anti-Defamation League, and other mainstream liberal groups—treated those two movements very differently. Their focus tended to be on the white supremacist movement, the Ku Klux Klan, racist skinheads, militia groups, so on and so forth.

If you look back at their material from that time, you'll see that there was really a division between the two. And that the Christian right—in particular the anti-LGBTQ stuff—was not considered hate. Racist anti-immigrant work was also not considered, broadly speaking, hate group activity. So one of the things we argued very early on was that, actually, you need to take a look at both of these political trends within the far right.

The location of the Shop, the center of the CHD's intelligence gathering from 1991 to 1997. Photo by Celina Flores.

When you look at them, it becomes very apparent that in order to achieve any kind of broader equality, in order to achieve a progressive or socialist agenda, in order to move forward, we need to fight both of those political currents. So that's what we did. And if you look at the Coalition for Human Dignity's research, you'll see very early on that we made a distinction between these two political currents, but also said that they had to be researched and they had to be fought and be struggled against. There were other groups who did this at a national level.

The second unique contribution I think the Coalition for Human Dignity made was that we argued that research should be local and should be carried out in local communities by local people. We tried to work with people to develop skills to research the far right. And some of that research involved infiltrating them: sending people to meetings, subscribing to their publications. We called this, broadly, having a research capacity, or an intelligence capacity. Because the far right was a social movement—it wasn't part of the state. Most of these people were organizing outside of government, outside of large corporations. They were in citizens' groups, grassroots, far-right organizations, which you later saw in the Tea Party. Because they were organized in that fashion, it gave us a unique opportunity to fight them politically, infiltrating them. We could do it in a way that could provide information to communities that were frequently attacked by these groups, so that they could defend themselves. We were not professional spies. That's not what we did.

We did training sessions, and at the height of our influence, the Coalition for Human Dignity maintained something called the Shop, which was an office that housed thirty filing cabinets full of primary and secondary sources on far-right groups in our area of responsibility, the Pacific Northwest. That's what it grew to be. We had a very specialized library of more than five hundred volumes. We had hundreds of video-tapes and audiotapes. And then we had databases full of license plates, from when we would send people to events to write down license plates, and then we'd have to run them through the Oregon DMV. This would take time, and it was very labor intensive.

There were, at that time, hundreds of small papers throughout the region that would include in them letters to the editor, stories by beat re-porters, so on and so forth. And if you wanted to get those stories, you had to subscribe to a clipping service, which would take, you know, keywords like "white supremacist," or "anti-immigration," or whatever. The service would have someone, very labor intensive, cut out the clippings, put them into a package, and mail them to us. Once we would get them, weeks later, we would index them and then put them into a database so that we could monitor and begin to understand what it was they were doing.

So my point here is that it was a very different information envi-ronment, a lot of volunteers and a lot of labor. So in order for us to be competent, we had to have funding, we had to have support, we had to have people with basic library science skills. So that's what we did.

ABBY LAYTON
Coalition for Human Dignity

I had joined the Coalition for Human Dignity about two weeks be-fore this episode happened: my daughter and two of her friends were coming home along SE Cesar Chavez Boulevard. They were between Hawthorne and Alder. A truckload of skinheads went by, they were—sieg heils, shouting nazi slogans. My daughter and her boyfriend turned around and noticed that they were coming back after them. So they took off running. The skinheads got out of the car and started chasing them with baseball bats, two-by-fours . . . Luckily my daughter knocked on someone's door. She screamed, "Help us, please!" Thank god, the woman, Mary Steiger, an elderly woman, opened the door and let my kids in. So my children were safe.

Later on that night, a group of skinheads went back to Mary Stei-ger's home and broke all of her lower-level windows, broke into her car, yelled death threats at her. The next day, she had a heart attack and had to be taken to the hospital.

Since the Coalition for Human Dignity was tracking so close-ly what was happening in these communities of hate, within days they knew exactly who had gone back to Mary Steiger's house and who had threatened my children. Scott Garl was the head of this group; we had him arrested, with evidence. We took him to court. We came to court, many of us with rainbow ribbons, and with good witnesses. He was put in prison for two and a half years.

M. TRELOR
Coalition for Human Dignity

So here are these terrified kids who ran to this house, and this older woman said, "Yeah, you can come in here." The truckload of nazis attacked that household right away, a household full of elderly people, fearful for their lives. They appealed to the police, who basically said, "Well, we can't do anything."

So somehow word got back to us, and we said, "Do you want us to sit on your front porch?" Mary Steiger said, "I want you in my front parlor! Wherever you best feel that you can guard my house. I haven't slept since then, because they'll drive by and they'll do stuff, and I'm scared out of my wits."

So we did. Some of us said, "Well, we're going to bring whatever is necessary to defend that household." And other people who were pacifists said, "Well, I'll just use my body," and we said, "That's okay." We did not try to tell people, "You must be armed," or "You must not be armed."

That was one of the other things that we did in conjunction with the public organizing. The household defense—we never took a penny, or we never tried to publicize that widely. We felt it had to be done, and the police would not do it. They just would not guard these houses that were under attack, that were under obvious attack! We did that, with members of ARA.

We did several others, including when Randall Krager tried to kill a Black man in the Northeast during an altercation at a convenience store. Krager jumped—and beat almost to death—a Black man. He was in the intensive care unit at Emanuel Hospital for a couple weeks. One of the women in his family appealed to us for defense of their house.

Again, we said, "Well, what do you want us to do?" And she said, "I want you sleeping in my front room, because I'm scared." People asked her, "Well, what should we bring?" She said, "You're gonna bring weapons, aren't you?" Those house defenses were one of the things that I think made things real for the members who had not been in direct confrontations.

So the violence increased. We were not attempting to ramp things up. But we always said we would defend ourselves in public actions. We trained fifty-plus people in basic martial arts self-defense, then we did our own security at events.

We were trying to get away from a more macho model of, "I'm gonna get tough, I'm gonna get weapons, I'm gonna attack these nazis." Well, that works at a certain level, but it also leads to a bad intragroup dynamic of, those are the people who will do the security, those are the people who have weapons, those are the people who will directly confront the nazis, and the rest of us will do our less important stuff. That's not a good dynamic. I won't say we had total success, but we did develop a number of people from having no skills to feeling, "Yes, I'm part of the security of this group and I won't back down."

We told the cops at our larger things, like at the March for Dignity and Diversity in 1990 during the trial of Metzger,[15] "We don't want you around." We didn't trust them, you know. They were going to do the wrong thing. They were not going to protect us.

JONATHAN MOZZOCHI
Coalition for Human Dignity

Part of that community defense project involved having a hotline where people could call in racist activity. At one point up on SE Belmont, there was a family of Vietnamese who were being attacked by racists. We mobilized a vigil to protect them. A former head of the Lesbian Community Project, Donna Red Wing, was one of the people who came and did the vigil there. So here you had antiracist Skinheads Against Racial Prejudice folks, along with a pretty powerful community leader in Donna Red Wing. It was a coalition of people coming together to fight against these folks, which I think was very unique. Outside of that, perhaps those communities didn't have a lot of interaction. But there they could.

Some of the antiracists had weapons, including firearms. So that stuff worked early on because the threat was very local, and the threat was a vigilante group, kind of like protecting folks from the Klan. So the Coalition for Human Dignity played an important role in that kind of community-based self-defense.

When we were doing this work, the Portland Police Bureau and Oregon state cops treated all of this stuff as gang activity. They understood everything through this very narrow lens of law and order and gangs. Anti Racist Action, a multiracial group fighting racists in the street, they were one gang. And East Side White Pride, or whoever, was another gang. We, of course, had a very different perspective on this.

There was one officer in particular—Loren Christensen—in the Portland Police Bureau who was the point person on all of this. He was, I think, the most important person in the State Gang Task Force—within which a lot of the police intelligence was collected on the racist right, as well as on Anti Racist Action and Skinheads Against Racial Prejudice—and Christensen was their guy. He, repeatedly in these early years, in the late 1980s and early 1990s, would attack Anti Racist Action and Skinheads Against Racial Prejudice as being violent gangs, no better than the racists: "This was angry youth off the rails and that we just have to have a firmer hand, and this will all go away." All of us said this is more than that, and it's different than that. We were constantly arguing with him in the press and elsewhere. It created an environment within which it was okay for the far right to attack people of color and to attack ARA and SHARP activists, because this guy's saying it's just a gang thing, right?

A March and Rally for

Dignity & Diversity

■ *Native Land Rights* ■ *Gender and Racial Equality* ■
■ *Religious Freedom — Fight anti-Semitism* ■ *Social and
Economic Justice* ■ *Lesbian and Gay Rights* ■
■ *No nazis or white supremacists* ■

Sunday ■ October 7, 1990

**Gather at the west end of Laurelhurst Park in Portland at 11:30 am.
March will begin at SE 31st & Pine, the site of
Mulugeta Seraw's murder in 1988.**

**Rally to follow at 2:00 pm, (rain or shine)
South Park Blocks, Portland State University.**

Speakers: ■ Tawna Sanchez, International Indian Treaty Council ■ Deni Yamauchi, Center for Democratic Renewal ■ Stu Albert, New Jewish Agenda ■ Cipriano Ferrell, PCUN ■ Kebo Drew, Radical Women ■ ■ Elliott Moffitt, Nez Perce Tribe ■ Joyce Harris, The Black Educational Center ■ and more ■

Entertainers: ■ Tribal Voice — John Trudell and Quiltman ■ Quadnivial ■ Hitting Birth ■ members of Sundunga ■ Portland Lesbian Choir ■ and more ■

*There will be childcare and activities for children, and food.
All events are wheelchair accessible.*
**This will be a peaceful event.
Please respect our alcohol- & drug-free environment.**

Stand Up for Yourself!
Stand Up for Your Neighbor!

For Further Information Call (503) 232-2159 or 232-1038.

March + Rally for
Dignity + Diversity
Portland, OR 10/7/90

Nazi skinheads best beware-- We're uniting everywhere!	No Nazis, no KKK No Fascist USA!
Racist, sexist Nazi Klan-- We will stop you, yes we can!	Hey-hey! Ho-ho! Nazi bigots got to go!
No to hate, no to fear-- We don't want the Nazis here!	Gay, straight, Black, white, Same struggle, same fight!

Flyer and suggested chants at the March for Dignity and Diversity, October 7, 1990. Courtesy of Portland State University Library Special Collections & Archives.

One of the things I did personally—that the Coalition for Human Dignity is not responsible for, but that I did—is I managed to get a hold of Loren Christensen's unredacted internal intelligence reports. I managed to get those over a period of about, I think, six months or a year. We used that information to have a more effective means of fighting these racist groups.

These intelligence reports—so you understand—every time a cop came up on a racist skinhead group and then interviewed them, or arrested them, or whatever, it would go into these summarized intelligence reports. The names, addresses, workplaces, Social Security numbers—it was just a wealth of data. I managed to get a constant, steady stream of those reports. And we used them to fight these guys. That's pretty provocative.

If there's anything that I would tell contemporary activists, it's this: push the envelope. You're going to need to do this kind of research. If you don't, you're relying on other outfits to do that intelligence gathering for you. If they do it, then it's going to be their political interpretation of what that stuff means. And if you're a progressive, if you're a leftist, you don't want that. We need to have control of our own intelligence. We need to have control of our own research. We wanted to know what they were eating for breakfast. We wanted to know everything about them. That makes it easier to fight them. And that's what we did. We did the research.

It was always tough. I'm by no means saying that spycraft is the only thing that groups should be doing. But I will say that if you're not doing it, then someone else is. And if that someone else has a political agenda that's not yours, then you allow them to frame your opposition. And we were never comfortable with that. We were never comfortable with that.

M. TRELOR
Coalition for Human Dignity

How do you deal with the media? There's a stance that's popular now, that I have some respect for but I don't agree with, that you should not talk to the mass media. We're not talking about community radio here, we're talking about the daily paper and the TV stations. That they can't be trusted and are entirely bought off. I think it gives that terrain away and says there could be no struggle there.

We decided early on that we would put out statements and say this is what we know, if you can contradict this, go ahead. If somebody was willing to work with us, we would give them more information, give them leads, give them interviews. If people were deliberately attacking us, we would deal with them with caution and/or not at all.

Let me give two examples of when that happened. First was *The Oregonian*, which had a reporter who was assigned to this, Maxine Bernstein. She was a dupe of the FBI. I use that term very carefully. The FBI was—through the Portland Police—issuing information about SHARP. *The Oregonian* wrote eleven, maybe twelve, articles that each time identified them as a gang.

Now, we had heard that there was going to be a picnic in Laurelhurst Park on Hitler's birthday. The boneheads announced that they were going to meet there, so SHARP, ARA, Lesbian Community Project, and Coalition for Human Dignity all said: we'll have a picnic there. Scot Nakagawa and I were there. We went over and talked to some of the other picnickers in the area, asked how everything was going. Everybody said, "Fine." So we left.

Shortly thereafter, fifty cops showed up and threatened to arrest everyone. Nobody got arrested, so far as I recall, but they harassed everybody and forced them to leave the park.

Then, *The Oregonian* wrote that the Portland police had busted up a neonazi rally in Laurelhurst Park. They could only have gotten that information from the Portland police and the FBI. They're just continually and deliberately getting this wrong. They're blurring the distinction between antiracist skinheads and neo-fascist skinheads. They're blurring the distinction between those of us who oppose the nazis and the nazis themselves.

We decided we had to do something. So we responded with an op-ed piece that they printed, where we pointed out they had gotten everything wrong. *The Oregonian* was embarrassed. They should have been ashamed, and they stopped calling SHARP a gang thereafter.

The daily or weekend skirmishes were going on where boneheads and SHARP and ARA were fighting each other in various clubs and on the streets. One of the nazi boneheads was called Bomber Dave, and he was the leader of a small group of boneheads, mainly sighted in Vancouver, Washington. He would come over here and he would attack people in Pioneer Square. He would attack tourists. He was a known violent

STOP THE LIES!!!!!

A.R.A.- Portland organized a "Never Again" picnic on April 20, 1990 in Laurelhurst Park. This event which was BLATANTLY anti-racist was reported in the Oregonian (compliments of the Portland police department) as "apparently to celebrate the anniversary of the birth of Adolph Hitler." This type of misrepresentation has to stop now! We cannot let the media continue to bury the Anti -Racist struggle!

Join us at the Oregonian Building 1320 S.W. Broadway at 1pm on Monday April 23, 1990 to
"SET THE RECORD STRAIGHT"
CONTACT A.R.A./ 1951 W. BURNSIDE BOX 1928/ PDX, OREGON 97209
phone 332-2382

1990 flyer, courtesy of Kelly Halliburton.

individual. Well, he was killed.

Immediately, the Portland police put out the word that SHARP had probably killed Bomber Dave. The media, of course, went crazy. SHARP said, "We didn't do this."

I don't have a problem with nazis being killed. However, I think there are ways of organizing that have a better effect than us going out and hunting them down.

We arranged for a media conference to occur on the footsteps of the Multnomah Public Library downtown. We did that because we were trying to confront the media with, "Here are these people that you've been talking about. Listen to them, let them talk themselves." We told the SHARPs, "Pick the people to show up who can get arrested—because that may happen. We'll be there with you. We're not worried about boneheads coming and shooting up a crowd of media people, but we do think it's likely the police will come and snatch you."

While that press conference was going on, the police had been slowly showing up, about four or five cars. And then, in the middle of it, they took off. It turned out that they just made the arrest of members of Bomber Dave's crew, who had, in fact, killed him because he was such an asshole. He'd been taking food from other people. He'd been stealing their money. He'd been doing all the usual bad-dude stuff, and being nazi boneheads, they kicked him to death.

KRISTA OLSEN
Coalition for Human Dignity

Within the Coalition, I would say that my biggest responsibility in the late '80s, early '90s, was a commitment I had made to our own internal antibigotry work, and to link issues to make sure that we were learning from our own individual struggles about ways that oppressions are layered. I wrote my thesis around the historical efforts to bring anti-oppression work into anti-oppression movements.

The work of actually showing up on the streets was essential. It was dangerous work. It was important to think about where violent resistance is appropriate and where the priority is keeping communities safe. Having folks who are more aggressive show up willing to face off with the bigoted right was important. Outnumbering the bigoted right was a huge thing. In the long run, that means a tremendous deal for people who are threatened and unsafe in that context, to know and see that there are allies.

Coalition for Human Dignity was more of an ally organization. My role, in part, was to point out the dynamics that gave rise to bias and left folks out. I came to that work as a young feminist—often the person to say, "Wow, this meeting has not had a lot of female voices participating." To give full credit, there were several men who helped found the organization and worked hard. Yet it was hard for women to move beyond the Xerox committee, which was photocopying back in the day. Some of my work was about trying to remind us to create more space—sometimes that meant taking a step back.

It takes extra work to bring in folks who aren't in your social circle. I think in the Coalition that tended to be a shortcoming. It partly came from losing phone numbers. And not all of us had phones. If you wanted to get in touch with me, you'd have to come throw things at my window or you would have to call Gillian, who would walk down the street and tell me something.

It always felt like there was something that was really urgent and had to happen right then, so it was hard to make space for discussions about integrating anti-oppression work. In the messy and urgent and imperfect work of fighting fascists in the street, and in that sense of urgency of people really, truly being in danger, we made lots of mistakes along the way and the way we treated each other, and the way we treated people who just came through the work briefly and then were like, "I'm out. This isn't very fun, this isn't very safe, this doesn't feel good. There's not a place for my voice." But good work got done.

How do we make sure that our organizing doesn't leave out the voices that might matter most in these times of everyday terror for many people? My perspective as an organizer also was informed by being a parent, and being a parent before many of my peers were, thinking about, "Okay, how can there still be space for me?" Like, "How can there be

Banner at the March for Dignity and Diversity, October 7, 1990. Photo by Kraig Scattarella, courtesy of *The Oregonian*.

space for me with a baby?"

I think about the amount of time I spent photocopying and wheat-pasting things. That's really how we got the word out. Some phone calls and things—but we spent a lot of time making photocopies and sticking things up on posts. The ability to mobilize lots of people makes our ability to organize spectacularly different.

I think that in the long run, we sell ourselves short as a political movement if we don't take time to step back. I think that that is a message that is relevant to the antifascist organizing happening now. It seems so urgent; there are lives on the line every day. Folks feel like sometimes the ends justify the means, and we need to rush forward. Sometimes that privileges more powerful voices and bigger bodies and folks who are less at risk because of the color of their skin or because of their gender identity.

In the Coalition for Human Dignity, it was sometimes seen as more expedient to just press on as an organization primarily made up of allies. Not to discount the work of people of color in the movement, but that organization particularly was a mostly white space. There was room for us to do more anti-bias work internally. Thirty years later, we continue to learn how to keep applying an equity lens to the work that we do and to keep trying to transform processes so they create space for new voices and for voices to hold the space more equitably.

JASON
ARA Portland

People from CHD made an effort to come to several of those early ARA meetings. They made themselves available. They were honest and up-front about consequences, about what things look like and what the risks were. They were really, really helpful, but also supportive. Those things work both ways. And then through coalition building, in like '91 or '90, everybody worked together to throw the biggest march and rally Portland had ever seen at that point. We almost got Public Enemy to play it. They didn't, but they gave us a shout-out on the radio!

It made a really strong bond that I still have to this day with a lot of those people. It's really, really cool. CHD was really solid about that. They rode that line really, really well. Jonathan [Mozzochi] never cared what anyone said about their support of us. They decided that it was a thing that needed to happen, and they were going to do it. Everyone from that community went all out, and we went all out on their behalf as well.

I'm going to give CHD so much credit, and the same with Northwest Communities [Against Hate] down in Eugene. These were people that wanted nothing to do with violence in a lot of ways, but they really knew that it was important to provide some cover. I think they believed in the work we were doing, confronting racists in the street. But the other part of that was that we very much reached out to them. We asked them their opinion: "How can we do this in a way that doesn't put you at more risk, or that actually supports you?" That was the big thing. That is something that is really lacking and frustrating for a lot of mainstream activists, and even radical activists, that a lot of things get done with disregard for other people's safety and more vulnerable communities. I felt that ARA had done a really frickin' good job of that. We really wanted to know what people thought, and then we listened to it. We also supported them and said, "We'll come do security at your event, but we'll also do whatever else. We'll come do childcare. We'll play music or we'll help with the sound, or anything that needs to be done." We also made a good effort to say that, "We'll do it the way you want us to do it. Do you want us to do it in a way that is very visible? Do you want it to be known that we're there supporting you and we're standing out front of your church that's come under attack for the last month and a half? Or would you rather have us very discreetly inside, or out front in cars where no one can see us?"

So then we would have larger meetings where people from each of these groups—Leonard Peltier Support Group, Radical Women, Lesbian Community Project—all these groups would be in the same meetings to talk about the churches that got attacked, bricks thrown through their windows. Or what happened to the people that got beat up over here or out in the outskirts. We all came together to talk about all this stuff, and worked on it. Many of us became friends with these people, such a diverse group. That diversity also helped us have communication with

WOMEN CALENDAR
OCTOBER 1990

BLACK CAMPUS ACTIVISTS IN THE 90's:
LEADING THE FIGHT AGAINST RIGHTWING HATE

Radical Women Monthly Meeting
Thursday, October 18, 6:30 p.m.
Standard Plaza, 1100 S.W. 6th Avenue
Conference Room B

Campuses are surging with debate and protest as Black students organize against entrenched university bias and student bigots who attack the gains of the 60's. Black students are advocating for more diversity in hiring, in student recruitment, and for a curriculum that includes the works and history of people of color, women, lesbians and gay men, and the poor. The role of campus activism on Black campuses will also be explored. *A light supper will be served for $3.00.* Everyone is welcome. For more information call 249-8067.

* * * *

R e d   R o s e   S c h o o l   8 - W e e k   C l a s s:
FASCISM: WHAT IT IS AND HOW TO FIGHT IT

Why are Nazi skinheads organizing now in Portland? What is the method behind the fascist "madness" of spewing hatred at Blacks, all people of color, women and lesbians and gays? Study fascism from Hitler's Third Reich to the U.S. in the 90's and how to *defeat* it. Lead by Radical Women and the Freedom Socialist Party.

Sundays, Oct. 14 to Dec. 2, 2:30 - 5pm, 4312 S.E. Stark
For information or to register call 249-8067

RADICAL WOMEN is the revolutionary wing of the women's movement and the feminist vanguard of the left. Immersed in the daily struggle against racism, sexism, antigay bigotry, and labor exploitation, RW's history and influence prove that women are decisive to the U.S. and to world revolution. **Join us.**

Portland Radical Women
1510 N.E. Brazee
Portland, OR 97212
(503) 249-8067

PORTLAND RADICAL WOMEN

labor donated 10/90

Courtesy of Portland State University Library Special Collections & University Archives.

other groups. These friendships that were made early on led to, of course, Jonathan [Mozzochi] calling me up and being like, "Hey, man, I gotta go dig through some trash, and I would really like to have a couple people with me." "You got it. Let's go!"

We made some risky endeavors to get information that was not available that would be available now. We had intel on everybody. It was crazy, because we were a little obsessed. But we knew it had to be done.

Someone would call us up and say, "Hey, my friend works at this Pizza Hut. This fucking nazi works there, and he's always fucking with her." So we would go to the Pizza Hut. We would just wait. When they get off work, we'd follow them home. Once we had their home, we could then disrupt their workplace. They didn't know we knew where they lived yet. So then we'd just stake it out, then follow them to another home and we'd stake that place out, and just start making connections. All of a sudden, we had this network scribbled out on a notepad that had like, twenty different addresses on it with the major, major hitters on their side.

All the Youth of Hitler guys in Milwaukie, Aryan Front, American Front—we had all these people's names and addresses, because we were patient. A lot of people wouldn't have that patience. They'd be like, "We've got to get them, let's go beat the shit out of those guys." Sometimes that would happen, and that's fine. But we're like, "Well, let's find out where they live." Then, when we knew that they were going to try and meet up somewhere, we could dismantle their car so they couldn't get there and make it really difficult for them to organize.

Our Friday nights would be like four of us getting together. And we'd go sit out in front of a house, drink a couple beers, and talk shit and listen to music and: "Someone's coming, here they go! Okay, let's follow them to the next house." And we'd just grab a bunch of Jolly Ranchers and go from house to house, putting them in their gas tanks the week before they were all supposed to go to Aryan Nations, so that they all had car trouble and they all had to pay a mechanic's bill. They didn't have as much income to take off for the weekend.

We were willing to do a lot of things that a lot of the other groups would not do. They didn't want to risk the physical scenario, much less getting caught and then having to answer to the police. "The Lesbian Community Project was found at the home of so and so." You know, that's not gonna go over so well. We were totally willing to do this, and we'd do it so you didn't have to.

I'm a white male. I'm gonna make myself a target. I'm not who they're going after. The right are going out of their way to attack vulnerable communities that are not attacking them. So for the left to go up and just straight up attack the right, there's nothing wrong with that. You're defending, physically defending, people that are . . . I'm not going to say they can't defend themselves, but they haven't chosen to enter the fight. They're just being themselves, and they're being attacked for that.

ARA flyers said, "If you want nazis to understand you, you have to speak their language." And it was a picture of a fist punching a nazi tattooed head. That's their game, which also explains why after three shows of getting stood up to, they quit coming to the shows. They didn't have the intimidation; they didn't have the power. As soon as it was a fair fight, they were gone!

There were three hundred of them in the Portland area in 1990, out in Beaverton, out in Milwaukie, out in deep Southeast. There were ten of us that were engaging them on a daily basis, and sometimes multiple different places on the same day. We would get in a car and drive to

Above: Kathleen Saadat and Donna Red Wing at Pioneer Square, 1996. Below: Courtesy of Portland State University Library Special Collections & University Archives, date and photographer unknown.

Beaverton, beat up a couple guys at the mall, and then we'd drive to Clackamas and beat up a couple people out there.

They thought there were tons of us. They thought we were everywhere.

M. TRELOR
Coalition for Human Dignity

I'm really critical of what we did and what I did. I think we failed in many ways.

But I think we succeeded in two ways. One, we left a little bit of a crumb trail for the future to say, "You can do open, direct confrontation to these people and win politically." The second thing was, we prevented the neonazi gangs and neonazi formations from cohering here in Portland. And the best example of that is with the American Front, which was a San Francisco–based group who had a fairly dynamic leader called Bob Heick. So Bob Heick announces he's moving to establish the American Front here in Portland. We had decided we would not allow any grouping to emerge. We attacked the American Front almost from the beginning of their existence here. They did some things that have not recurred but gave us pause then and should give people pause now. They demonstrated in front of an abortion clinic. That'll get them support from the theocratic right. They did an action in front of a lesbian poetry reading. They called for a public gathering in downtown Portland, which they pulled off, though we disrupted it.

We went after Bob Heick. We destroyed his living situation. He ended up appealing to the Portland police because he said, "My house has been attacked three times, they've destroyed it!" Yeah, we did that. We said, "If you come to Portland, we will make your life hell." And we made his life hell. We made it impossible for him to live in Portland. The American Front fizzled out here in Portland. That was what we were looking to stop, and I think we succeeded on that limited level.

Here's a failure on our part and on the part of the community as well. A couple members of the Lesbian Community Project started the Homophobic Violence Reporting Line. [See Appendix A. –Eds.] This is before hate crimes existed as a federal thing and before anybody was tracking them. Unfortunately, a member of the community here in Portland, Azalea Cooley, a Black lesbian who worked for the Multnomah County Corrections Department, decided to start faking hate crime incidents and asking for community support, which she got. There were marches, rallies, and stuff. Initially, she told people, "I can't talk about this publicly, word will get out," et cetera. But then she was on the front cover of *Willamette Week*. There were a lot of stories about it.

The problem was, she was staging all of these things. She was burning

The Portland Alliance

VOLUME 13, NUMBER 6   PROGRESSIVE COMMUNITY NEWS   JUNE 1993

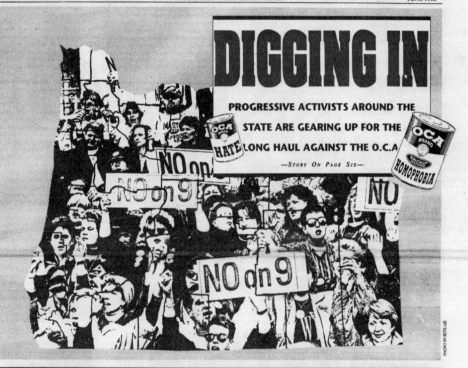

DIGGING IN

PROGRESSIVE ACTIVISTS AROUND THE STATE ARE GEARING UP FOR THE LONG HAUL AGAINST THE O.C.A.

—STORY ON PAGE SIX—

PHOTO BY BETTE LEE

After last fall's defeat of the Oregon Citizens Alliance's Ballot Measure 9, many observed that the election was actually a victory for the O.C.A. in all but the most technical sense. The O.C.A. removed the last traces of doubt as to its power to influence state politics, and the vote pinpointed for the O.C.A. those regions of the state most sympathetic to its message of fear and exclusion.

Now the O.C.A. is systematically working to claim those areas as its own. June's round of local "Son of 9" measures would do to city and county charters what Measure 9 would have done to the state constitution: single out gays and lesbians as undeserving of the level of civil rights enjoyed by other Oregonians.

Springfield and Cornelius have already passed versions of the O.C.A.'s initiative, which it has watered down "to accomodate some of the concerns of the middle-of-the-road voters, and still accomplish our intent of stopping the homosexual political agenda." The O.C.A. has initially targeted 32 additional cities and counties, of which four counties and two cities will put the measure to a vote at the end of this month.

Win or lose, these elections represent only the earliest efforts in what will surely be a long struggle—the struggle to develop a proactive movement for human dignity and human rights throughout our state.

On page six the *Alliance* takes a look at the organizing work currently being done in three Oregon communities.

Northwest Alliance for Alternative Media and Education
2807 S.E. Stark
Portland, OR 97214

Complimentary Copy — Please Subscribe!

ADDRESS CORRECTION REQUESTED

DATED MATERIAL—DO NOT DELAY

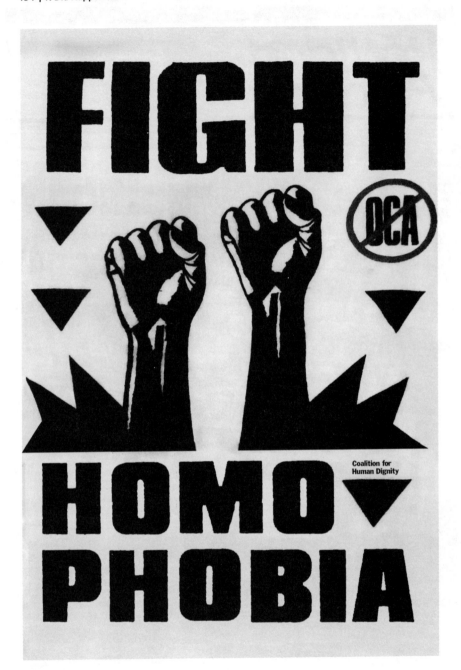

Coalition for Human Dignity poster, 1992. Courtesy of Jonathan Mozzochi.

little crosses in her front yard. She'd appealed to us for help. Two of our Black organizers had gone and investigated, then they came back and said, "This isn't real, we gotta stay away from her." The error on our part was that we did not tell anybody else. For that, I apologized then, I apologize now. It took the FBI setting up surveillance cameras to catch her. So when she was outed by the FBI and also by the Portland police ... when that came forth, dozens if not hundreds of people basically washed their hands of political work and organizing for a while. She had an entire support committee set up around herself. You could only feel for those people, as to how disillusioned they were. At least three separate groupings disbanded shortly thereafter because of the effect of this. We should have dealt with that amongst ourselves.

SCOT NAKAGAWA
Coalition for Human Dignity and ACT UP Portland

The story told backwards now is that the Coalition and other groups basically ended the rise of white supremacist groups in Oregon in the '90s. That's not at all true. We were part of an effort that broke the back of the neonazi skinhead youth movement, which was a particular faction of the right. White nationalist organizing here continued. It's continuing now.

Many of the young people who are in skinhead groups have transitioned into professional neonazi organizations and other kinds of white nationalist and alt-right formations. You know, around 1996, the bombing of the Oklahoma City federal building, the Alfred P. Murrah Federal Building in Oklahoma City, occurred. Timothy McVeigh is famously blamed for that bombing and was prosecuted for it. That bombing caused so much carnage, so much damage. Children died, there was a childcare facility within the building. Hundreds of people were affected. That finally got the federal government to put white nationalist groups, and Christian Patriot groups in particular, at the top of their FBI watch list. They recognized that their own assets, their own interests were at stake. So they escalated surveillance and repression of the violent arm of the white nationalist movement. It forced that movement underground.

But they continued organizing. Obama was like a shot of adrenaline in the arm of the Islamophobic faction of the right. So those organizations grew in number and in support until the Trump election, when his ascendancy basically turned on the green light. Movements that had gone underground and become alienated from mainstream politics decided to step out into the light of day and began organizing and vying for power. They believed their time had come and that Donald Trump's election was an indication of it.

The CHD attacked the cultural landscape. We knew that whoever owns the cultural landscape owns a very important tool to define ideology at that time. We put up posters, we spray-painted out nazi graffiti, we put on concerts, we did things like that that would interrupt the life of the alternative music scene and the life of young people in the city of Portland. We were assertive about it. We were in the media. We were in the news cycle. The story about the fight against white supremacy in the state of Oregon was listed among the top two stories of the twentieth century by *The Oregonian*. We put the story in your face and we forced people to have to deal with it. We took young people and marched them up and down the bus malls, downtown Portland, to protest neonazis, so that people would begin to see that this was a real problem. They could not just go to work. We were in their faces. At KBOO, there used to be a show called *Boneheads and Bigots: Confronting the Politics of Fear* that I hosted along with a couple of other people. It was a monthly radio show where we reported on what was happening on the neonazi right, and we would name culprits and give people their phone numbers or home addresses or other information to get them mobilized. That kind of thing, I think, really made a difference.

I also used to be a member of ACT UP. ACT UP activists put their lives on the line, they put their bodies on the line, in order to make the case that something needed to be done about the AIDS crisis. If it were not for ACT UP, I do not honestly believe we would have made the kind of progress we finally were able to make under the Reagan administration, the Bush administration, to do something, to make some funding available to start to deal with prevention and treatment of HIV and AIDS. These kinds of things happen because people didn't just take a picture or send an email. It happened because they *took action*, and they worked with people one on one, in person, and mobilized people in groups, in order to really change the way that people are going to experience their day-to-day lives.

There's one other thing I would offer people, which I think might be an interesting thing for people to undertake. This is not that hard, right? The CHD once organized this big rally called We Are Not Afraid. At that rally, we brought together the broadest coalition possible of people who could speak to the problem of white supremacist violence in the city of Portland and the state of Oregon. Thousands of people came. We made these buttons, and the buttons that we made had the names on it of children who had been killed in white supremacist incidents. Black churches were being burned down. People of color were being victimized. It was happening now. It wasn't the '60s, it wasn't the '50s. It was the 1990s. So we put the names of people who had been victimized in that way on these buttons, and we pinned them to pieces of paper that told the story of that person. And we asked people to wear the button to work. And when they got there, there's a name on your collar, on a button that is not that person's name. People would ask, "Why do you have this name on your collar?" They could answer by telling them that person's story and saying this was a six-year-old Black boy in some city in the state of

Coalition for Human Dignity graphic, 1992.

Georgia whose house was burned to the ground before the fire department responded, because the fire department did not respond regularly to fires in Black neighborhoods.

There are ways that you can get those stories in front of people. Those are the kinds of things people should be thinking about. But those of us who are able to take action need to do so, and need to do so assertively and boldly, and we need to do it in public.

ROLLING
BACK
CIVIL
RIGHTS

The Oregon Citizens' Alliance at Religious War

S. L. Gardiner

$7.00

Coalition for Human Dignity
Portland • Oregon

The Oregon
WITNESS
Vol. 2 No. 1 — The Journal of the Coalition for Human Dignity — July, 1992

The OCA:

A Case Study

in

Organized Bigotry

2nd Edition
Funded by the Oregon Democracy Project

Some of the hundred–plus publications issued by the Coalition for Human Dignity: *Rolling Back Civil Rights* (1992), *The Oregon Witness* vol. 2:1 (1992), *The Dignity Report* vol. 1:2 (1993), *The Northwest Imperative* (1994)

The Dignity Report

A journal of investigation and analysis dedicated to exposing right-wing attacks on civil and human rights.

A Publication of the Coalition for Human Dignity Research Department • July 1, 1993 · Vol.1 / No.2

In This Issue

Around the Region

- Clean Sweep for Bigotry in Oregon Election Returns 1
- White Supremacists Organize Around Weaver Trial 2
- White Supremacists Take up Anti-Gay Banner 2
- Racist Sentenced for Murder 3
- Christian Coalition in the Northwest 3
- Oregon Christian Coalition Membership Drive 4
- Gay Agenda in Lynden, Washington 4
- Ballot Box Bigotry on Horizon 4
- OCA Petition Drive in Estacada, Oregon 5
- Veneta, Oregon Takes Stand Against OCA 5
- Computer Bulletin Board Hosts Holocaust Revisionists 5
- Prokop Comes Out 5
- Oregon House Compromises on Gay Rights Bill 6
- Traditional Values Coalition Attacks Sex Education 6

National

- Pat Buchanan Heads Up "American Cause" 7
- Conference to Feature Beam, Peters and Temple 7

International

- Neo-Nazis Storm Negotiations in South Africa 8
- Racist Skinheads Riot in Ottawa, Canada 8

Clean Sweep for Bigotry

When all of the votes were counted in the 29 June mail-in ballot, six of six anti-gay, anti-civil rights measures passed by margins ranging as wide as 46%. The measures, sponsored by the Oregon Citizens' Alliance, were approved by voters in Douglas, Josephine, Klamath and Linn Counties and in the cities of Canby and Junction City.

The election was closest in the Lane County town of Junction City (population: 3,740), where the measure passed by a margin of only three votes, 631 to

628. The election was particularly divisive in Junction City where the OCA's No Special Rights Committee distributed propaganda linking homosexuals to the Nazi movement and where vehement OCA supporters brandished hand-lettered signs saying "Keep Private Practices From Becoming Public Policy" and "PRO-HETERO." At the other extreme Douglas County voters approved a similar measure by a margin of 21,633 to 7,812, the anti-gay position garnering more than 73% of votes cast.

Election Results

Canby				
Measure 3-2	YES	1,961 (55.7%)	NO	1,556 (44.3%)
Measure 9	YES	2,429 (54.3%)	NO	2,048 (45.7%)
Junction City				
Measure 20-01	YES	631 (50.1%)	NO	628 (49.9%)
Measure 9	YES	902 (55.1%)	NO	735 (44.9%)
Douglas County				
Measure 10-01	YES	21,633 (73.5%)	NO	7,812 (26.5%)
Measure 9	YES	27,356 (59.9%)	NO	18,317 (40.1%)
Measure 8	YES	23,180 (61.2%)	NO	14,720 (38.8%)
Josephine County				
Measure 17-1	YES	13,830 (60.8%)	NO	8,923 (39.2%)
Measure 9	YES	19,541 (58.7%)	NO	13,754 (41.3%)
Measure 8	YES	17,582 (65.3%)	NO	9,323 (34.7%)
Klamath County				
Measure 18-1	YES	11,304 (65.9%)	NO	5,856 (34.1%)
Measure 9	YES	16,229 (59.8%)	NO	10,908 (40.2%)
Measure 8	YES	13,636 (61.2%)	NO	8,650 (38.8%)
Linn County				
Measure 22-01	YES	18,197 (69%)	NO	8,153 (31%)
Measure 9	YES	27,187 (60%)	NO	18,090 (40%)
Measure 8	YES	20,608 (59.4%)	NO	14,089 (40.6%)

A comparison of results from the November 1992 anti-gay Measure 9, the 1988 OCA-sponsored Measure 8, which rescinded an executive order banning discrimination based on sexual orientation in public employment in the state of Oregon, and results from the most recent anti-gay initiatives.

The Dignity Report — Page 1

THE
NORTHWEST IMPERATIVE

Documenting A Decade Of Hate

Robert Crawford
S. L. Gardner
Jonathan Mozzochi

COALITION FOR HUMAN DIGNITY
PORTLAND, OREGON

NORTHWEST COALITION AGAINST MALICIOUS HARASSMENT
SEATTLE, WASHINGTON

Coalition for Human Dignity Fact Sheet:

The Neo-Nazi Movement in the Pacific Northwest

The neo-Nazi and white supremacist movement in Oregon and the Pacific Northwest has received a good deal of attention in the years since November of 1988, when Ethiopian student Mulugeta Seraw was murdered by racist skinheads in Portland. In the aftermath of the murder and during the subsequent civil trial of professional neo-Nazi Tom Metzger, Portland-area activists began to systematically monitor and oppose the bigoted violence and racist, anti-Semitic ideology of local supremacists. Those involved in the effort quickly came to realize that the scope of the problem was both greater than anyone had guessed, and that it was growing at an alarming rate. Further, it was also realized that there was no integrated analysis of the political, social, cultural and legal impact of neo-Nazi activities in Oregon. This topical report is the briefest possible summary of such an analysis as it has been developed by the Coalition for Human Dignity over the last four years of anti-Nazi activism and opposition research.

Hate Crimes

When most people think of the white supremacist movement in Oregon, they think of neo-Nazi skinheads. This is understandable: with their shaved heads and jackboots and a tendency toward violence, the racist skins are an obvious presence. It is also unfortunate to the extent that it has lead some people to consider the neo-Nazi movement as another form of "youth gang." This is unfortunate because the white supremacist movement is composed of a broad variety of organizations that cannot be understood in such terms.

Still, as a point of departure, the idea of a "hate crime," a crime motivated by racial, ethnic, religious, or homophobic bigotry needs to be explored.

First, the statistics . . .

In the one-year period beginning May 1988 and ending May 1989, the Metropolitan Human Relations Commission (MHRC) documented 84 bias-motivated crimes in the city of Portland. The following year that number rose to 149, and increase of 56%. The situation statewide is no more encouraging, with 343 hate crimes being reported between January and December of 1990. In 1991 and the first half of 1992 the numbers continued to increase, with each week seeming to bring in a record number of incidents. There were ten cross burnings in southeast Portland alone during the summer of 1992.

Then an explanation . . .

Law enforcement officials are quick to point out that increases in the rate of reported crimes may indicate increased reporting, and in this case that is certainly true, since the hate crimes law in Oregon is still relatively new. Still, behind the raw numbers are two vital facts: 1) the numbers represent actual human victims, individuals with hopes and dreams and lives to live, and 2) the impact of every act of bigoted violence extends far beyond the immediate affect on the individual victim.

To put it another way, the harm done by hate crimes is done not just to the individual victim, but to her or his entire community and beyond. Every act of bigoted violence tends to escalate the level of fear within the community under attack, and it is this kind of fear that organized neo-Nazis feed upon, using it as a weapon and as a recruiting device. The message is that if you inspire fear, then you need not be afraid. Such messages can have a powerful appeal to young people.

The White Supremacist Movement

While feeding off of the fear generated by hate crimes, neo-Nazi and white supremacist groups do not confine their activities to street violence. Such groups attempt are primarily political, intent on radically changing the nature of the society in which we live so that it fits into their own vision of a racist utopia. A brief sketch of the sorts of groups involved in white supremacist activity in Oregon is indicative.

The white supremacist movement encompasses a broad array of organizations, publishing houses, pseudo-scientists, electoral fronts and individuals for whom race and the struggle between racial groups is the prime motivating factor. For these groups and individuals race becomes the very foundation of society and political organization. They perceive other races as, through there very existence, a threat to the continued purity, and hence the continued existence of the white race. There is thus a coherent logic behind the ideology of genocide, for once race and racial purity become the ultimate grounds of social organization, then the removal

---

Patriot Games
Jack McLamb & Citizen Militias

by

Robert Crawford
S. L. Gardiner
Jonathan Mozzochi

Seattle Preparedness Expo '94: a collection of 2nd Amendment extremists, Christian Patriot ideologues, alternative medicine gurus, ultra right-wing book dealers, anti-Semitic conspiracy theorists, militia organizers and military surplus venders.

September 10, 1994, the second day of the Expo, some three hundred supporters gather at the Seattle Center Exposition Hall to hear retired Phoenix, Arizona police officer Gerald "Jack" McLamb talk about a conspiracy to enslave the American people in a diabolical New World Order. Playing on themes that have been developed over the years in the so-called Christian Patriot movement,[1] McLamb proceeds to tell the appreciative audience about the extent and nature of the enemy they face and the need to prepare for the "coming storm," to thank all assembled for their help in recruiting law enforcement officers and soldiers into the movement, and to encourage the formation of citizen militias.[2]

A former conscientious salesman from California,[3] McLamb is the self-appointed ambassador and evangelist from the Christian Patriot movement to the law enforcement community. His Aid & Abet Police Newsletter and the various reports issued by the American Citizen and Lawmen Association (ACLA) and Police Against the New World Order target police officers and soldiers, attempting to "re-educate" them in the ways of Christian Patriot conspiracy theories.

Face-to-face McLamb is a large, smarmy man who wears his police uniform at public appearances.[4] His consistent theme is both simple and disturbing: if police officers refuse to enforce the law, then the government—a cabal of demonic elitists in the Christian Patriot view—is rendered impotent. Speaking informally at his booth at the Seattle

---

CHD Factsheet: The Neo-Nazi Movement in the Pacific Northwest (date unknown), Patriot Games (1994), Guns & Gavels (1996), The Dignity Report vol. 5:2 (1998)

GUNS & GAVELS

COMMON LAW COURTS, MILITIAS & WHITE SUPREMACY

Devin Burghart
Robert Crawford

COALITION FOR HUMAN DIGNITY
PORTLAND, OREGON

Volume 5, Issue 2
Spring 1998

The Dignity Report

10 YEARS IN DEFENSE OF DEMOCRACY AND CIVIL RIGHTS

Did the Birmingham Bomber Sleep Here?

A Special Focus on the Anti-Abortion Movement

Which Side Are You On?
The "Pro-Life" Movement Responds to Clinic Violence *by Will Offley*

Pro-Life or Pro-White-Life?
The Far Right, Eric Rudolph and a Link to the Olympics Bombing *by Leonard Zeskind*

Wrath of Angels: The American Abortion War
Reviewed by Leonard Zeskind

Plus Volksfront • Anti-Immigrant Activism • The Far Right in Eastern Washington

And... CHD Nabs Famed Holocaust Denier for the Board of Deputies of British Jews

STEVEN GARDINER
Coalition for Human Dignity

We were constantly confronting, and being confronted by, political vigilantes who we knew to be violent—they had proven themselves to be. We made strategic alliances with community organizations, neighborhood associations in Portland, but also groups around the Northwest as we expanded out of Portland to do work in Idaho, Washington, rural Oregon, in coalition with groups there. We started specializing, after a year or two, in doing the research. This is not academic research; this was definitely opposition. How can we find out who these folks are and suggest ways to minimize their impact?

So that might be having political strategy conversations with SHARP skins to say, "Look, you guys are doing great work. Let's look at your overall politics. What about misogyny? What about anti-queer stuff? You know, do you really want that hanging around your neck when you're trying to do this antiracist work? It's not enough just to be anti-nazi."

We subscribed to and read right-wing publications, trying as best as possible not to have to pay for them. We sent people to rallies or we went to rallies, if it was a public event, or places where we knew were not necessarily nazi space but where we expected to find them. That would be punk shows, gun shows, and what became to be called "preparedness expos," where survivalists gathered together to trade tips and buy mineral supplements and bayonets.

We debriefed people who didn't want to be nazis anymore. We spent a lot of time with anyone who wanted to come out. Asking them, why did they get in? And what kinds of activities were the groups involved in, what are your biggest concerns, and so on. And again, like talking with SHARPs, when it came to ex-nazis, we were like, "If you were once a nazi, it's not enough just to say, 'I'm no longer a nazi.' You can't be neutral in this particular fight. It's not ethically tenable. If you're going to come out, you're going to come all the way out and tell what you know."

This strength was really a willingness of a half a dozen people or so to continue changing tactics until we would find something that would work. We'll try this, we'll try that, and to then say, okay, we think this will work. But we're not going to do this on our own. We can do research on our own. We weren't trying to be right, we were trying to have an impact. And so then we would go to community organizations, usually the most impacted.

That might be the Jewish community, if this is a Holocaust-denial situation. Or the Black community, if this is a situation with street intimidation. Or the queer community, if this was an OCA thing. We would say, "We're thinking about doing this. What do you think?" Or, "What

---

Portland ACT UP flyer, 1989. Courtesy of the Oregon Historical Society.

ACCORDING TO THE OREGON DEPARTMENT OF HUMAN RESOURCES
AS OF NOVEMBER 29th, 1988 THERE WERE 463 CONFIRMED CASES OF AIDS,
270 DEATHS AND COUNTING........

ANGRY ABOUT AIDS, AND IT"S IMPACT ON THE GAY AND LESBIAN
COMMUNITY? DO YOU NEED A STRUCTURED OUTLET FOR THAT ANGER? DO YOU
WANT TO BE PART OF THE NATIONAL AIDS ACTIVIST MOVEMENT?

JOIN THE PORTLAND CHAPTER OF ACT UP, THE AIDS COALITION TO
UNLEASH POWER. NOW IN FORMATION, WE ARE COMMITTED TO NON-VIOLENT, DIRECT
ACTION TO END THE AIDS CRISIS. WE ARE PRO-GAY & LESBIAN, ANTI-RACIST AND
PRO-FEMINIST. AND WE NEED YOU!!

MEETING SCHEDULE:

WED., NOVEMBER 30th	7:00-8:30 p.m.
MON., DECEMBER 5th	6:00-7:00 p.m.
TUE., DECEMBER 13th	7:00-8:30 p.m.
TUE., DECEMBER 20th	7:00-8:30 p.m.

ALL OF THE ABOVE MEETINGS WILL TAKE PLACE AT THE MULTNOMAH CENTRAL LIBRARY
801 S.W. 10th at Taylor.

IF YOU ARE UNABLE TO ATTEND THESE MEETINGS BUT WOULD LIKE TO BE INFORMED
ABOUT ACT UP ACTIONS, OR SIMPLY WANT MORE INFORMATION PLEASE CALL 224-8809.

ACT-UP

AIDS COALITION TO UNLEASH POWER

would be helpful to you?" So we tried to do movement-facing partnerships to inform our activities.

The most effective things were direct interventions. That included SHARP/ARA-style confrontation, but it also included—if they had a public event—to show up with many more people than they did and confront them more rhetorically. That included outing them. This was a strategy to make them visible in the community. So to call up employers and say, "Look, you know, you have a nazi working for you, doing customer service, who has visible swastika tattoos, do you really want that?" We had a known violent skinhead who was living in an apartment complex where there were vulnerable people. We would call up the landlord and say, "Look, this is a person with a history of violence. Within the applicable fair-housing laws, do you really want this person living in your space?" And usually what they would do is they would look at it and say, "Huh, this person is having a party every weekend and trashing the walls with hammer blows ... You know, maybe we have good cause to ask them to go elsewhere."

I wouldn't say that we always succeeded. I mean, a lot of us were pretty young back then. There's a certain arrogance of youth that sometimes made us think that we were smarter than everyone else. And we certainly spent a lot of time figuring things out about the right reading their newsletters, and so in a certain sense, especially in a pre-Internet time, we did know more about what was going on with the right than anyone else in the Northwest, by virtue of having fourteen filing cabinets full of their newsletters. That doesn't necessarily translate into winning.

We won some fights and we lost others.

Opposite: 1989 flyer, courtesy of Kelly Halliburton.
Pages 176–77: March for Dignity and Diversity, October 7, 1990. Photo by John Klicker.

ROCKPORT RECORDS & USAMBA
PRESENT

AN EXHIBIT OF ANTI-RACIST ART
with Poetry, Music, Video and Performance Art

NOON - 6PM
SEPT 23 & 24
ROCKPORT RECORDS
203 SW 9TH

FREE Admission.......A Benefit For
COALITION FOR HUMAN DIGNITY

Chapter 7

Sharper Times
On the Streets with the
Skinheads Against Racial Prejudice

In the late '80s, a young skinhead named Mark Newman came to Portland as a SHARP, a Skinhead Against Racial Prejudice. According to veteran antiracist skinhead Tom, "There were already antiracist skinheads here. He didn't bring that. He brought the name SHARP, the first antiracist skinhead crew. He brought the glue to help us organize into something."

Most SHARPs were in their late teens or early twenties. During interviews, many of them mentioned uneasy relationships with family or being kicked out of their homes. They had only the skills and training they gave each other, read about, or amassed on the streets fighting boneheads. By their own admission, they drank and used drugs freely, creating a fragile balancing act between their antiracist, humanitarian ideals and the violence with which they delivered them.

Across the country, activists fighting the white power racists faced an uphill battle with the media, and the Portland SHARPs were no exception. SHARP's formation, based on loose principles of antiracism, brotherhood, and camaraderie, was easily characterized as a gang, both by outsiders and insiders. They were not officially organized into a nonprofit like the Coalition for Human Dignity or nationally networked like Anti Racist Action, and that made them especially vulnerable to press depictions as skinhead-on-skinhead violence.

SHARP members spent their time fighting "the bad guys" for a public who, under the influence of the media that was fed information by cops like Loren Christensen, eventually lumped in them with the nazi skinheads they despised. Disillusionment in this environment is inevitable.

Portland SHARPs, October 7, 1990. Photo by Coyote Amrich.

MICHAEL CLARK
SHARP

ARA used to meet in the apartment next door to mine, downtown. And we would all party. I really didn't think about things on a political level. I thought about them on a commonsense level: this is my family and we look out for each other. Your own belief system coincides a little bit with this person's, and theirs rubs off on you, or they're stronger and tougher and you want to emulate them. And that is, especially when you're young, how your beliefs evolve, right? It's like what you choose to be exposed to and what your parents expose you to. I'm not gonna act like I was altruistic or something. That antiracist mindset rubbed off on me from the people I was around, who understood that it was a more serious issue. I bought into that, and I was more than happy to go help make a difference. I wasn't, like, leading the charge that this is some moral and ethical positive thing. I wish that I could say I was, that would be cool, but that wasn't exactly what happened.

Anti Racist Action was really political, and politics always made me crazy. I believe in antiracism 100 percent, and I believe it takes what it takes, but one of the things for me personally that kept me from getting more involved in ARA was too many rules. I'm an old-timer and I'm kind of slow. So I can't get woke all at once. I'll say it was . . . morally intimidating. You couldn't call a girl the B-word. You had to be okay with everyone being gay. You had to be okay with everything. Which I don't have any issue with now. But it was so cut-and-dried. It felt like I was gonna take on a belief system that I really hadn't even processed on my own yet.

There are a lot of skinheads that I've been friends with for a long time that were members of ARA and who really worked within the parameters of how to portray yourself and what to get caught doing and what not to get caught doing. Then SHARP came around; it was kind of the same thing, but you could be violent if it was under these circumstances, so that was a little better. [Laughter.] Over time, so many cliques branched off, because people needed a place to stand by the things that they were really behind, without all the clutter of the social movement.

So I tended over time to gravitate from the more political and organized stuff to, "We're two-tone, we're working class, we're not dealing with your nazi BS. And if you look at me sideways, I get to punch you in the face." [Laughter.] Which was what I needed at the time.

Tom T., circa 1991. Photo courtesy of Jon Bair.

TOM T.
SHARP, ARA, and the Portland Baldies

My introduction to skinhead was SHARP. I met those guys and they started explaining the culture. I moved out of my family's house at a really young age, and the family side of SHARP really provided a place for me to belong and to be looked after. I came in around '89. I shaved in with SHARP in Portland.

There was a big protest that I think CHD organized on Hawthorne, in front of a house where a lot of nazis lived. At 20th and Hawthorne over by that 7-Eleven. Randy Krager, who later became the founder of Volksfront, and a bunch of other nazis were there.

Later that day, we fucked their fucking shit up. We threw shit through their windows, bricks and whatnot, and then we left. A few of us came back several hours later, and they surrounded the car. They started blowing out our windows, hit two of my friends with sticks. We took off. One of them had to go to the hospital because he was split from the front of his forehead to the back of his head.

Then we went back and two people that ended up getting hit—one with a hammer and I think maybe another one with a pipe—filed a complaint with the police. They were both female nazis. That allegedly all happened inside the 7-Eleven, if that even happened. I never went inside

Silkscreened SHARP patch. Courtesy of Jon Bair.

there, but I got pulled over driving away. I was seventeen.

Then later on, I was arrested at the Tom Metzger trial and was subsequently charged with two counts of assault to which after a plea bargain landed me sixteen months in the state prison system. I was seventeen when it happened. I was eighteen by the time I was tried, convicted, and sentenced.

To the best of my knowledge, I was the first antiracist skinhead in Oregon to hit the prison system. That would have been in 1990. Within an hour of landing in Oregon State Correctional Institution, I was in the chow hall, eating food. Kyle Brewster walked right up to my fucking table and was like, "Are you Tom?" And I said, "Yup." And he said, "Get up. Those were my friends."

I ended up grabbing him. We were, like, face to face, kind of grabbing each other. Then people yelled, "Cops!" so we broke away. Within an hour, he had sent somebody into my cell, this guy named Warren, who beat me pretty good. I was bloody from my head to my waistline and

SHARPs, downtown Portland, 1992. Photo by Coyote Amrich.

soaked into my jeans. So that gives you, like, an idea how bad this dude beat my ass.

Luckily, I was coached by my stepdad. After I had a smoke, I walked to that guy's cell. When I walked out of my cell, most of the unit—I found out later that I was on the unit that housed most of the white supremacists because it said "skinhead" in my file—they were beating on the railings. "Death to the SHARP! Death to the SHARP! Death to the SHARP!" Hundreds of people.

I walked over to his cell, all bloody, and opened up the door, and I was like, "Come on out, man." And he's like, "What?" I put my fists up and I was like, "We're gonna get it. We're gonna get some. You're gonna finish it right now." After a little bit of back-and-forth, he's like, "Look, dude, I already beat your ass." I'm like, "Well, you're gonna do it again. In front of everybody else." He's like, "Nope, you got my respect. You and I got no problem."

Later the cops noticed I was bloody—I didn't even have a change of clothes yet, I hadn't even been in prison that long—and they sent me to the hole. Then they went, "Oh, shit. We put this guy on a white power unit." They then sent me to Eastern Oregon Correctional Institution for a sixteen-month sentence.

I don't know what the impact was as far as determination, but I know who I was when I walked into that prison, and I was determined to walk out that same person. I never denounced what I was, who I was, what I stood for. Mostly I just tried to do my own time. Towards the end of my stay at Eastern Oregon Correctional Institution, which is the same prison where Jon Bair would end up, it was the Latinos that saved me, that backed me up when Rude Brood ran up on me on the weight pile—they were finally going to do something to me after months of threats.

I jumped up off the weight pile and then, like, all these Latinos came behind them, and they're like, "You're not doing this." I had a friend that was Latino that I played pinochle with, and he backed me up. That's how I got through the rest of my time, really. I can't be 100 percent, but I'm pretty sure that the guys that helped me out there were Norteños. I don't know if I'd have made it through without those guys.

Ironically, on the other side of the prison, Steven Strasser was doing his time, but we never crossed paths. Steve Strasser was the third person convicted in the Mulugeta Seraw murder. That guy's been a ghost. From what I understand, he did his time pretty quiet, and out of prison, he just disappeared.

By the time I got out of prison, SHARP wasn't really a thing anymore. People were just kind of independent. The original Baldies came from Minneapolis to Portland and gave us a lot of support through the early days, and there was a Portland version of that starting up. I instantly jumped into that because of the political praxis with the Baldies in the history of ARA. SHARP was nonpolitical. The Baldies, their lens, you know, you've got racism, but you also have sexism, homophobia, transphobia—all the tenets of ARA—and that made sense to me. So we started up the Baldies.

I got out like late '91, early '92. The Portland version of Baldies was a thing at least through '96. Bovver Boys came in around '94. We were all friends and we hung out, but that's their story to tell.

IRAN
SHARP affiliate

JACKSON
SHARP

Iran: I grew up around the remnants of the Black Panther movement in Portland. Even though my family wasn't a part of that, they would eat in my family's restaurant, I would listen. I thought, when confronted with a situation where someone was trying to beat me for my color, I had to fight. But that's not exactly how it started, because I was a pacifist at first. The lack of protection from police and the indifference of the people

---

SHARP getting arrested during Rodney King protest, Pioneer Courthouse Square, May 2, 1992. Photo by Coyote Amrich.

Portland SHARPs, circa 1990, photographer unknown.
Photo courtesy of Jon Bair.

around me drove me to be a fighter where I hadn't been one before.

Jackson: One day, I was on my way to work. I saw Iran being confronted by these nazis. This one, he ran up on him, and Iran grabbed him very simply by the head and the crotch and picked him up—this is at Pioneer Square—threw him to the ground so hard that the bricks shook and he bounced back to his feet. He was unconscious, but he was on his feet for just a moment. It was the oddest thing. And then he collapsed.

Iran: I remember that happening. It was June 29, 1989. It was my birthday. I was going to go see *Do the Right Thing* at the Guild Theatre. It was a fight; it was the rare occasion where gangsters were fighting against nazis.

I was crossing Pioneer Square, and this guy turned around and ran up in my face. His exact words were, "Martin Luther King was a faggot," and he tried to take a swing at me. I grabbed him by his crotch and turned him upside down and bounced his head off the pavement. At that point, because I wasn't expecting to get in the situation, I wasn't mentally present to actually see what happened to him. I just know that he was incapacitated.

Jackson: It's funny that you mentioned the gangsters, because that first night after I shaved my head, I got jumped by some Bloods across from Pioneer Square. They knocked me unconscious. They just thought I was a nazi. [Laughing.]

The beginning of my path to become an antiracist skinhead was a combination of punk rock and skateboards, which I was into by the age of twelve. I started to get a little older. I wanted to go to see these bands I'd listened to on tapes and records in person. However, going to punk rock shows was a dangerous endeavor in Portland, because of the amount of nazi skinheads that showed up to any show. It wasn't until I met some antiracist skinheads and I was told about the history and the roots of it that I realized that was something that I wanted to be.

I started hanging out with skinheads and learning more about it and listening to Oi and ska music, and I was already into hardcore. Iran remembers when I transitioned from being a long-haired punk rocker to a skinhead.

There was an incident early on. Mark Newman—who brought SHARP up from LA—and I think it was Egghead ended up wanting to go to the hospital. Mark got a ride with a police officer. The police officer looked at his arm, because he had a crucified skin on his arm, and he asked him, "Are you a skinhead?" Mark said, "Yeah."

Of course, the police officer's assuming that Mark's a nazi. And the police officer said, "Well, you know, what you guys don't realize is that at least half the police force is on your guys' side."

Iran, circa 1991.

Iran: I wasn't a skinhead. I had three guys that I could trust that were Native American that would sometimes fight alongside me. I had a lot of other people who liked the fact that they felt safe around me because I wasn't just fighting the nazis, I was fighting the racist rednecks, too. It was nothing to be standing around the corner, or in front of a club or something like that, and a bunch of rednecks drive by and say, "Hey, nigger."

Once I started fighting back, I would say things back to them that would be sort of wimpy. It would make them positive that they would have good results if they got out of their car and came up to me—which always ended poorly for them. Later on, they would drive by and yell, "Hey, fag." And so I would say, "Yeah, you want to fuck?" They'd go, "What?" And they'd jump out of their car, and that would be their mistake. The nazis were no different. After a while, you know, I started wearing a dress around downtown just to bait them.

Jackson: I remember that. I remember what Iran's talking about. In fact, there's a really good window into that time period that's been preserved by the Dead Kennedys: "Night of the Living Rednecks," where Jello Biafra describes an incident where he was in Northwest Portland getting jumped by rednecks.

In Southeast Portland, I saw East Side White Pride all the time, every day. They were driving around in a in a black-primer Chevy Nova with "white power" spray-painted on the side and baseball bats. They had a spotlight mounted to the side. That was Southeast Portland.

Iran: Portland—really up until Mulugeta Seraw got killed—Portland was really indifferent to racism. I'd be hanging out with people and they would say, "I like you. You're better than other Black guys."

And you know me, I would say, "How many other Black guys you know?"

"You're just like us. You know, there's niggers, and there's Black guys."

In the beginning, I wasn't like I am now. I would be thrown for a loop, and I would just spend less time around that person. If that person ran into a situation when they were in trouble, I'd let them stay in trouble. I was hanging out in a club called Skoochie's, and the reason why I went there in the first place was I saw a news story on TV about how the nightclub wasn't allowing Black people in.

It's the same thing that affected the hip-hop scene later on when it started emerging in Portland; they started creating dress codes. They could really come in and shut you down, and they did, in the '90s. With a few places that were getting a Black crowd, one place downtown and one place on Belmont that is now a grocery store—that was a restaurant that had dancing in it. So even in the '90s, Portland was still pretty racist.

I feel like if my great-grandchildren or great-great-grandchildren have to face the same things that I faced, that Jackson has faced, everything that I pushed back against was a failure. It should end now. I just don't want my great- or my great-great-grandchildren to be dealing with the same nonsense that I'm still dealing with, or you're dealing with, or anybody of color in this country is dealing with.

PAN NESBITT
Portland ARA and SHARP

I have a deep hate for nazis. And in the early ARA/SHARP days for me, I didn't even think of those peckerwoods as people. That was my mentality. I didn't give a fuck what I did. I didn't care what happened to them. It took me until my older days to realize that they're people too and that they're misled and that there's like a systemic cultural system that creates this. There's pity to be had for them. But as a kid, they were just my enemy.

It's a weird thing, because I could easily melt in with a bunch of peckerwoods; I can easily melt in with a bunch of white people. But my dream would be a day where there wasn't racism, you know. So I try to

Portland SHARP zine, 1991. Courtesy of Pan Nesbitt.

S.H.A.R.P.

SKINHEADS AGAINST RACIAL PREDJUDICE

Confronting The Racist Problem Head on!

Don't be apathetic to the Racist problem. It's not enough just to say you're Anti-Racist. Toleration of the Racist allows them to multiply and further imploy their tactics of fear. Don't let their Bald heads and millitiant dress scare you. Anyone who belives they are superior to another race are the one's who are inferior .Take a stand against Racism!
        Skinhead or not, write to SHARP today to find out what you can do to stop the spread of
              the Nazi menace in America.

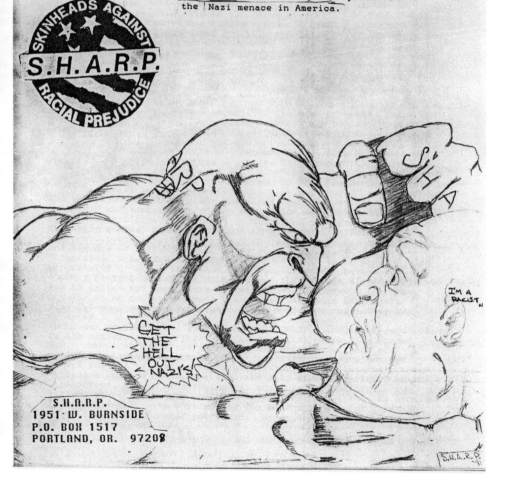

live that way. On the flip side of that, I blast the fact that I'm Jewish. Everybody in the world knows I'm Jewish. I'm not religious, by any means, but Jewish by ancestry, for sure.

My first gang was in the third grade. My dad and I were watching *West Side Story*. My dad was a poor Brooklyn Jew and was a greaser in the '50s. So we watched *West Side Story*, and afterwards, he pulls out a cigar box, shows me his switchblade and pictures of him as a greaser and his old brass belt buckle. They used to sharpen the four corners so they could swing it in the fight and shit. I didn't know that about my dad.

Next day, all the misfits at school, all the poor kids, man, we were the Westside Falcons. That was our school mascot, and we lived on the west side of town. That gang mentality was playful then, but then my dad died. My mom took me in. It was real hard for her, I think.

So my mom's a lesbian, right? And as a kid, I couldn't go to where she lived when my dad was alive, because men weren't allowed. Women that she dated didn't like men; they were men haters. I had to sit in the back of a truck because I was a boy. I just never learned what a man was. I needed to become a man, and I was alone a lot. I needed a family.

After Mulugeta Seraw was murdered, images of skinheads were all over the news, in the newspaper, and, hate them as you must, they fucking look tough. You know, that look: boots, rolled-up jeans, flight jacket, Harrington whatever. And I remember sort of wishing that they weren't fucking peckerwoods. I wish they weren't nazis, because that would be something I would be into. Right?

And then within a year or two, there it is: SHARP. Prior to SHARP, there was a crew called SCAR, which was Skinheads Committed Against Racism, but they had disbanded; they got absorbed by SHARP, I think, when Mark brought SHARP to Portland.

I don't know if I joined as much as hung out. You could have said I was ARA as much as I was SHARP, initially. But I gravitated towards the skinheads, and the crew of guys that I hung out with, we all got clean and sober about thirteen, fourteen years old. We—we're going to meetings together—Jon, Mike Clark, we basically came up together and shaved down together, ran with SHARP from probably '89 to '92. And then it got too political.

We used to make fun of the peckerwoods because they were just the foot soldiers of the right. We became the foot soldiers of the left. We had to apologize a lot for violence and for doing what we thought was right. "Why do you fight nazis?" Why wouldn't you? What kind of a fucking question is that? Why do I need to validate that?

I think we wanted to stop being asked. Then, you know, doing security for marches is cool, protesting outside of homes and businesses where nazis are working is cool. But I wanted to just beat them up. It's actions, not words. Do what you say. That's turned into my life motto.

It's weird how fast it went by, how much time has gone by so quickly.

Above: Pan Nesbitt (second from left) and friends at 1990 national SHARP/ARA convergence, downtown Portland. Photo courtesy of Pan Nesbitt. Below: Portland antiracist skinheads, Michael Clark on left, 1992. Photo by Coyote Amrich.

I remember a lot back then. I was the younger kid in the background, just observing. And then Banks got killed, and I moved to LA, and I got a whole different orientation down in LA of gang life. When I came back and we started Rose City Bovver Boys, it was just straight gang life. Antiracist. What Rose City was about was fucking dressing sharp and kicking ass. We wanted to be hard as nails, but the best dressed. We were smashing nazis, keeping them out.

The violence that we did as kids, we were the snowplow. After us came the people that could actually create real change. With the nazis around, nobody could do anything, because they were in fear all the time. And I know that, like, when the Baldies first came out, one of the big lessons that I learned was that we don't have to apologize for beating up the nazis. That, to me, was really empowering. We don't talk. We don't debate the subject. We don't go, "Well, have you ever thought about not being white pride?" No, just fucking smash you. I mean, smash on sight.

I feel like there's integrity there, too, though. You know who I am. I know who you are. The only people that really matter at the end of the day is your core group of people. I mean, it sucks. But that's gang life. That's the ruthless part of it. I feel like we set the tone for a lot of change. I'm proud of that. We did quality work. I come across talking about all the violent shit. But there's so much more to it. We did so much more.

Opposite: Portland SHARP at Rodney King protest, downtown Portland, May 2, 1992. Following four pages: Antiracist Portland skinheads, 1992. All photos by Coyote Amrich.

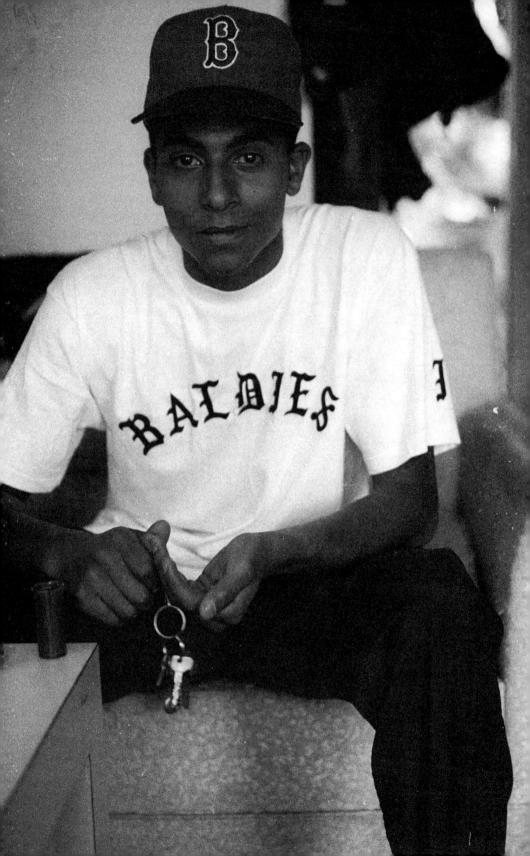

Chapter 8

This Is My City
The Story of Jon Bair

Activists succeeded in clearing the streets and show spaces of overt neonazi presence. For most residents of Portland, this felt like the menace had quickly disappeared. Antiracist skinheads knew better, and they moved from a defensive to an offensive strategy. While the Coalition for Human Dignity focused on strategies like research, community defense, and building an increasingly larger network of information and support, Portland antiracist skinheads took it upon themselves to find the remaining boneheads and fight them, wherever, whenever. Here's how it worked: someone would see a bonehead at a convenience store, make a call on the payphone, and antiracist skinheads would pile in a car to prowl the surrounding neighborhood, following leads to find the nazis.

Boneheads were still around, but they were no longer highly visible. It was no longer safe for young neonazis to wear their uniform. Many had grown their hair out. Most nazi skinhead activity took place in the outer reaches of Southeast Portland and Vancouver, Washington. Show spaces that had previously lived in fear of nazi skins now felt comfortable turning them away at the door or kicking them out at the smallest signs of trouble. The alliance between the CHD and antiracist punks and skinheads effectively forced the

Jon Bair, 1992. Photo by Coyote Amrich.

boneheads to cede the cultural landscape of the alternative youth scene to SHARP and ARA.

The opposing groups were in frequent contact, calling and threatening each other. The continual mutual harassment included frequent hit-and-run brawls and sporadic, targeted threats and street altercations. As the boneheads moved to a defensive footing, they set down their bats and picked up firearms; antiracist skinheads followed suit. Drive-bys and firebombings became common. The ongoing hostilities between racists and SHARPs consumed the two groups.

On New Year's Eve 1992, young antiracist skinhead Jon Bair jumped into a car with other Portland Baldies and went to fight a carload of young white men who believed in the extermination of the majority of the people on our planet.

JON BAIR
Portland Baldies

I grew up in Northeast Portland. I think my parents might describe me as kind of a wild kid. I was a skater. I did really well up through middle school, and in high school I took a dive and got more interested in skateboarding and hanging out and less interested in doing homework. I became interested in politics while I was in high school.

In my community of skateboarders—looking back—some of us became involved in the antiracist movement, some of those guys became involved in the racist movement, and some of those guys got into a lot of drugs and alcohol. So in the early days in Portland, the racist and not-racist groups—we all knew each other. We all had been to some of the same schools or dated some of the same people. That's something that is very different now than I think it was then.

Erin Yanke: Were you actually a SHARP?
When people would ask, I would say yes, because the acronym is, you know, Skinheads Against Racial Prejudice. But in Portland, [SHARP] was a specific group that I was actually not a member of. I was in a group called the Baldies.

There was SHARP, there was ARA, there was Coalition for Human Dignity. There were drinking groups like Spy Club and Ale Crew. There were a lot of different cliques of, I'd say, five to fifteen people that had some different interests and some differences of opinion. But when it mattered, we would all be united.

ARA had a lot to do with that. ARA had four points of unity that we thought were very important. One was, when it came to racists and their organizing and their activities, we go where they go. So if they're

Jon Bair in high school, 1988.

doing a parade or a demonstration, we're there, too. We never wanted to avoid them or let them have the streets.

The next one was, we don't rely on the cops or the courts to do our work for us. In my opinion, the police exist to protect the powerful, and our groups existed to protect those without power. Our motivations were very different right from the beginning. We were aware of that, the police were aware of that, and that affected all of our interactions.

The third was nonsectarian defense of other antifascists. So, there's a lot of different antiracist and antifascist groups. For example, there's like super communist groups, and that's not my thing. But if those guys are fighting racists, we'd be there.

The last one was that we support abortion rights and reproductive freedom. I think in this day and age, we could expand on that into the LGBTQ and the trans community. They're another vulnerable population that definitely gets persecuted and abused, and I think we would stick up for them, too.

The group that I was a part of started in Minneapolis; then I was part of a smaller group that was an offshoot here in Portland. But yes, in the antiracist skinhead world, we become connected—actually all over the world—pretty quickly. That was something I really enjoyed about the culture. I think I was the last one among my group of friends to really join the group. The progression for me was kind of slow and natural.

I worked since a very young age, and I had a house that I rented when I was very young. My house was the main house where a lot of the activity happened and where I got more deeply involved. The day-to-day of it was music, parties, drinking. And all of this happened long before I was twenty-one. We didn't hang out in bars; we weren't allowed to go in bars. We did a lot of stuff like going to thrift stores, going to record stores. There were house parties, and there were friends.

Sometimes we'd get attacked by people who thought we were nazis, you know, and it was a lot of trying to explain our position, and ultimately, at least in my neighborhood, we formed some alliances with some of the other groups. Early on, it was a lot of drama all the time.

What happened for me is on New Year's, New Year's Eve of 1992, my friends and I were drinking, we were at a party. I don't know who called who, but there was some nazi groups we'd been fighting regularly. People were talking to them on the phone, and threats were being exchanged back and forth. We're all drunk. That's part of the story, too. So we decided we'd go out and meet them for a "fistfight." We went out and it was snowy and icy out everywhere.

They drove up. They pointed a gun at us out the window. We got back in the car, and then they were following us. Nobody could drive fast, because everyone's tires were slipping. This is the middle of the night. There's no traffic around. So we had this weird following-each-other thing around the streets for a while and slipping around the corners. I remember we were trying to decide what to do, like, should we go past the police station? And we were like, no way. One of the guys I was with said, "All right, I'm just going to fight the guy. Pull over and I'll fight the guy."

We pulled into the parking lot. He got out and stood up. They came with their car and they just ran him over, right in front of us. We thought he'd been killed. But what happened was, he got pinned under the car and just slid on ice. He wasn't even hurt very bad. The next thing I remember, there's a lot of yelling, there's a lot of screaming, people are screaming that they're shooting at us. People are screaming, "Shoot the gun!"

I had a rifle with us in the car. I pointed it in their general direction and fired it a few times. At that point, my friend who I thought had been killed jumped up and got back in the car with us, and we drove off.

Later, we all kind of split up, we did different things. Ultimately,

Above: Pan Nesbitt and Jon Bair at antiwar protest in 1991. Courtesy of Jon Bair.
Below: Portland Baldies, 1992. Photo by Coyote Amrich.

3835 SE 32nd, known as the 32nd house, was an antiracist skinhead house from 1989 through 1993 that was rented by Jon Bair. Above photo by Coyote Amrich. Photo below courtesy of Jon Bair, 1992.

I was arrested and questioned and released. Before I was released, the detectives said, "You know, it's a shame that that kid lost his life out there." And I was like, "Oh my god!" It just hit me like a ton of bricks. But they released me and they told me that they knew who did it. They had the person locked up and that the person was cooperating with them. I surmised which of my friends was locked up, and I definitely knew that he wasn't cooperating with them. I basically had some time to think about what to do.

You know, I was twenty years old. I thought about running away. I tried to think about what my little brother would think, what my parents might think. I thought if I do that, they'll definitely think I'm guilty, that I did this thing on purpose. Ultimately, I made the decision to turn myself in. So I did.

I went and talked to the detective, and I made a complete confession. I told them everything that I did, and for me, it was important to just tell them my part. They wanted to know what everybody else did, and I kept it to me. Then they let me call my parents, and I called my dad, and that was the toughest phone call of my life. I tried to tell him what was going on a little bit. He was kind of confused. And he was like, "Did you talk to the police?" And I was like, "Yeah, I've been talking to them all day." He's like, "Oh my god, do not talk to the police." Good advice. It was a little bit late. But I did what I needed to do to be right for me.

Obviously, that was a huge turning point in my life. I think I was in jail for about six months before I was offered and accepted the plea bargain that I took. I spent my twenties in prison and on parole.

I would say that I had a not very good relationship with my parents at that age. I had my own feelings about the ways I thought they weren't great. I thought that everything that I was doing with my friends was really great.

I can tell you that when I went to prison, my parents came and visited me every single month for all the years that I was in, and twice on every month there was a holiday, and drove, no matter how far it was. A lot of my friends, a lot of my brotherhood, evaporated. Not completely—but that was a huge wake-up call for me. My family that I thought were so crappy, they were really there for me to the best of their ability. My friends weren't present as much.

I can't put that all on everybody else, because I dropped off, too. When I went to prison, I didn't know what to do with myself. I didn't know what I wanted to do. I didn't know what I should do. I really isolated myself for a long time. But today, I have friends. I'm not entrenched in activism. But I have friends that go back twenty years. I have friends that go back thirty years. This is my city. I grew up here. I've got a lot of love and support here.

MICHAEL CLARK
SHARP

Jon and I were good friends, and he lived with me for a while in high school when he was having a hard time with his parents.

I don't think it [the Eric Banks shooting] needed to happen. The police thought I was there. My cousin drove a car very similar to one that was there that night, and his door got kicked in New Year's Day. I got a call: "What the hell did you do last night?! The police just kicked in my door looking for you!" Blah, blah, blah. "I told them I didn't know where you were."

I spent the day calling around going, "What the hell happened last night?" I would have been there, but I was a little too high on LSD to leave the house, you know. [Laughs.] So I definitely wasn't in any shape to do anything. It just—everybody was loaded, and it just worked out the way that it did. It was a hard time. I was really sad to see Jon go to prison.

It definitely put us on the map in a different way, at a different level than I think we had been before. We have a reputation now—we have for a long time—as being somewhere that's not going to put up with your shit. SHARP is out setting a boundary in the community, saying: this is what we want our living space to look like, and we're willing to stand up for it.

JON BAIR
Portland Baldies

I said that I rented a house when I was like seventeen. It became the house where we had the wild parties and the big events, and we became kind of a target. Everyone pretty soon knew that was the SHARP house, and the house had been shot up one time. Molotov cocktails thrown at it another time. We had a lot of noise complaints in the neighborhood, and we had a strained relationship with our neighbors, and the police had been there a bunch of times.

At my pretrial, I wanted to defend why I would have ever bought a firearm or own one. I owned a rifle that I bought legally, that ended up being the weapon I used, that I decided, when drunk, to take with me when we went to go meet these guys to fight. So I was in court and I was describing how we lived in this house and it had all these problems, there'd been all this police activity. And the reason I bought the firearm was to defend our home, to defend my home.

I called the two officers to the stand who I dealt with in the neighborhood. They got on the stand. Each of them said they'd never seen me before in their life. They didn't know who I was. They had nothing

ID NO. 203039   DATE 010293
SHERIFF'S OFFICE
MULTNOMAH CO., OREGON
CORRECTIONS DIVISION

ID NO. 203039   DATE 010293
SHERIFF'S OFFICE
MULTNOMAH CO., OREGON
CORRECTIONS DIVISION

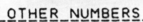

OTHER NUMBERS

SCARS-MARKS-TATTOOS

:SHARPS ** PPDS #924959

None found

03039

DEPARTMENT OF CORRECTIONS
INMATE IDENTIFICATION

BAIR, JON

DOB
03/15/72

Eye
BROWN

Ht
66

Wt
135

Hair
BLACK

SID
10306907

06/16/93

on file of any incidents, including my claim the house had been shot up, including my claim the house had been Molotov cocktailed. No records of any of that existed.

That broke my heart, because I realized that I was fighting a system that was corrupt. I didn't like the police. But I still believed at age twenty that they played by the rules, that they had to follow the rules. When they got on the stand and lied to my face in front of the judge and everybody on an oath before God and all that, I knew that they were going to screw me.

The officer had been at my house dozens of times. We were naive; we would ham it up for these guys. We'd take pictures; we'd let them take our pictures. We'd make up our own little hand signs and throw our hand signs for the pictures. Of course, all this stuff was just going into files that could later be used against us.

I'm not a big, tough guy—thought I was pretty average. But when I got to the penitentiary, I was like, "Oh, I'm a small guy." That was pretty intimidating. There was about a week, I think, where people didn't know who I was. People were friendly. I was trying to get the hang of things.

Then the first newspaper article about my conviction came out, and people started learning who I was. There were some nazi groups in the penitentiary where I was, and they immediately started giving me a hard time, harassing me, threatening me a little. The white people that I was friends with, for the most part, basically said, "Hey, you seem like a nice guy. I don't want to have the kind of problems that you have. So don't talk to me anymore. Sorry if that seems harsh, but that's the way it is."

So I found myself very scared. Very alone, not knowing what to do. People would confront me, I would swallow my pride and would walk away. It's just very, very scary for a while. At that time, they offered college classes for inmates, or GED programs, stuff like that. I requested a work position in the college. I got a job as a teacher's assistant for English as a Second Language. I also busied myself with college and reading, you know, I tried to busy myself in as many ways as I could, that I felt were safe. But ultimately, what saved me is the guys I was working with, the Hispanic community doing English as a Second Language.

They started to wonder why I was different, why I always ate by myself and why I never went outside. I was all pale, and they were wondering if I was a child molester or what the deal was. When they learned about who I was, they basically said, "Look, we're going to make you an honorary Mexican. You're going to be with us now. We're going to take you under our wing, but you look terrible. Starting today, you have to go outside every day. You have to start lifting weights." They had certain ways that they did their clothes, and they said, "You're part of our group. You do your pleats this way," and they brought me into their community.

Honestly, it was wonderful. It was a type of community that I felt really comfortable in and I could relate to. I don't know what it's like now, but it was a multiracial community. We had fun, and they kept me safe. I started getting healthy and I started feeling better about myself. That was another real turning point for me. So that was my experience with the Mexican Mafia. They liked me and they kept me safe. I was able to keep my nose clean while I was in.

Eventually I earned minimum custody and I went to a work camp where people go out on work crews and pick up litter and stuff like that. That was wonderful. That was such a different vibe. In the big penitentiary, you are housed with people who will never get out. Some of those people are crazy, and some of them don't care. So when I got to the work crews, I felt like I could breathe a big sigh of relief. Everybody at the minimum-security facilities is looking forward to going home and being reunited with their families.

I was in Baker City, Oregon, which is very far from Portland. Then I got out. I didn't realize how weird that would be. There's a lot of things I had to kind of readapt to, like, in prison, there's no darkness, there's always lights on. So sleeping in darkness was kind of like, whoa, that's crazy.

Erin: You were in prison from what year to what year?
I was first arrested on the last day of 1992. I did over four years, but not by very much, because I earned some good time. I got out in '97. After I got out, I had five years of post-prison supervision.

I had no priors before this happened. I had never had any documented police contact. So, in 1992, I fell in a really unique place on the sentencing grid. When I pled guilty to first-degree manslaughter—which is what I did—they gave me the maximum that they could give me at the time, according to the grid block, which was sixty months.

Since Measure 11, I think that changed to, like, ten years with no good time.[16] Maybe that's changed again, I don't know. I used to hang my hat on that, like, "Well, they sentenced me to the maximum allowed by law and they wouldn't listen to any of my mitigating factors." But I recognize now, as an adult, with the experience that I have, had I been a person of color or a person who didn't speak English or looked different than the status quo, I don't think I would have been offered a plea bargain. I think it would have gone to trial, and I think it would have lost. So there is that.

This is not the kind of thing that I ever would have wanted to be involved in. It's just what happened. And it definitely has shaped my life. I have different feelings about all of it. It's important to me to not regret the past or shut the door on it. I hope that sharing my experience can help others. But I also wish that that never happened. I wish I never got in the vehicle. If I could go back in time, I absolutely would do a lot of

things differently. But you know, we move forward from where we're at.

I'm not allowed to own any firearms. It's not legal for me to, but I don't want to, because I don't want to shoot anybody. If I could go back in time and do something differently, it would be: not have a gun. Those guys pointed a weapon at us. Maybe they would have shot us. I don't know.

In this country, racists and nazis, they kill people. It's not uncommon. It's just not something I ever wanted to be a part of. I wanted to stand up to the bad guys, protect the vulnerable, feel good about myself, have fun, listen to music, have friends—those are the things I wanted to do.

One of the guys who killed Mulugeta Seraw had just been crowned homecoming king at Grant High School. A lot of the guys who were involved in the racist groups were pretty typical white guys that you'd see in your neighborhood. Some of the young people today hear about those stories and they think that these guys were, like, these crazy nazi punks—they weren't. They were pretty normal white guys. They weren't very different from the Proud Boys and the Patriot Prayer types—more so the Proud Boys—but they were that kind of guy.

They had a similar kind of relationship with the police in that they seem to be—from my perspective—favored. I believe the police exist to protect the powerful, and our groups existed to protect those who don't have power. So the motivations are really different right from the beginning, which puts us at odds with the police. White supremacy is not a threat to the police. People who hold racist views, they're not a threat to law enforcement. So it makes sense that they'd be treated as less of a threat. Those things are really similar.

I remember in the early '90s thinking that we will fight these guys and we will run them out of town. We wanted to take back the punk scene and get them out of downtown. We thought, if we can run them out, then they'll be gone. It seems like we put all this energy and all this effort into this direction, and then here we are thirty years later, and I feel like things have changed a little bit.

One thing that occurs to me—and I don't know if everyone else from the scene or the old guys would agree with me—but the work that we did, including the violence in getting the racists out of the Portland area and not having a visible presence, especially in downtown, really paved the way for an open and free queer community to rise up and exist in Portland. From my perspective, I see a direct correlation.

I've had people tell me, "All violence is wrong, and all violence is bad," and sometimes that's frustrating, because the person who's telling me that might not realize that they are someone who's enjoying a privilege and a position where they directly have benefited from the violence that happened before. I'm not advocating violence when I say that. We have all benefited from violence in some way or another.

That's where the organization was really important, because the

Jon Bair (second from left) at Eastern Oregon Correctional Institution, 1995.

skinhead groups were pretty violent. There were other groups that did different things—that gathered information and found out where people lived and where people worked. There were other groups that put on events and hosted parties or whatever. But in the scene, there was room for all different kinds of people. Not everybody had to be a fighter. Not everybody had to be an organizer.

When I turned myself in, I honestly didn't think that I would survive my prison sentence. I just felt that's what I had to do to be right with myself, to be right with the world, the universe, God. But I did. Today, I've been sober for eight and a half years. That's been really good for me. I have an amazing wife who is also sober with me. We're parents to five kids that we have part-time. Being an antiracist skinhead isn't my whole story. Mostly, I'm a father. We're a nice, modern mixed family. The kids have different biological relations; the older ones are out on their own. I'm a grandfather, actually.

When my kids were little, I still had this idea that I'd be murdered. I was convinced that I'd be murdered. I just—I carried that fear with me for a lot of years. The way I responded to that was I always thought, "Okay, I want to make sure that I always tell my kids that I love them. I want to make sure that I hug them a lot." So even though it started from a morbid motivation, I ended up having really great relationships with all my kids. I got to be the kind of father that is my ideal.

I'm the parent of a trans teenage girl. That's been a really eye-opening and new experience for me. She came to me at one point and was talking to me about it, and she said, "You know, it's really important to me, Dad, that I transition sooner rather than later." And I was like, "Why is that?" And she said, "Well, if I can't pass, I'm such and such percent more likely to get physically attacked, such and such more likely to get murdered, such and such less likely to ever find a partner or have love."

How awesome is it that I get to be a supportive parent for her through this process and see where it leads, because this is new territory for me. I know trans people in my community, and I have some friends who are trans, and a lot of them don't have good relationships with their parents, especially fathers. So I've really been very lucky to be in this position. I think a lot of people believe if trans people didn't want to be targeted that they should just quit being trans and quit dressing how they dress. If you think for one minute that a teenager would choose to be something that makes them hated, that makes them a target, that makes them ostracized and alone and hated—no way. Nobody would choose that. Those teenagers who are trans and are going down that road and facing all of the dangers, I think they're the bravest people, you know? People just need to be able to be who they are.

My other kids are amazing, too. Life is pretty amazing.

Chapter 9

Less Booted, More Suited
The End of the
Coalition for Human Dignity

Bonehead hate crimes continued throughout the '90s. After three separate attacks in 1993, two Black men and an Indigenous man suffered serious lasting injuries from skinhead assaults. So it's not that violence itself disappeared from Portland, but that racist skinheads retreated from open displays of menace on the streets. Where in 1990, punks could expect to run for their lives just trying to go to a show or the corner store, by 1993, attacks became more like infrequent ambushes from a car of neonazis. As for the homophobic Christian Right, the Oregon Citizens Alliance petered out following leader Lon Mabon's unsuccessful run for US Senate in 1996.

City leaders, the media, and sometimes antiracist activists began to promote the idea that we had "won." The single-minded focus on a specific kind of racist—the young neonazi skinhead—gave the false impression that once the streets were cleared of the violent white gangs, racism was solved and "Skin City" was no more. As contradictory as it sounds, the success of the Coalition for Human Dignity and other groups in eradicating the visible presence of racist skinheads played a role in the CHD's demise.

With finite resources available to support leftist causes, CHD's

Coalition for Human Dignity's 1996 board meeting. Photo by Julie Keefe.

funders became swayed by the dominant media narrative of triumph and directed their dollars elsewhere. This seductive conclusion has had dangerous long-term consequences. CHD's research work on white nationalist and Christian Identity groups consistently showed how they were embedded throughout Oregon and the Pacific Northwest. That message had little resonance with mainstream politicians, media, and the voting public.

Short on funds and casting about for solutions, in 1998—ten years after the death of Mulugeta Seraw—the Coalition for Human Dignity migrated to Seattle to share resources with the Northwest Coalition Against Malicious Harassment. After a short time, the two groups merged to become the Northwest Coalition for Human Dignity.

JONATHAN MOZZOCHI
Coalition for Human Dignity

How to measure the impact of the intelligence aspects of our work was always a challenge, especially for dealing with funders who liked quantitative results. Some elements of what we did were necessarily secret. But you could see and measure other parts of our work. For instance, our publications reflected a quality of research on the far right that the SPLC and ADL could not match. Theoretically, we also insisted that the Christian right and white supremacist movement operated in a parallel manner; they were different, but related.

From 1989 to 1993, we were building CHD into a regional think tank that also had an operational arm; we succeeded in doing that. If we had never carried out the opposition research in Portland, I think things would have been worse; I also think there was much more we could have done that could have made things better.

We were self-consciously a group defending democracy and civil rights against political forces that were intent on dismantling them. There was a view that what we did was misguided and extreme. You could read this in local publications like *The Oregonian*, *Willamette Week*, or the now-defunct *PDXS*. We really didn't take such nonsense seriously, because for me, and I think most CHD activists, it really didn't matter at what stage bigoted groups were in their development, how incipient or inchoate their influence, only that in a racist, exploitive, and patriarchal society such movements will always be with us and therefore must always be fought. From there, one has to evaluate their relative strengths, connections to centers of power, and what kind of threat they posed to vulnerable communities. And then take appropriate action. What is effective or not is the important question, not whether one should fight them. In a certain sense, the only way to prove if white nationalists were a threat was if they came to power: if they came to power, then we would

Northwest Coalition Against Malicious Harassment buttons. Courtesy of the Wing Luke Museum of the Asian Pacific American Experience.

have been proved ineffective.

The best evidence that our research and intelligence was useful and effective comes from activists themselves and the communities most impacted by far-right violence. By this measure, we were extremely effective at assisting activists in Portland during the early 1990s.

I left the CHD in, I think, 1998. I was always very singularly focused on research and intelligence. That was my role. At some point, folks in the Coalition wanted to take a different tack. They wanted to do different stuff that perhaps didn't rely on a research-driven mechanism. We became more of a think tank. For me, personally, when I was training judges in how to understand the arcane arguments of Christian Patriots around the Fourteenth Amendment to the Constitution, this was not very effective, at least for me.

The office moved to Seattle, and then the folks who ran it for a couple years after that merged it with the Northwest Coalition Against Malicious Harassment. They were a more establishment kind of outfit. They had cops on their boards, and stuff like that. I didn't really have anything to do with it. Those were not my politics.

Today, Rose City Antifa, Pacific Northwest Anti Fascist Workers Collective, Eugene Antifa, and the groups that protect, like, Planned Parenthood clinics know very well the importance of intelligence. You need to watch these folks, and then you need to organize against them. Today, groups are carrying that out through doxing, through deplatforming. They're very effective, and they're effective in ways that we really never could be. I have a great deal of respect for that work.

I think, you know, all of these local groups, all over the United States and Europe and elsewhere, need—well, what do they need? They need platters of brownies. They need political protection, too. In a very real sense, they're on the front lines. I would say one thing, not a criticism, doing intelligence work online is one form of research-driven politics. But the other form is human intelligence, where you actually have people go to their meetings. Where people befriend these folks so that we can steal their membership list, so we can have a better idea of what the internal culture of their politics are with them and what their political organizations are. So we can have an understanding of where the funding comes from. So we can track and monitor, for instance, when they're supporting a far-right candidacy, you know, months before the guy is going to run for office. We need to have that information.

Contemporary fight-the-right groups are far more effective at signals intelligence in utilizing the Internet. But perhaps not quite as good as we were developing people to infiltrate those groups. We need to do both.

When I speak to contemporary stuff, it's as a ghost, someone outside the movement and from the past. Two contributions that I think were unique to the Coalition for Human Dignity: the radical one, which concentrates on the role of the Christian right, and the white nationalist movement within the far right, and how those were the pillars of an American style of fascism. If fascism were to come to power, it would come to power through them. We always needed to fight those elements. In addition to everything else we're doing—just in addition—there always needed to be that element on our side that was dedicated to fighting them.

And the second: the research-driven model that we use was our second unique contribution. We said local communities have it within their power to monitor their own racists, with local people who know best what's going on in their communities. We became a regional source to knit together all of that research and all of that monitoring. And that meant training and working with hundreds of people in different communities who were tracking all of these groups.

So that required foundation backing, it required really labor-intensive work like maintaining these legal files, these filing cabinets—physical files, newspaper clippings, all of this. You're setting up a whole office, so you need funding. The third thing, I don't think you need an office to do this anymore. Antifa and other antifascist groups understand that. They're right. So what that also means is that you don't necessarily need a foundation-driven approach to this. Maybe we're better off not having foundations involved in this directly. Perhaps there's a new model? I would argue that there is, that it's developing and it's emerging.

DEVIN BURGHART
Coalition for Human Dignity

Our jobs have always been really to try to help inform people about what's coming. So I don't know if that makes us sound like prophets or Cassandras. Making sure that people know what's coming down the pike. And that's always an uphill battle.

It requires a lot of really hard work to have the data to show them, "Look. Here's the details. We can tell you exactly what's happening, how many people are doing it, what's going on, what to look for, how you prepare for it." The fight against white supremacy is a marathon, not a sprint. It is a long-term struggle to fight racism and bigotry in all its various forms. In this fight, we need all the allies we can get. So even though we might politically disagree with everyone on everything, now is not the time to be sectarian. Everyone who wants to get involved in the fight to deal with racism and bigotry, to try to stomp out the threat of rising white nationalism, can and should be welcome.

We need to keep in mind that everyone has their roles. There are places for everyone in this fight. If you do not feel comfortable with direct action and being on the front lines confronting white nationalists when they protest, there are plenty of other ways in which you can get involved and do your part, whether it's conducting research or helping organize.

There are local activists who—they come from a wide range of backgrounds, but they're bartenders. They have experienced a tremendous amount of Proud Boy and other white nationalist activity, disrupting the venues in which they work. So they've organized a rapid response network for when white nationalists show up in their community. They'll let everyone else in the area know what's going on, so that they can be prepared to react accordingly. That's organizing a community that is susceptible to white nationalist incursions. They prepared themselves. It's that kind of stuff. It's organizing in the places that are vulnerable to white nationalist activity, not ceding them and creating a vacuum where white nationalists can come in.

So that means organizing a big tent, organizing across tactics. It means organizing widely politically. And I think it also means making sure that you're doing that kind of innovation to come up with ways in which different folks can fit in and figure out where they feel most comfortable taking on the very uncomfortable struggle of dealing with the larger question of white supremacy in our society.

The Northwest Coalition Against Malicious Harassment was formed a couple years before CHD. It was formed by a former Catholic priest by the name of Bill Wassmuth from Coeur D'Alene who participated in a lot of the early responses to the Aryan Nations. In fact, he had his house blown up by the Aryan Nations and barely survived one of their assassination attempts on them.

Bill was an ally and close supporter of CHD in the many years that

Northwest Coalition Against Malicious Harassment inaugural conference, North Idaho College, Bill Wassmuth at podium. Anderson Photo, 1987.

he was the head of the Northwest Coalition Against Malicious Harassment. They were doing a lot of the organizing work by the early 1990s, and CHD was doing a lot of the research work. That was really how things were working throughout the mid-'90s up until Bill ended up having to step down from his role as executive director at the Northwest Coalition, because he had ALS.

With Bill stepping down, the merger between the two groups removed some of the duplication of efforts and brought everything under one house. Coalition for Human Dignity and the Northwest Coalition Against Malicious Harassment merged and became the Northwest Coalition for Human Dignity. They stayed active up until the early 2000s. I think what was really detrimental to the organization as it got newly formed was, in part, a perception in the Pacific Northwest that the problem was gone.

I'm talking specifically about when the Southern Poverty Law Center came in and sued the Aryan Nations.[17] They won and took over their compound. This gave the impression to a lot of folks around the region that the problem of white supremacy in the Northwest had been, in effect, litigated away. It was—unintentionally, I assume—a blow to efforts to organize and to fundraise for a newly merged organization that was trying to do that kind of work, because there was no longer the same kind of urgency that groups like the Aryan Nations provided around the region.

NWCHD started running out of money; they also started losing interest, which meant that the large network of grassroots local community groups that they'd helped build up around the region started to slowly wither and die at their height. I think in the five- or six-state region, they had over 125 local groups on the ground that were doing work to counter white nationalism, but a lot of those folks stopped doing it after the Aryan Nations trial. They thought that they had won or they moved on to doing diversity work in local communities and had given up doing a lot of the programmatic work around fighting white nationalist or militia-type activities. Those external events helped make it really hard for the organization to continue as it was. That's what eventually led to the organization closing up.

CHD is an organization that means so much to me and so many people that I know. It has played an integral role in the larger community of antifascists and inspiring and supporting the work that so many people have done for so many years. I can't even count how many people that are still doing this work today either worked at CHD or had had contact with CHD. It really was a magical place in providing that inspiration and the kind of spark that allowed people to continue doing this work over the long haul. That's something that not a lot of organizations can tout.

I'm really proud to have played as small a part as I did of that. So many people deserve a lot more credit than they ever got back in the day. It's an important part of the region's history that often gets overlooked, in part because it was in a period where there wasn't a lot of online activity. It took a lot of foresight and tenacity to get it to where it was, and you've gotta give it up for those folks. They were amazing. So it was really important, both to Portland, but, I think, to the work across the country as a whole, and also CHD played a really interesting and important role internationally.

The work of the CHD fed into an international network of similar organizations doing work to monitor white supremacist activity in their countries. Members from CHD participated with other organizations like Search Light in the UK, Expo in Sweden, other folks in Germany and France and other parts across Europe, sharing information, ideas, and intelligence. The work wasn't just Portland-based, it had a local, a regional, a national, and an international perspective. It was really important.

So like when the Center for New Community and the Coalition for Human Dignity worked together on a project to counter white power music called the Turn It Down Campaign, that project eventually became modeled and taken to Germany, where they did a campaign and made a website called TurnItDown.de. They specifically modeled the kind of campaign we were doing in the United States back there in Germany and tried to replicate the successes that we've had. So from small grassroots organizations, the ripples extended all the way across the globe, and they impacted a lot of different people doing a lot of amazing work to counter white nationalism.

ABBY LAYTON
Coalition for Human Dignity

What I recall, at the end of Coalition for Human Dignity, is that we just got broke. [Laughter.] I don't think that was any one thing. People were starting to go off on their own, in different directions. Like, a couple of the people got good jobs with other groups that weren't in Portland, doing this same work in a bigger arena.

We did it. We actually pushed a whole population of brown-shirted people marching through Southeast Portland, goose-stepping, doing Heil Hitlers—we actually, over a period of three or four years, got them to leave. By being incredibly consistent and knowing the facts, knowing who people were. I think our success really came from inclusion. It came from spreading the word, from informing every group.

We went into high schools in teams to teach tolerance in rural Oregon. My team member was a Japanese woman whose family was interned during the Japanese internment.

Something that Eric Ward taught me, it's very important to see these movements as woven into society. They're not separate things. One of the studies that helped me understand hate, anti-Semitism, and racism is a study that was done by Christopher Browning, written up in a book called *Ordinary Men*. He went into Poland and researched how many people participated in rounding up Jews to kill them. There's this kind of myth that people were forced. What he showed was that 84 percent, or something like that, made a gleeful decision to round up and kill Jews.

I want people to know that there's a great threat here. That these people really are dangerous. The work can be—can get very, very scary. It can get life-and-death. I want to encourage each person to find their own place in it. You don't have to force yourself past where you feel at your edge. Just go to where your edge is. You know, that'll be enough.

You don't have to not be afraid. But just hold your own hand and do what's right. Get your friends to hold your hand. Do it together. But don't back down, because we want to be able to say never again. We want to be able to say that out loud together.

It really is, truthfully, scary. And traumatizing. I was willing to risk my life doing this. And you know, I'm not really a big risk taker. It was just really super important to me, the work. I still feel so impassioned, about the work, about life in general, and about the gift of meeting them when I did.

So I will never give up. I love people. I love human beings. I want them to flourish, and be happy, and experience love the way that I experience love. As human beings, we have a whole lot of work to do. We're all completely interconnected, we all need each other so much, and that misconstruance of human capacity in love is heartbreaking, and it's just

WHITE SUPREMACY

IN THE 90s

IN 1983 AND 1984, PETER LAKE INFILTRATED THE ORDER, A
WHITE SUPREMACIST GROUP. COME SEE PETER LAKE AT
PSU AND HEAR HIM SPEAK ABOUT HIS EXPERIENCES.

MAY 11 1990
NOON • ROOM 338
SMITH MEMORIAL CENTER
PRESENTED BY THE PSU SPEAKERS BOARD
POSTER DESIGNED BY GREG NEEDHAM/DESIGN TYPOGRAPHY

association • ku klux klan • white ary
erican police association • white ary
ront • nazi skinheads • white americ
n youth movement • nazi skinheads •
e order • white knights • national fror
association • ku klux klan • white ary
erican police association • white ary
ront • nazi skinheads • white americ
youth movement • nazi skinheads •
white knights • national fror
 association • ku klux klan • white ary
police association • white ary
nazi skinheads • white americ
movement • nazi skinheads
e order • white knights • national fror
ku klux klan • white ary
erican police association • white ary
ront • nazi skinheads • white americ
n youth movement • nazi skinheads
e order • white knights • national fror
association • ku klux klan • white ary
erican police association • white ary
ront • nazi skinheads • white americ
n youth movement • nazi skinheads
e order • white knights • national fror
association • ku klux klan • white ary
erican police association • white ary
ront • nazi skinheads • white americ
n youth movement • nazi skinheads

what we gotta keep working on.

I don't see it as any worse or any better. I see it as pretty much the same as it ever was. This is a ripple effect, right? Everything that we did in the Coalition, there's a ripple effect. So we helped millions of people by doing that work. I'm so proud of that work. I'm more proud of the work I did with the Coalition for Human Dignity than just about anything I've ever done in my life. I look back on my life, being seventy, when I see those pictures of us doing that work, I feel like my life was worth living.

STEVEN GARDINER
Coalition for Human Dignity

We won a battle. But this older generation of thought leaders emerged and set an ideological agenda that was, as they said at the time, "less booted, more suited." It was more about a strategy for capturing public policy, particularly around issues linked to immigration, which they strategically came to understand as the single biggest threat to what they see as white identity, what they refer to as white genocide, because of the demographic shifts in the United States. It doesn't mean that they don't continue to be anti-queer, anti-Black, and so on. They are. It's just, "Step back from that, and focus on immigration."

The thing to keep in mind is that white supremacy is a broad spectrum of groups. It's not just a few folks that you will see on the streets. It's people who work for think tanks like American Renaissance; it's people who are giving funds to Holocaust denial groups; it's people who are fellow travelers in the world of Make America Great Again, who would never consider themselves to be fascist.

But when you start looking at their views, their desire for a more militarized state, their protectionist ideas that are linked—even when they don't admit it openly—to white identity, you're looking at very disturbing tendencies. This has changed, of course, partially because of the Internet and partially because of the size of the movement and its fight to stay in power.

When the most egregious examples show up, there are three things that you need to do.

One, you need to protect the vulnerable. Figure out who's going to be most vulnerable, and talk to them about what they want to see, and try to come up with some kind of consensus, get as many people on board, as many communities as possible.

Two, don't ignore them, but don't aggrandize them. There's no point in fighting just to fight. Pick ground to stand and fight smart. By "fight" here, I mean all of the things that you can do to publicly show up and send a message that Portland isn't a place where these folks are welcome.

The third thing is, there has to be relentless pressure on the city and county, the local governments, not to do anything that indicates toleration of these organizations, particularly any hint of collaboration with law enforcement with these kinds of political organizations. It shouldn't even be an issue, because law enforcement shouldn't be collaborating with political organizations of any stripe, other than in the way they would interact with the public. So when they're having secret meetings with representatives of one far-right faction or another, this is clearly beyond the pale and should be called out. Anyone who won't take a stand against this should be called out in the strongest possible terms. This is a no-go when you have a chief of police, or a sheriff, or a city council person who won't take a stand on this.

These folks are dangerous. People need to protect themselves, protect their personal information. It doesn't mean you need, necessarily, to do things in secret. It means you work in groups where you figure out who is vulnerable and who can confront the politics relatively safely, and so on.

Keep in mind that you need to know who you're dealing with. It's not usually useful to engage in hyperbole. If someone is a neonazi in the sense that they're literally, you know, wearing swastikas and calling for genocide, then you can call them a neonazi. If they're not, call them something more accurate. Otherwise, your argument loses cohesion and it loses traction. Be accurate.

Those are two principles that we had back in the '90s that remain important today. The tendency is to engage polemically; much more effective—in the long term—is to get

Northwest Coalition Against Malicious Harassment
P.O. Box 16776, Seattle, WA 98116
Ph: (206) 233-9136 Fax (206) 233-0611
ncamh@aol.com

An evolution of logos.

your facts straight about who you're dealing with, which faction. Then you can use that strategically to say, okay, maybe we can't get the broadest coalition to fight some more mainstream-seeming group. But when it's this more extreme "group," we can get even more folks on board and make that coalition as broad as possible, as long as you don't compromise the most vulnerable. Never try to get a coalition that is so broad that it includes people, for example, who would throw the queer community under the bus.

The work continues to be urgent today. It's everyone's problem, to the extent that we care about the kind of society that we live in and recognize that there are large-scale trends that are pushing the politics, making it more vibrant on the far right. Those are demography, the ways in which the demographics of the United States are changing. Those are migration, that is going to be driven increasingly by climate change, militarization, and authoritarianism—the typical responses of states when they feel their legitimacy is being challenged, and identity threat, as they perceive it.

So I anticipate the state increasing moves towards authoritarianism, in the name of fighting "nazis." In fact, historically, those state resources have usually been used much more broadly and much more intensely against communities of color.

What I hope for is the possibility of a real multiracial democracy that is grounded in principles that don't marginalize women, or queer folks, or migrants. I think these are possibilities, but they're not assured. There's that great MLK line: "The arc of history is long, but it bends towards justice." We like to say, "The arc of history is long, and it bends towards those who pull the hardest."

LEONARD ZESKIND
Center for Democratic Renewal

This is a huge issue, and it's not going away quickly. Look, we have a fight on our hands. And people are pretending that it's four minutes of battle and they'll get it done. And we've got to get prepared for, you know, the next generation of battles, and we're not doing it. We need not only more intelligence gathering but smarter. We have to act like there's a battle going on and build towards tomorrow.

Multiyear funding would help. That would be one thing that would help a lot. Doing things aimed at tomorrow's young people. That's what would help getting ready; we're fighting the battles now that we have to fight—because we have to fight them.

The white supremacists have been organizing against immigrants since David Duke did the "Klan Border Watch," where he staged a militia of armed white supremacists on the border with Mexico in 1977. Aryan Nations in the 1980s used to hand out maps about the big immigration

When
Hate
Groups
Come
to Town

A Handbook of Effective
Community Responses

Second Edition
Revised and Updated

STUDENTS
UNITED
Against
RACISM
Mont. College Studen

**Published
by the
Center for
Democratic Renewal**

The Center for Democratic Renewal (formerly Klanwatch) was a parent organization for the early CHD. Leonard Zeskind was their research director and also a CHD board member. 1992 edition. Courtesy of Jonathan Mozzochi.

flow with big red arrows in '83 and '84. I picked up a copy in rural Kansas. And that has been their agenda for a long time. They have been paying attention to the calendar; they know with certainty that there's a battle to come. And they've been acting like it.

You hear that with their slogan that "immigration is white genocide"—because white people will lose their power through majority dominance. Now, frankly, I think that's a good thing. But there's a lot of white people who agree with them—I think the number is 55 percent. That's a high percentage of white people who think Black people are oppressing them. There's massive misinformation and false consciousness out there. On the coasts, it's not as easy to see. But this battle is going to get tough when a majority of people are no longer white, when they're a minority in a nation of minorities.

Celina Flores: I saw recently that the number of babies of color was larger this year than white babies.

You bet, red rider, that's what's coming down the pike. White people are dispossessed, and white nationalists have been saying that since '72. Now they've got a chance to say, "Yeah, there's more of them than there are of us. They are destroying our culture." And they're fighting, and they have followers.

We think we're gonna beat it out of them. No, we've got to get education out, into every hand. It's a battle for hearts and minds.

SCOT NAKAGAWA
Coalition for Human Dignity and ACT UP Portland

In order to embrace this very difficult future that faces us right now, can we move forward together? Or do we have to move forward separately? Is it just simply not possible for us to move forward together? If we move forward separately, our ability to contend with the multiple history-changing crises we are likely to experience over the next twenty and thirty years—partly driven by climate change—then we are incredibly out of luck. We need to try to figure out how we resolve these problems together.

But in order to do that, we need to start to try to understand what we mean when we say "we." We have been very, very carefully taught by our racist society to think about race comparatively, to think, like, "Whites have it one way, and Blacks have it another way, and Asians have it in another way." And maybe there's even, like, a hierarchy of oppressions, where one group's suffering way more than another group.

But the thing that we ought to be doing, I think, is giving up on

Anti-OCA graphic from the *Oregon Witness*, 1992.

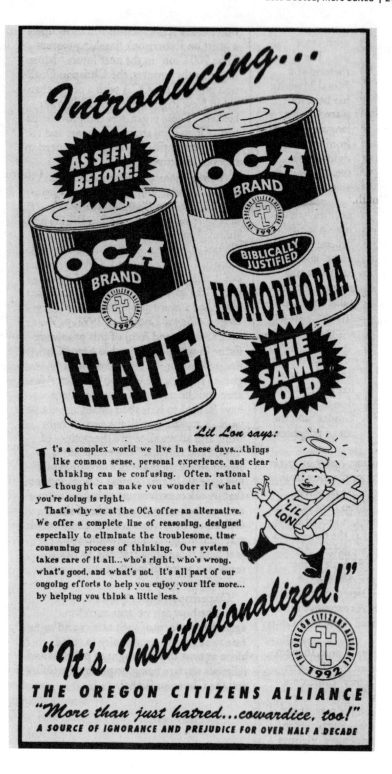

the master's way of seeing the world. Race is a comparative system of categorization. To start to think about race relationally, how is it that my experience affects your experience that affects the next person's experience? So that we understand that each of us in our way, as we go through the world, are impacting one another within this—a system of relationships. So that in order to be able to dismantle racial hierarchies, we need to work together. If we don't, we're constantly going to butt up against one another.

Asian Americans learned this lesson really well in recent years, because of the way in which we've been stereotyped as "model minorities," and we are beginning to figure out how to pivot in order to address it. In order for there to be model minorities, they have to be problem minorities. Historically speaking, the Asian American model minority has been particularly used to present African Americans as a problem minority, to say that, "If this one group can climb out of poverty and experience this kind of success," they say, "in American society, then groups that haven't done this must be, in some way, broken." And they use that to justify attacks on civil rights and ending programs like Aid to Families with Dependent Children, that were created in order to try to address the problem of inequality and entrenched poverty that exists in this country.

So, for Asian Americans, being cast as superhuman is still not human. You're still a perpetual foreigner, you're still very vulnerable to prejudice, scapegoating, and targeting, because you're not viewed as "one of us," you're this special group that somehow has characteristics that makes you super competitive and perhaps even a threat to white interests. What it means for certain Asian American minority groups, certain immigrant groups, is that their poverty becomes invisiblized by the mean experience of the group. So the model minority myth is not to the benefit of Asian Americans generally, even if it may be an advantage in certain forms of employment. The reality, though, is that once you're hired, Asian Americans are the least likely to be promoted into executive positions. Because that model minority myth is the stereotype that applies to the most highly exploitable worker: one who never complains, who works super hard, who's very self-sacrificing, and who's a technical worker.

I'm almost sixty years old. I've been around for a while. I've been doing this since I was seventeen. It's never been my experience that most people are checked in. Most people are attempting to deal with the day-to-day reality they're in and to make it as comfortable and happy for themselves as possible.

At the moment, we need to change minds about a bunch of different things. And it's really difficult to do that, because for the last forty years or so, people on the left of American politics have been subjected to the worst kind of marginalization and attacks. Left-wing institutions have been destroyed. We on the left are relatively anemic, not as well organized, not as robustly informed by think tanks and true radical foundations and idea-producing institutions that would help us address this historical moment.

You know, identity politics is a really important reaction to that singularizing, totalizing worldview that allows authoritarian regimes to develop. Native Americans, African Americans, and new immigrants in the United States basically live under authoritarian regimes. They are excluded and persecuted in ways that people who are in the mainstream of American society are not. When we talk about "protect and serve" as a guiding principle of our police force—protect whom against whom? Serve whom against whom? This is always the most important question.

So those of us who are excluded fought for inclusion. We were able to put a lie to those grand narratives, but we had no narratives to offer as alternatives. We need to be able to start to develop those narratives of our own. We need to be able to start to talk about the future that we want and become more future-oriented and not just reacting against what others are doing to oppress us. We're trying to do that now, under really difficult circumstances.

We have now approached a point in time where what we've learned from the past is not good enough to inform the future. We need to start to develop new tools, new ideas, and new visions for change. And we need to do so incredibly rapidly, because it is a race against time.

The white nationalists, the Christian nationalists, are vying for power. There is the real possibility of the business right and the white nationalist right forming the kind of alliance that the Christian right and the business right now have. When the near right and the far right merge, the problems we will face will grow far greater than they are now. And so we are in a race against time.

So were we successful? I'm not sure. We did what we had to do under the circumstances, and given the extent to which we were pummeled and marginalized, it was not contingent on us to be able to put forward visions of change that would supplant those of the hegemony, of those in power. But now that we've reached this point, it is our responsibility. It's up to us. Nobody else is going to do it for us. We are the ones we've been waiting for. And this is our time.

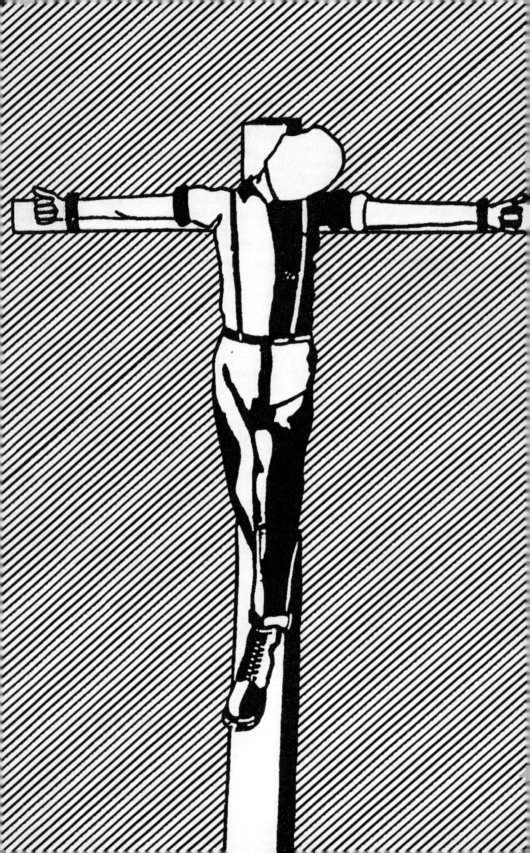

Chapter 10
Nothing Is Final

To an outside eye, the Portland of 1996 looked much the same as the Portland that spilled the blood of Mulugeta Seraw in 1988. But the city was changing. Shuttered storefronts along Alberta Street masked the increasing rents, evictions, and gentrification occurring in Northeast Portland. There were still nightly rock shows at the stately building on SE Pine and 9th, but the venerable Pine Street Theatre had been rebranded as La Luna, and Elliott Smith and Team Dresch replaced headliners like Poison Idea and the Accüsed.

Compared to Seattle and San Francisco, houses were relatively cheap, and a basement room in a group house still rented for about $100 a month. For the many new residents drawn to Portland in the late 1990s, the fears and risks of getting jumped by a carload of racist skinheads were ghosts of a reality that had ruled a bygone scene.

But the veterans of the front lines told a different story. Jon Bair and a few other seasoned SHARPs were still in prison. Many hadn't survived. Some were in recovery, in addiction, or somewhere in between. The antiracist skinhead scene splintered into smaller and smaller factions—crews like the Bovver Boys, PUB, Unity, and Intensify. Portland ARA organizer Jason described this shift as, "The energy changed and it became much more street oriented. It became

---

The two-tone crucified skinhead is a longstanding symbol in the antiracist, working-class, skinhead community and is meant to relay their societal persecution. This concept was immortalized by Agnostic Front on their 1989 *Live at CBGB* record with their cover of the song "Crucified."

more of, 'How do we get *out* of the political?' Everybody was like, 'We're just going to fight them in the street, and keep it there.'" The CHD had pulled up stakes out of Portland and was phasing into a nonprofit existence. After driving the violent right wing underground, survivors of that era could begin to assess what their lives felt like when they weren't fighting to stay alive—how to heal and move on.

Like many youthful coalitions with no money, little experience, limited mentorship, and lots of energy, the big tent that brought in punks, skinheads, and the CHD proved to be a fragile alliance. The movement rhetoric needed to evolve beyond the simple and effective shared principle of "nazis out." But the disparate groups had no strategy for moving forward together, aside from a general and fiercely held agreement that racist, homophobic, and anti-immigrant boneheads should be evicted from the city. The excitement of uniting was not enough to sustain—much less build—a decades-long campaign to fight oppression in all its forms.

JASON
Portland ARA

I want to say that when Eric Banks was shot, most of them believed that our side had killed one of them without hesitation. In some ways, that really worked in our favor, because it quieted things down. But it changed the way they operated.

They started moving further out. They grew out their hair. They changed the way they dressed. They started recruiting in a different format. They went online, and they started being more secretive. And this is what has led to the resurgence now, the way that they changed their operating procedures.

We changed because of that, too. We knew a lot of what they were going to do. There were some inside voices who gave us some info. We started working in other forums to slow them down, and it made their recruiting and organizing efforts difficult, and it really made their street presence difficult. We were still doing it.

ARA was just me and my girlfriend at that point. There were still really, really political shows going on—Resist was huge, Deprived was great. They were still killing it, doing a lot of stuff. Then Deprived became Defiance. They never stopped doing what they were doing; it was through music, instead of through this political apparatus.

ARA nationally still had a lot of stuff going on, but it totally got hijacked in '91, '92, by the Trotskyists. They tried to hijack it from us in '91. They came in with a big contingent and tried to get us to vote to ratify all these things. And we were like: this isn't us. We're not a left-wing, political organization. We're antiracist activists. We see a bigger picture, and so we're willing to work with the people, but you're not going to come in and take over our meetings, and you're not going to take over our structure.

They did that in many places. I think Cincinnati was one that had a huge antiracist skinhead punk scene that was ARA, and it became a very left-wing, communist-leaning political organization. They just took it from them.

Many of us, you know, were socialists or communists, and that was fine, but we weren't going to be a political component. We were here to fight racism, homophobia, sexism. We did not want to lose focus on that. So everybody was like: we're just going to fight them in the street and keep it there.

JORIN
Portland ARA

I do not regret our use of violence back then. I do think that it had its intended effect. I think that the fascists now are doing a much better job using Antifa's willingness to use violence against them. That strategy may not be as effective now as it was then.

I personally believe that the narrative that the fascists are using—around Antifa just being violent thugs that are anti–free speech—needs to be more carefully addressed. Something that we didn't do a good job of—increasing public approval of our side—needs to be done more. I don't think getting in an argument with your average civilian about the definition of violence is very helpful. On the other hand, fully committing to violence in the sphere of public opinion is not necessarily helpful.

I think some of the things that we didn't adequately succeed in before—getting the message out to young people that fascism is not a viable option for them—are still really important. The use of the Internet is something that fascist organizations in this country do really well. There's a lot of potential there to organize around people's minds rather than just their physical bodies.

Thinking about these things, a lot of sadness comes up for me. We're looking back at this not just from a historical perspective. We are back in a place where the threat of fascism in Portland and around this country is not only alive, but perhaps more viable than it was even in the late '80s and '90s, which boggles my mind. I think it is really important that people are doing things to fight fascism. We cannot be fighting with each other over minutiae of tactics, when the far bigger threat is well-organized and becoming only more savvy and motivated by the current political system.

CHINA
Portland ARA and SHARP affiliate

By the mid-'90s, I was somewhere else. This fight started in the '80s for me, and I stepped out probably '92, '93. There was a point that I realized that nobody was listening to me, because I was a kid with nowhere to live. I didn't have any education. I was also a Black girl. Nobody was listening to me. I was getting police brutality; I was getting skinhead brutality. I had to be strong as fuck, okay? I had to be so strong. But I realized that— at a point, that I needed to go to college. So I went to college.

I would tell young activists, keep your head. Keep your values, but take care of yourself. Go get a medical checkup. Eat right. Go to school— not that Western education is the answer to everything, but having that piece of paper behind your name gives validity to some of the stuff that you're saying. It took me many years to graduate, but I realized I had to live, you know?

I'd say if you're a white activist, keep up the fight. If you're a person of color, if you're Black, if you're disabled, if you're somebody that is in danger—I don't think you need to be up there on the front lines all the time. Find other ways to do the work, but take care of yourself.

We've been fighting this for a long time in America. I'm gonna say five hundred years. There's people watching you, they're taking heart. But ultimately, if you're not taking care of yourself, nobody's really going to care about you.

Let some of these privileged white kids and white people that see what's wrong, let them stand up and do some of the fighting. It really needs to be addressed by white people, people with privilege, white privilege.

This is a part of my life. I'm glad that I was a part of it. I'm not really connected with what's going on right now. I'm a mom; I do other stuff. But I definitely see Antifa as a continuation of what we started. I'm proud of them. I'm glad that they are doing the work that they're doing. I mean, I feel like they shouldn't have to be there putting themselves out there like that at this point. We already did that thirty years ago. And now they're having to do it again.

People in the city were initially like, "Yeah, nazism is wrong," and now everybody acts like there's two sides to the Proud Boys and Antifa, and it's garbage. There isn't two sides.

KELLY HALLIBURTON
Portland ARA

Against this backdrop of a really fractured society and this war environment where there were almost daily demonstrations downtown—against that backdrop, a lot of us took a holistic approach to the problems that we were facing. A lot of the people organizing back then were a little older than us, but we were a bunch of eighteen- and nineteen-year-olds, and you get a bunch of politically charged eighteen- and nineteen-year-old punk rockers and put them all in a room, you're bound to have a lot of petty disagreements, and egos are going to come to the fore.

Kelly Halliburton playing in Deprived, 1991.

Then there were some elements starting to incorporate themselves into the ARA culture that we didn't mesh with very well. The early incarnations of the Portland SHARP scene, there's a lot of homophobia and a lot of nationalism. The only thing some of these guys and us could really agree on was that we hated nazis. That was it.

They wanted to fight. They were very violent. It was great that they were on our side, but politically in nearly every other aspect, we didn't really get along. I don't want to say by any means that that was everyone.

There was some really, really cool people associated with the SHARP and the skinhead culture in Portland at that time—some of these guys I'm still friends with thirty-some years later—but between the political grandstanding that we were seeing on some fronts and being labeled dirty crusties and "flag burners," or whatever they were calling us at the time, we had to walk away.

We all continued within activism, but we were more focused on the musical part of things, and that was important in its own way, too. There was a point where we stopped being part of organized group-oriented activism and started concentrating more on information dissemination.

I think we were part of a culture that made Portland the way it is now, for better or worse. We're the butt of everyone's jokes. A lot of that came as a direct result of some of the things that my culture was pushing for back then. These are things that mattered: antiracism, this feeling that other life forms can feel pain and fear, and maybe you should think about that when you make your dietary or fashion choices, or the homophobia

228 | It Did Happen Here

that we've been raised to accept our whole lives. There weren't a lot of other people at that time, outside of our culture, it seemed, that were really thinking along those same lines.

I know there were other groups, of course. We didn't know the older activist types. We were young, we were punk rockers, and we were finding our place. We'd grown up in a climate where we were constantly told that we were freaks and we were wrong. And we were arguing with our parents and the people around us. And at that magic point in the late '80s, we found each other.

We found some strength in that and some unity. It was pretty great, you know? We were trying to articulate complex social and political themes, and we did the best that we could. I'm sure we were totally insufferable.

PETER LITTLE
Antiracist skinhead

I came into the antiracist skinhead scene in the mid to late '90s. I'd been living in Newberg, Oregon. Newberg at the time was a rough place to live if you didn't fit the mold of conservative Christian or came from the wrong side of the tracks.

I ended up leaving town after a friend of mine went to jail on a Measure 11, defending some of us from anti-gay bullying, and moved into Portland. I had begun to identify with the antiracist skinhead scene, and been drawn to the subcultural elements, and was basically taken in by those folks at sixteen years old. I was homeless and jobless, thrown out of my house by my parents. They took me in, gave me a place to live, took care of me.

There's very little political education in the antiracist skinhead scene except for "We don't like racists and we don't like nazis." That's useful and has a draw; it was a draw to me. It was a draw to other young folks who intuitively got antifascism, and it appealed to them.

I think it also had drawbacks. There's a difference between strategic militance and militance for its own sake. Without some political development, it's very easy to direct that energy in ways that become self-defeating, self-destructive, or just aren't effective.

At that point, the movement itself had really diminished. You didn't have CHD. You didn't have ARA. You didn't have the organizational and broader social movement context. In the absence of that social movement, there was a lot of self-destructive behavior, a lot of infighting.

I tend to understand the role of CHD and ARA as, like—there were a lot of political radical veterans in there. I think they played a significant role, both in providing the important social base outside of the

1998 flyer courtesy of the Black Studies Department Collection, Portland State University Library Special Collections & University Archives.

No More Nazi Skinheads!

Eastside White Pride '88

FACE THE AGGRESSION

Anti-Racist Vigil

Mark the 10th Anniversary of the murder of PSU student Mulugeta Seraw in SE Portland by Nazi skinheads.

Thurs. Nov. 12
8 pm
SE 31st & Pine
(where Seraw was killed)

There will be speakers and Oregon Spotlight will release a report on the state of Nazi skinheads in Portland in 1998.

For more information call Oregon Spotlight (503) 725-8502

subcultures to sustain support, and to defend the young militants. They did a good job in helping to cultivate a level of political understanding, consciousness, and awareness that would hopefully allow that militance to be utilized in more thoughtful and productive ways.

MICHAEL CLARK
SHARP

By my recollection, it just seems like some things lost steam, based on heavy politics. And so much shifting, because there were a lot of different crews. I want to own that at least like 80 percent of what I had going on at that time was ego-based. I wanted people to look up to me. I wanted to be a tough guy for a reason. I wanted to stand up for something. I wanted to have something to offer people coming after me. I just want to own that.

So, across many groups, I definitely saw membership change. People stepped away from certain groups that they couldn't mesh with ideologically.

I think that we set a precedent where nazis weren't tolerated, wherever they were at. Different groups did that in different ways. I can tell you that the people I hung out with—if you brought some nazi BS to me or the crew that I ran with, or the people that we hung around with, you might get your face cut off with a broken pint glass, you might end up getting your head stomped in by ten guys. You definitely were going to get something broken. And you're going to hear that what you were bringing to the table was unacceptable.

So to have that power, to step from a position of "Am I safe here? Do I need to watch my back here?" to "Anybody who's bringing that better watch their back!" was huge and powerful. It did get to the point to where if you walked through downtown with an Iron Cross, you might be in trouble. If you spouted off some racist shit. If you talked smack: "Oh, you skinheads. You think you're so tough." Well, then, we were into showing you why we thought we were.

One of the things, too, that people forget about: think about 1986. Most people's parents hadn't gone to school with a person of color. Right? We're no more than two generations away from segregation. Two generations is not a long time. There's definitely a lot of growth to be had still. Anybody who's out doing that work, I think should be praised. I don't think that there is a right or wrong way to do it. Really.

I don't fault people for not wanting to be violent. But I'm also thankful that there's people who are willing to do that when it needs to be done. It's really hard to be a person with the heart and the mind to be a natural-born critical thinker, that puts two, plus two, plus two together and goes, "Oh, shit, we're in trouble. Who's going to do something about this?" And then steps up to the plate.

I'm very empathetic and very proud of people who are able to do that. We're seeing a little bit more of that now. Remember that those people are struggling, and that they're coming into their own, and that they're right. Give them the support they need instead of trying to steal the power that they've taken. Most people aren't going to understand Antifa. I do share that message with people regularly: "Hey, dude, you know, you don't ever step up to anything that puts your life in danger. You're a family man, that's great. Until you stand for something, shut up. Let them do what they need to do." Right?

The daily involvement for me dissipated the bigger my drug and alcohol problem got. [Laughter.] I got a little too messed up behind some drugs and some booze to hang on to my altruistic, good-guy persona. I went south pretty fast. I'm not going to go into how gangs or crews are run, but there's definitely a lot of politics and a lot of democracy. Sometimes things don't quite go your way.

We had some issues around someone beating a woman. I couldn't really let it go, and I got a little busy with it. I went against the grain of following directions, which is something I've always been pretty good at. Long story short, I disrespected people. I got violent behind it. And that was pretty much the beginning of the end for me.

I was getting really into cocaine, heroin, and methamphetamines. Drinking a fifth or a half-gallon a day to take the edge off. My nickname was "Psycho." I was known for getting really intoxicated and starting fights we didn't need to be in. That's a lot of energy for a crew to deal with. To be handling every fight you get yourself into, every crew that you start a fight with, that we're supposed to be affiliated with. It gets to be a lot, so I had to go, which was reasonable.

Broke my heart at the time. I went down the toilet pretty bad. May 17, 2006, was the day I walked out of a detox center, and I've been sober ever since. For me, violence and ego was a lifestyle that served me like a broken tool. It did a lot of good. But like most things, I ended up abusing it. That part of me is so linked to drugs and alcohol that I really have to have a commitment to not be violent.

One thing that really helped was in '07 I got custody of my six-year-old daughter. So I became a single parent, and for the first time in my life, I was the responsible adult. Which was pretty funny, because I was thirty-four. [Laughter.] Life looks a lot different today.

Even though it would be nice, we're not all going to get woke all at once. We got to be patient with people. The human capacity for change is actually really small. Right? Fake it till you make it isn't good enough. Change is uncomfortable. And the best change is the most uncomfortable.

Take the things that you really believe in. Take those things, get behind them 100 percent, and make the change where you can. That's the connection, right? Masses of uncommitted numbers don't change a thing.

We think of antiracism and antifascism as, like, this altruistic, all-encompassing thing. People who are participating and active in that and making a difference are still people and still have a lot going on. It's a big commitment to make that a part of what you do. And so I want to express gratitude for people who are carrying the torch. Walking through the fear about doing the right thing in the face of a bunch of idiots who wouldn't know the right thing if it bit them in the ass.

Portland protester, date unknown. Photo by Dean Guernsey.

Chapter 11

Together Against

The people who generously shared histories, memories, and stories acted from a fierce combination of love and optimism. But at the heart of this story lies a brutal violence. The murder of Mulugeta Seraw was a heinous act that no one could deny. But the city created an environment where such a death was inevitable by ignoring repeated reports of the growing racist threat and then by responding with incarceration and lawsuits. The ongoing violence of the city leaders is hard to see, expressed as it is by neglect. A deliberate, consistent failure to recognize hate crimes, like those experienced by Scot Nakagawa and Hock-Seng "Sam" Chin, is an expression of the violence of social exclusion. Putting law enforcement in charge of responding to a social crisis like nationally organized hate groups assaulting citizens is an example of a city weaponizing its police against its citizens instead of taking responsibility both for the problem of why neonazi skinheads proliferated and for coming up with a response. While it's historically accurate that the city of Portland had numerous reactions to the murder of Mulugeta Seraw, with rallies, school assemblies, street sign memorials, the imprisonment of the murderers, and the trial of Tom Metzger, Portland city leaders' basic response—of denial, diffusion, covering up, and weaponizing police—persists. Without a

---

Button assemblage from the McKenzie River Gathering's 1996 annual report.

deep commitment to human dignity, in the end it is the speech of the police baton that reverberates.

How do we end a story that's on a continuum? This is a story about coalition, about different people and groups who stood together to fight intolerance. What did we learn from the groups who generously shared their stories?

Mulugeta Seraw taught us that no one is safe when white supremacists are unchecked. We can't ignore them, even when the police and the city deny that there is a problem.

From the Coalition for Human Dignity we learned the role of queer people in bridging communities, the value of building and maintaining connection across different organizations, the importance of local research as a support for local activism, and ways to show up to protect citizens in allyship. We learned that training in self-defense is community defense, that owning political mistakes supports integrity, and that neglecting internal equity diminishes group longevity.

The Baldies and Anti Racist Action taught us how we can build a national network against hate out of a group of friends—also, how to stand up, come together, and turn the tide from reaction to direct action. From Skinheads Against Racial Prejudice we learned that to be bold is effective, but the price of living with violence and conflict without wider community understanding and support can be higher than we can afford.

How can we create an environment of unity and listening? From the long years since, we have learned that we need to expand our thinking, that immediate local solutions may appear to be effective while they are actually driving problems underground or to the suburbs. This story ends with the demise of the big-tent coalition that came together in 1988. ARA and SHARP split apart, and the Coalition for Human Dignity merged itself out of existence. The small group of friends who fought nazis in the streets, organized protests and house defenses, and stood together against white nationalist violence left a legacy.

Of the survivors of these groups, of the ones we interviewed, almost all of them have carried the work and wisdom of that coalition into their present-day work. They are still fighting, still holding out a hand in welcome.

SCOT NAKAGAWA
Coalition for Human Dignity and ACT UP Portland

In order to be successful in organizing and mobilizing, you have to polarize people. So you choose an issue, and you polarize people around it. When you choose that issue, and when you think about who the interested parties are that you need to mobilize in order to be able to win the day, you need to think really carefully about where you put more polarizing things, so you're not polarizing things with too few people and too few assets on your side. The right has been really, really effective at polarizing things in places where they have more bodies than we do. Even if we can defeat something—like we did with Ballot Measure 9—they were still able to build their forces and build their base to be a more powerful force going forward.

There's hope, you know, but there's also just being real about what's out there. The struggle has always been there. It doesn't have to be a totally bad deal. It feels a little bit like sometimes you're on a runaway roller coaster. There are ups and downs and twists and turns, and you're never quite sure what's going to come next. You don't seem to ever be in control. We have a choice in that situation: you can either grab onto the rails and white-knuckle it with your eyes closed and hope for the best, waiting for the ride to end, or you can throw your hands up in the air, open your eyes and go "wheee," and try to embrace the moment and recognize that it's an opportunity to feel alive, to be a part of what's happening in the world, and to do something.

A very small percentage of people can make a really huge difference. Really, really huge difference. In fact, minorities always are really the leading edge of change, right? It's almost never the case that the majority of people reach for radical change. Those kinds of radical changes are inspired by tiny minorities of people who are in an environment in which many, many people are checked out and not offering any kind of resistance. If you have 10 to 20 percent of the people on your side, that's a huge number relative to the most significant movements for change in the United States, in our history.

The legacy of white supremacy today is structural racism, which is the way that society is organized. The fact that communities are located where they are relative to services, the pattern of investment, the representation that people of color enjoy within various different kinds of institutions—it is cultural, it's political, it's economic, it dictates where you live, it tells a variety of things about you. People don't often know that the one most powerful determinant of one's success in life is your original zip code. So in a segregated society like ours, that makes race a really big difference. That system of inequality continues, but that's a historical construct. Nobody who is alive now was part of creating that. That original blueprint was created by entirely different people.

The thing is that while we were not the architects of structural racism, we are its inheritors. And we don't all inherit the same thing as a result of this legacy. Some of us inherit real assets and privileges, and others of us have inherited terrible disadvantages. In our lifetimes, we get to determine whether or not we will pass that legacy on to yet another generation. In order to avoid doing that, we need to understand that we have to take on antiracism as a first principle in progressive politics and do so at all times. Because our future is contingent on our being able to work together.

PETER LITTLE
Antiracist skinhead

I think I was lucky in that a few years after hanging around the antiracist skinhead scene, I was craving and looking for something more, politically. I ended up connecting with the newly formed IWW branch here. I managed to connect with a couple of old CHD members, who began to mentor me and help me develop politically, and also helped me develop some political engagement and vision outside of the subcultural context of the punk and antiracist skinhead scene.

That was rare at the time. I don't think there were a lot of other folks from my generation, in the subculture, who had the same kind of mentoring. It's important to acknowledge that in a lot of the folks who came out of ARA and into and out of SHARP and the antiracist skinhead scene, there were folks feeling wary and suspicious of the left. Feeling like they had been used when needed but also—I wouldn't say forgotten—but maybe people feeling some caution and suspicion towards the organized left due to dynamics that existed at the height of that movement moment.

I was involved in some political groupings who had been thinking about the ongoing significance of fascism. We'd been monitoring anti-immigrant groups around town and been organizing around Volksfront and Hammerskins, who both were still the two predominant forces at the time when there was this big national Hammerskins event here in town with a big rally. Lent's Park was near the house of one of the primary leaders of Volksfront. It was out of the organizing around that event that what became Rose City Antifa was eventually born.

I still think that there's a very, very subcultural thread in the antifascist movement. In some ways, I think building countercultures is valuable, because it's a home for kids from the Island of the Misfit Toys, right? It also can offer different values than the dominant culture. Hopefully, those subcultures embrace values that lead towards freedom, and that they combat the more destructive elements of mass culture. But I think subculture can be limiting. In my era, the role of women in antiracist skinhead subculture really became sidelined due to macho culture.

1996 flyer courtesy of Jonathan Mozzochi.

If we're looking at the limitations of the moment that we're in, and the limitations of the moment that I was brought up in, there's a strong tendency to conflate militance with radicalism. That if it's militant, it must be radical. I think that that's a dangerous assumption and can be a costly assumption.

A subculture can create a space where an alternative world concept develops. It can create a space for people to feel at home, to unify, to come together. But the question of fascism is fascism as a *mass politic*. I think to confront that, there will need to be the kind of military component of engaging it.

These folks think and act in military ways; they have no qualms about force and power. In fact, that's one of the essential threads of fascism, is that force can be its own justification. So I think that a militant component needs to be a part of it. But you can't defeat these people militarily.

First, they're much better organized than we are in that way. They're much better armed than we are in that way. They have a greater capacity to win over elements of the armed forces and the police.

Second, as long as capitalism exists, it will continue to create the potential basis for a fascist movement. The decline of the privileges of whiteness is a real thing right now—that is the product of neoliberalism. So I think the political questions need to supersede the military ones. I think that the risk of where we're at right now is a militance with a real underdevelopment of the political element.

How do we create an alternative world vision that appeals to enough of society that we can win over some of the potential base of fascists but also defeat capitalism in a way that begins to limit the actual conditions that breed the fascist response?

One of the amazing things about the Internet is that anybody can find their "tribe." Right? That's powerful for, like, queer youth in some isolated, remote place. It's powerful, I think, for all sorts of people. It's also potent for young white men and women both, who are seeing a decline in what they believed were their entitlements. I think that there's something significant there. It raises the question for me of where the antifascist movement is going. Saying, this is about a vision of a better world. One that actually addresses what's going on in society—here's the culprits, here's the issues.

Fascism can't be defeated by a subculture if a subculture places militance over politics—politics being development of critical capacities of all participants in the movement to engage whatever potential they have, and also the ability to collectively evaluate and engage in tactics and strategy.

It's a long list of folks who brought me up, or who came up with me, who are now dead. Addiction and trauma—there are pretty significant reasons for that. Any antifascist struggle will be confronted by violence and will have to have a capacity to defend itself.

I think it raises the importance of a social movement that can care for the people who are wounded by those consequences. A lot of that violence, and a lot of that militance, may not have been productive or worthwhile, you know, which is a painful thing to look back on when you think about people you know and love who are no longer here.

Some of what worries me is that a lot of the antifascist movement right now is engaged in doxing—which I think can be valuable, maintaining intelligence and information on these people. On the other hand, there is mass confrontation, but I think that it's very easy for mass confrontation to be reduced—either by the state, by the forces that we oppose, or both—into something that just becomes scripted and also costly. It can backfire on the movement itself if it's not engaged thoughtfully.

Back in my day it was, you see a nazi, you go at them. That was the rule. I'm a very small person, arguably dumb enough to be willing to live by that rule, which led to a lot of physical injuries. But that eliminates broad swaths of people who are antifascists from being able to engage, and, like, it isn't always the smartest thing to do—confront somebody physically just because you see them somewhere. What I see as the tactics of the past are in many ways the scariest—and some of the most admirable—for the courage that they require, but also some of the easiest for both the state and the fascists to adapt and to respond to. On that terrain, both the state and the fascists will always have the upper hand. If it's a question of military engagement with fascists—knowing that the state is a third player that sometimes will stand aside and let both sides go at it, will sometimes be happy to offer one side an advantage against the other, but who in the end, I think, do oppose both sides.

I think another dangerous political assumption that we run up against is that the state and the fascists are the same thing, that the state sympathizes with the fascists. I think an understanding of history is important there. The Order was an armed paramilitary group in the Pacific Northwest who assassinated a Jewish talk show host, robbed banks, and funneled millions of dollars into the radical white supremacist movement. The state opposed those people, because they were dangerous. They [the Order] were willing to break the law, and they were looking for a revolutionary struggle to overthrow the existing state of affairs.

The state realizes this. It doesn't mean that the state won't, at times, take hands off them if they feel that it's advantageous, but we can't assume the state and the fascists are one and the same. The straight head-on confrontation in the streets is actually relatively easy for the state to manage in most situations. There are times where it gets out of their control.

But looking at the past few years in Portland, I think the state has started to figure out how to contain it, at times to even utilize it to their advantage: "We're the only thing standing between both of these folks and you." When four hundred people are kettled, it's a great opportunity to identify who's there. So on the question of tactics, it seems that there's an entire array that would require a broader anticapitalist strategy—more than symbolic or momentary alignments with other sectors of the working class that are in movement. That is absolutely going to be necessary to confront this.

CECIL PRESCOD
Coalition for Human Dignity

I've been doing some reflecting as I get older. People move on to different aspects of their lives. That's why I think it's so important to not only share the information you have, but also to recognize that for each generation, those things are new and they need to confront them in their own unique ways. I think generally, young people are open to ideas, and that's something that the right has used very, very well.

I never felt as if, "Oh, we won," or that things are over. We need to continue the education. But also, we need to do political organizing on the ground. One thing that the Coalition did very well focused on the Oregon Citizens Alliance, OCA: how they were organizing, and also how they were doing political education, how they were running for school boards and things like that. That's the type of thing we need to continue doing, to respond to, and not forget that it is so important. Sometimes we wait until someone is murdered, or someone is elected president, and say,

Cecil Prescod, 2022. Photo by Celina Flores.

"Oh, we got to do something." Well, by that time it's too late to respond to that in an effective way.

What we need to do is basic research, basic organizing, one on one, running for school board, paying attention to what's being promoted on social media, and things like that. So it's different, but yet the same. It's the same struggle. And it manifests itself in different ways. But it's never over.

What are some basic things that we can agree on? A very great thing about the Coalition was the name: Coalition for Human Dignity. The idea of human dignity is a baseline of agreement, and then we build up from that point. Oftentimes, we talk about who we are against, but there we are saying who we are *for*.

So I think the first thing is, recognize there are differences. But recognize there are some basic agreements. That will take work. You have to agree to listen and agree to be solid, to hear the other person. Recognize that people's stories are different. And for me to recognize that there is no right or wrong—that person's truth is true for them. I need to respect it. We need to come to an agreement that we will respect one another.

There's different levels of commitment and different ways in which you can be a part of the movement, and all of it's very important. To recognize it, to celebrate it, and to appreciate one another—what the tasks and the callings of each person are. You have the people who write and publish and the people who will be in the street. The people who are willing to take risks should be appreciated.

It's really important for people to know that they are going to be misunderstood. And they're going to be mislabeled. That's a reality. That's what's going to happen. You have to be aware of that. You have to remain focused on what you're doing and your goal.

You know who you are and what you are fighting for. Maintain that focus. And also, you need time to relax and to breathe. And to be able to build community and support one another, because it's hard work. We need to find ways to nurture, to be aware of one another. To spend time and take care of one another. It's important to struggle, but also remember what we're struggling for. We have to take care of ourselves so we can be here for the long haul.

ERIC WARD
Coalition for Human Dignity

People often ask me, "What does community defense look like?" The best way to answer that is to ask *yourself*, "What does community defense *feel* like?"

The way that it often feels is joyous, celebratory, empowering, and beautiful. The best way to tell if one has been successful is the feeling that is evoked at the end of an action, right? If one feels frustrated, if they feel angry, if they feel grief, it likely means we weren't successful at community defense.

If people are able to realize that they've won a victory, demobilize, go home, and allow the entire city to feel what folks on the streets are feeling, that is successful community defense. It is often a hard place to find, particularly for those who are engaged in direct action or street protest. There is an adrenaline rush that comes from street confrontation, and that adrenaline rush can be somewhat addictive.

Too often, our tactics are driven by the addiction to adrenaline rather than the knowledge that our role is to allow our communities to feel joyous, safe. One of the key lessons we learned in the '90s was to ensure that we were really reflecting the joy that our communities needed to experience—on the other side of being challenged by white nationalists and other folks committed to intimidating vulnerable communities.

It's a really important conversation, both then and today.

I think the Coalition for Human Dignity helped shape our understanding of what it really meant to take on white nationalism. We couldn't just be concerned about the subculture fight that was happening. We also had to understand that hate groups didn't come to town bringing racism or anti-Semitism, homophobia, or other forms of bigotry to our community. These hate groups simply organized the bigotry that already existed.

The Coalition for Human Dignity and other leaders really helped us understand that we needed to move from subculture to both challenging institutions and diminishing this white nationalist social movement that was seeking to reshape all the gains we had made in civil rights over the last fifty years. We have to be cautious and understand that the past should help us by informing what we might do, but it shouldn't be the decision maker. The decision maker is always the current political and social reality, and the culture of a community. Those are the things we have to be responsive to, in terms of shaping strategy and tactics and fighting hate.

One of the lessons is that we didn't build political power. I don't mean just electoral power, I mean community power, economic power, cultural power. We didn't consistently build a constituency that would allow movement against bigotry, to challenge policies and rules that create space for organized bigotry.

That is from an understanding that who is elected in government—who holds positions of power in our community—matters in these moments of crisis. Power absolutely matters, and the democratic institutions, regardless of whether we think they're perfect or imperfect, actually do matter, and we need to pay attention to that.

The second lesson is around subculture. Many of us came out of subculture. So when we created an antibigotry movement, of course, that antibigotry movement resembled the subculture. Subcultures are not effective in this moment.

This is a moment where white nationalism is on the rise. It has not peaked yet. What we know about white nationalism and other forms of authoritarian and totalitarian movements is that they are dependent on mass base. It means we have to respond in scale. That means we need more people involved.

Subcultures are not good containers for mass base organizing. How do we move out of subculture and into culture? It is our role to challenge and to influence Portland's culture, not just our own political subculture at this moment.

The third is—I didn't learn this lesson until recently, and I learned it here in Portland from street protesters—find joy in resistance. It is so important that we not replicate the toxic masculinity that we are experiencing from white nationalists and the alt-right, that we don't try to respond in kind, that we lead with our values. The August 2019 protest showed

Eric Ward, in *Facing the Fear Together,* a promotional video for the Northwest Coalition Against Malicious Harassment, 1997.

that we can effectively respond to toxic masculinity through joy, through celebration, through spectacle.[18] I really am thankful for the women and nonbinary leaders out there who really brought that home to us. It was an incredible gift we saw in very impactful ways that not only inspired people on the political left, but I think inspired people across the city. That is a huge victory.

What we should understand is that the white nationalist movement does not go back into a jar. It will continue to grow and expand.

We are at a time of huge debates in our society around identity. Who are we, as Americans? What will America look like? We are in a space where people are really contemplating what demographic change means. With significant demographic change comes demographic anxiety. We've not yet figured out how to deal with that anxiety and those who choose to exploit that anxiety.

We live in a time in the United States where many Americans, not just vulnerable communities, are experiencing vast income inequality for the first time. I do not—as an African American who has grown up under vast income inequality—I do not wish that upon anyone. We understand the stresses that that brings. We know it leaves people vulnerable to other messages as they try to understand why they've been abandoned in this society.

That income inequality—that anxiety around demographic change, and the fact that we are debating what it means to be American—is a perfect storm. In that storm, the white nationalist movement has brought its bigotry, and it will continue to recruit members until we build enough infrastructure and movement to start competing for that same constituency.

That is the next challenge for those who oppose authoritarianism and totalitarianism and who seek to create an inclusive America that's people-centered, transparent, and accountable. It's time for us to get out of our subcultures.

Start door knocking, start sitting down with Americans and convincing them that there is another America that can speak to the needs of all of us. We aren't trying to start a race war. We're trying to end one.

Pages 260–61: Photo by Celina Flores.

1960

FOREVER FREE FRO

NOTES ON INTERVIEWS, SOURCES, AND RESEARCH

The *It Did Happen Here* production team edited interviews for readability and clarity; we tried to retain each person's individual speech and language style. To hear the voices of many of the activists from *It Did Happen Here,* listen to the podcast at itdidhappenherepodcast.com.

A small team, headed up by the podcast producers, conducted the bulk of the interviews in 2019 and early 2020. Several participants made themselves available for follow-up interviews and clarifications during the production of the podcast, and we thank them for their generosity of spirit. Some interviews were conducted after the podcast finished its initial eleven-episode run in January 2020. There were a few significant figures we were unable to interview; some we couldn't find, some were unwilling to talk, and some have passed on. Particularly missed are the elder wisdoms of Susan Wheeler and Stew Albert of the CHD, and the Lesbian Community Project's Donna Red Wing.

None of the people who brought you this story are trained historians or researchers, but for almost all of us, this book holds a piece of our own histories. We discovered that this story exists in an information shadow—pre-Internet but not yet digitized into easily accessible archives. In our research, we frequently relied on the Oregon Historical Society and the Multnomah County Library archives of Portland's daily newspaper, *The Oregonian.* The Elinor Langer research collection on white supremacy in America at the University of Oregon was also a tremendous help.

However, time and time again, as we sought to verify events we experienced or remembered, we came up against paywalls: academic paywalls, archive paywalls, journalism paywalls. And one source—*The Oregonian*—we did not trust to be invested in portraying a truth that served everyone.

The Oregonian was founded in 1850 as a weekly newspaper by Thomas Jefferson Dryer, a staunch Whig with a propensity for strong drink and an unspoken agenda to "attract settlers, sell lots, boost business and trade, attract investment and establish Portland's economic supremacy above all others." Additionally, as historian Harry Stein notes at the *Oregon Encyclopedia* website, "The paper long stood for the established order, state and city growth, private and public regional investment, and efforts to establish and maintain Portland's supremacy over regional rivals."

Today, *The Oregonian* is owned by the usual nesting-doll arrangement of corporations: Advance Publications, who owns directly or through subsidiaries the Discovery Channel, Condé Nast, the digital news website *Wired,* Lycos, Angelfire, and Tripod; the company is also the majority shareholder in Reddit.

The paper is published by Oregonian Media Group, whose president, John Maher, also currently serves as the cochair of the Portland Business Alliance, whose mission statement includes this sentence: "The Alliance advocates for *business* at all levels of government to support commerce, community health and the region's overall prosperity" (emphasis ours). *The*

Oregonian has stayed true to its settler, capitalist, colonizer roots.

Media can be subtle; it's important to be aware of who controls the messages we consume. The power of the press to influence public opinion is enormous. The people fighting white power racists had an uphill battle with the press, a situation that remains unchanged.

It's not just *The Oregonian*. Oregon Public Broadcasting on October 8, 2021, ran an in-depth interview with Jon Bair about the shooting that landed him in prison. Our conversation with Jon afterward revealed that OPB rejected his lived version of events in favor of the police report—most of which was based on the bonehead version of events.

Jon said, "At one point, the reporter was talking with me in the parking lot where the incident took place. I kept telling him how the cars were positioned, and he kept going back to the nazi's tires being against the curb, and I was like, 'Well, that's not how I remember it.' But he kept circling back, so I was like, 'No, that's not what happened.'

"And he said, 'Well it's in all the police reports.'

"And at that point I reminded him that no cops ever saw the scene in any way, shape, or form. By the time any cops got there, both cars were long gone. I suppose that was a red flag, that he would blindly trust the reports to be the gospel truth. He did hear me, but I was stunned at the lack of clarity on his part, and I found it betrayed his own implicit bias. Put that in the book, HAHA!"

Lived experience is valid, real, and shifting. In adapting the podcast version of these oral histories into a book, we worked to present an experienced-based people's history of a struggle that has touched many of us. We have seen very little of our shared experiences represented anywhere in mainstream culture. We acknowledge the impact on our process of conflicting accounts of events, the aforementioned paywalls, a thirty-year time gap, and the strong anti-antiracist bias of mainstream and alternative media at the time. We have done our best to verify the claims and facts stated throughout the interviews.

Throughout the process of collaborating on this history, we made a deliberate choice to focus on antiracists. These antifascist communities are our communities of friends, comrades, respected longtime organizers, and other people living in resistance to white supremacy with whom we feel a sense of kinship. We offer *It Did Happen Here* as our version of what it was like to live through those years, to try to make a difference with few resources, to strive to be safe while protecting the vulnerable and targeted, and to maintain mental and physical health enough to continue. Our accountability lies with those who offered us the great gift and trust of their deeply personal histories, their time, and ultimately, their continued friendship and authentic connection.

All gratitude to those who came before, and to those who shared stories and images so we could make this book. Stay vigilant. Make your own media. Look after each other. Thanks for reading.

Appendix A:
HOMOPHOBIC VIOLENCE DOCUMENTATION PROJECT

The Homophobic Violence Documentation Project, also known as the Homophobic Violence Reporting Line,[1] was a twenty-four-hour hotline where survivors or witnesses could report incidents of homophobic violence in order to track patterns of increased attacks against queer Portlanders. Homophobic violence denial was prevalent in both the media and within the city, especially the police department. Donna Red Wing, the executive director of the Lesbian Community Project (LCP), along with Gillian of the LCP and the Coalition for Human Dignity and Scot Nakagawa of ACT UP Portland and the CHD, conceived and carried out a simple and effective program whereby local activists were able to collect and use data to show consistent attacks on queer people across Portland.

Scot Nakagawa and Donna Red Wing gave several talks in a citywide campaign to promote the project and recruit volunteers willing to help protect the human rights of queer people by staffing the hotline. Gillian described how the LCP printed stickers with the name and number of the hotline and stuck them up in areas where queers were most vulnerable. These stickers were shared across activist groups. The LCP also printed cards with the same information, which they left at local gay bars, and they took out ads in *Just Out* and other gay media.[2]

In 1990, the right-wing religious group the Oregon Citizens Alliance mounted the statewide Ballot Measure 9, which would have reversed existing (and scant) civil rights protections for non-heterosexuals; it would have declared homosexuality "abnormal, wrong, unnatural, and perverse," the equivalent of "necrophilia, bestiality and pedophilia," and would have barred queer people from public employment. Though this ballot measure lost in the Portland general election, it was immensely popular, garnering 638,527 votes in favor. (Similar measures passed in several counties across rural Oregon, sparking the birth of the still-active Rural Organizing Project.) In this political environment, homophobic street violence spiked.

An example of a practice police frequently described as "just a robbery" actually had a name: "Roll a Troll." Gillian recounted how a group of ten or so nazis would hang out by gay bars at closing time and jump men as they exited, beating and robbing them.

Homophobic Violence Reporting Line form, courtesy of Portland State University Library Special Collections & University Archives.

P. O. BOX 5931
PORTLAND, OR 97228   HOMOPHOBIC VIOLENCE REPORTING LINE file#: _____

Operator's Initials: _____   Date of Call: _____

Date/Time of Incident: _____   City/Area: _____   State: _____
Setting: _____
Caller is: A. Victim   B. Witness   C. Friend   D. Other _____
Victim(s):

N	Sex	Orientation	Age	Race	Other identifying info
	M / F	homo / het / bi / TV / TS			
	M / F	homo / het / bi / TV / TS			
	M / F	homo / het / bi / TV / TS			
	M / F	homo / het / bi / TV / TS			

Perpetrator(s):

N	Sex	Orientation	Age	Race	Other identifying info
	M / F	homo / het / bi / TV / TS			
	M / F	homo / het / bi / TV / TS			
	M / F	homo / het / bi / TV / TS			
	M / F	homo / het / bi / TV / TS			

Type of Incident (circle all that apply):

A. anti lesbian/gay language   B. verbal threats   C. chased, menaced   D. punched/hit/kicked
E. attacked with weapons   F. sexual assault   G. robbery   H. vandalism
I. unjustified arrest/summons   J. arson   K. fired from job   L. followed/watched
M. obscene/harassing phone call   N. intimidation   O. grabbed   P. objects thrown
Other: _____

Physical Injury to Victim: A. none B. minor C. moderate D. serious E. treated/discharged F. hospitalized E. death

Does caller believe incident motivated by victim's sexual orientation?   Y   N   Unsure (explain in narrative)

Police response: _____ Notified   _____ Not Notified
                        A. adequate   B. inadequate   C. more than adequate (for B and C, explain in narrative)

What happened to Perpetrator(s): A. not found/arrested B. arrested C. indicted D. sentenced E. outcome pending

Crisis Line Response: A. referral   B. counseling   C. referral not available   D. set support info   E. other _____
                      follow up (explain) _____

Caller referred by: A. lesbian/gay organization   B. sticker campaign   C. lesbian/gay media
                      D. non-lesbian/gay organization   E. other _____

Optional: Name: _____   Phone: _____
                                                                          revised 2/23/92

Gillian called the category a "homophobic robbery," because bone-heads were explicitly targeting gays—easy targets at ten versus one. Gay and queer people were—and still are—far less likely to go to the police with complaints about violence. Until the 1991 launch of the hotline, such crimes remained unreported. The mainstream narrative promulgated by local media relied only on police reports, and thus promoted the idea that such attacks were rare and not necessarily related to the survivors' sexuality.

A bare-bones project with one paid staff person and lots of volunteer support, the Homophobic Violence Reporting Line was an example of politicized, community-based research essential for the LCP and the CHD to build evidence to share with the wider public about urgent local threats presented by ongoing right-wing hate crimes. Beginning early in 1991, hotline volunteers collected raw data from survivors of anti-queer violence using an uncomplicated, plain-language questionnaire. On March 19 of 1992, after noticing a marked increase in violence during the Measure 9 campaign, the LCP held a press conference to present the first six months of hotline data, collected between July and December of 1991. Gillian recalls, "There was a feeling we were under attack. People were happy we were doing it, but I remember the press being skeptical." Willamette Week and The Oregonian gave pushback, she said, responding with things like, "Well, how do you know it's because they were gay? There's violence everywhere."

According to a March 20, 1992, Oregonian report on the press release, over one hundred hate crimes were reported via the hotline in its first six months, listing as victims twenty-four gay-identified men and forty-eight lesbian-identified women who experienced events that ranged "from threatening calls at home, obscene and sexual catcalls on the street and antihomosexual graffiti painted on business walls to thrown bottles, physical attacks and arson. Thirty-two of the incidents involved the use of antihomosexual language. There were eleven reports of verbal threats made in person and ten reports of harassing or obscene phone calls." The article also recounts, "A gay man reported that he was followed by several men who called him names, attacked him from behind and hit and kicked him while he was lying on the sidewalk. The man's eyeglasses broke, and the attackers ground his face into the glass. He required hospitalization and surgery." [3]

As Scot Nakagawa explained, "It was part of a much broader effort to get aggregated data, because the Portland police were trying to make the argument at the time that there were no neonazi skinheads in Portland. They also claimed that the most victimized group of people by race, in terms of hate crimes, were white people. And so we were eventually able to disprove that, by demonstrating that there were a variety of ways in which people of color being subjected to hate crimes were different—the character of the crime, the way crimes were committed, and the intensity of the violence."

Appendix B:
THE HOLOCAUST DENIER

In the 1990s and up into the 2000s, Portland anti-Semites repeatedly invited bogus English historian David Irving to the Portland area to share Irving's false and disproven history denying the occurrence of the Holocaust. Bringing this Holocaust denier to Portland involved lots of grassroots activity by local anti-Semites: securing a venue, paying the speaker, funding a plane ticket, printing flyers, and actually getting people in the door to hear his words. These efforts identified local anti-Semites, which was helpful information for the researchers of the Coalition for Human Dignity.

Resistance to these events became a fruitful place to organize broad groups of people outside of their usual confines, involving Jewish groups, progressive Christians, and other more mainstream civil rights organizations who came to stand with antiracist skinheads, punks, and activists against anti-Semitic historical revisionism.

The ongoing fight to deny a platform to Irving was frequently referenced by several CHD participants as examples of their most successful campaigns.

David Irving made six visits to speak in Portland in the Portland area: 1992, 1994, 1995, 1998, 2009, 2011, and 2012 (shut down).

STEVE WASSERSTROM
Coalition for Human Dignity

David Irving was increasingly active as a Holocaust denier on the international scene in the '80s. Some of these local groups, we knew who they were, invited him to come repeatedly to Portland. They would organize these events by word of mouth, but we had people who could find out where these events were going to take place. Then we would organize demonstrations to bring as much attention, to make life as difficult for them as possible.

We couldn't, and wouldn't, and never did debate them. There was a universal consensus among people who work with these kind of groups that you don't debate Holocaust deniers. If you debate them, then you give them legitimacy. So we weren't going to do that. But short of that, we could bring people out to see that they were in their community and that they were organizing the community. The crescendo event took place at Mount Hood Community College. It was quite a large event of theirs.

David Irving was brought to trial in London for denying the Holocaust. There was a good book and then movie made about the case.[1] When Irving was brought to trial, they had to demonstrate that he was in fact a neonazi, an extreme right-wing activist. So they collected witness statements from a number of us from around North America who had actually heard what he had to say. I submitted one of those, and he was convicted. It's just an example of something that we did that helped have what we think of as a positive outcome.

So one of the big differences between what we were doing then and what is happening now is there's much more organization, much more powers of communication and transportation, et cetera, on the part of these hate groups, but there is also considerably more awareness and higher degrees of activism around the country. That's Antifa, but also more middle-of-the-road kinds of groups—the Anti-Defamation League, the Southern Poverty Law Center, the Western States Center, and many, many other groups from the center to the left. They're very active online. There are indie journalists who follow these hate groups and put their materials online. There are many, many ways in which these folks cannot do things in secret anymore. That's a far cry from where we were in the '90s.

It's not encouraging, because we're talking about a kind of culture war that's ongoing and escalating. The powers that are pushing back are considerable. And Antifa is part of that, and faith communities are part of that. Enlightened folks of all kinds are now aware of how white nationalism has become entrenched in North America and is unsettlingly close to all of us. There are elements in the Trump White House—who were there for a number of years—who are connected to white nationalist groups and were being encouraged by white nationalists. So that's changed the equation in many ways. There was a now-notorious statement that came out of the White House that there are "good people on both sides" and encouragements of that sort. It's hard not to think of it as correlated politically to certain parties.

We don't want these folks in our downtown, in the courthouse, the square, or anywhere on the street, spewing their hate. In many cases, we're not talking about groups who are literal neonazis or virtual nazis. We're talking about hardcore hate groups, organized and marching in our streets. What people can do is show up. Rose City Antifa and other groups who monitor these groups make clear when they're going to have rallies. Bookmark those sites, and find out when events are coming, and show up. My ideal would be that many, many more Portlanders of good, good faith would show up at these events of these activists and never let them come and have any degree of comfort, spouting hate in our streets.

Engaging with the folks who are on their side—I don't think it's productive to debate, they have already established their commitments to

E12 ■. 3M   METRO/NORTHWEST

Anna Rasmus (left) and Shelly Shapiro display a book that shows the original construction plans for the gas chambers at Auschwitz.

Group blasts revisionist historian Irving

■ Holocaust survivors say David
Irving represents white

from Irving's writing is that some
may view it as little more than an alternative view of historical facts

to Americans who want to see another side in every controversy,"
Shapiro said. "There is no other side.

refuted by a number of sourc
"This all would be laughab

News coverage from *The Oregonian*, October 1992.

violence and hate. But the community at large can make it clear that this
is not what we want in our community. More generally, we don't want
large expressions of hate, particularly if it's connected to violence. And
there's lots of other kinds of work to do—academic work, scholarly work,
and political work of all kinds. But when they organize intentionally to
come to the streets, then I think it's important for our community to
show up in as large a number as possible.

The police have protected them and ushered them, and there have
literally been threats of violence. Law enforcement organizations have
come out in a large force and kept them separate. But part of the effect is
that they have protection. This is a bind. I'm not saying, "Oh, we should
unleash violence in the streets," but I'm concerned with the way that law
enforcement has been managing these events in such a way that these
folks feel protected and comfortable coming back.

Folks who work actively in this area do not, generally, shy away from
comparisons with the 1930s in Germany. We are hearing those more and
more now. And while I think that's still alarmist, we do know that there

are precedents of increasing authoritarianism, and this kind of street hate activism is part of a package of a slide into authoritarianism. It's not clear how many folks have had their consciousness raised sufficiently to understand how much closer we're getting to that world, and therefore how much more work everybody needs to do to stop it.

ABBY LAYTON
Coalition for Human Dignity

Let me give you an example of something I think we did very well. It's 1993, '94, somewhere in there. David Irving was the most prominent Holocaust denier in the world. We found out that he was, again, coming to Portland. Mount Hood Community College had given them their speaking room to speak in. The first thing I did was write an editorial and call the police and get everybody on board and that whole thing.

There was an *Oregonian* editor at the time named Phil Stanford.[2] He picked up on this and started writing editorials in our newspaper about how, "Maybe we should listen to this guy, David Irving. You know, maybe he's right, maybe not that many people died during the Holocaust." This is in our *Oregonian* editorial, first thing on the column. So we had to then organize in a broad base of all faith communities, all political communities, and start answering that editorial. Stanford doubled down, and he went on to write two more editorials. So what we did, besides organizing every community, I invited in Anna Rasmus, who created the movie *The Nasty Girl* [*Das Schreckliche Mädchen*, 1990], which is a film about her hometown in Germany during World War II and how she went back there and started exposing nazis in her community. It's a brilliant movie. So Anna came, and with her came Shelly Shapiro, who was head of the Holocaust Center in Albany, New York. We did a four-day symposium. I had them speak at Lewis & Clark College. We also went out and did a peaceful demonstration while he was actually speaking. Over two hundred people stood there and sang, and had presence. And of course, the police showed up in all of their riot gear and deadly clubs against us.

Appendix C:
BERHANU V. METZGER

Tom Metzger was a national figure in neonazi politics. He was head of the hate group White Aryan Resistance, an adherent of the racist Christian Identity ideology, and a high-ranking leader of the California chapter of the Ku Klux Klan. After the three skinheads pled guilty without trial for the death of Mulugeta Seraw, the Southern Poverty Law Center (SPLC), represented by lawyer Morris Dees, sued Tom Metzger for his support and influence over the killers in a civil suit

ens
ger
lash

unty
of force,
s, two
urthouse

macist Tom
tland on Mon-
his opponents
movement.
d the Multno-
l surveillance
d, part of an
to ensure the

d inside the
prospective
retired attor-
aid that they
2, head of the
They were

was spent in
preparations
Multnomah
L. Haggerty
2k.

three Skin-
ir the court-
cealed weap-
ling assault

nd two Port-
'er and Ken
1e family of

Police frisk a line of Sharps seeking entrance to the Multnomah County Courthouse,on Monday before the trial of white
supremacist Tom Metzger. Below, Metzger questions a
potential juror during the first day of his trial.

The Oregonian/TOM TREICK

■ SKINHEADS BRISTLE: While the Metzger
trial began inside the courtroom, rival
groups of Skinheads glared and chanted at
each other outside.   Page A12

■ LEGAL BRIEF: The Portland chapter of
the National Lawyers' Guild has filed a
legal brief in the Metzger case that centr

zations attempting to organize and recruit
Skinheads nationwide.

Metzger has acknowledged knowing the
individuals the suit refers to as his agents
but says he didn't incite them. He also has
claimed in pretrial papers that Seraw and
two of his Ethiopian friends. who were

Mainstream news coverage of antiracist skinheads consistently highlighted their potential for violence. *The Oregonian*, October 9, 1990.

brought by Mulugeta's uncle Engedaw Berhanu.

Elinor Langer describes Engedaw Berhanu as, "An idealist, a man
of principle," and continues, "Berhanu was not interested in money,
but he did want to honor Mulugeta. The world should know his true
story. In time Engedaw contacted a California office of the NAACP and
began exploring the possibility of a civil lawsuit."[1] Both the NAACP
and an Ethiopian lawyer suggested that Berhanu contact the SPLC; he
put in a call to attorney Morris Dees. "We're already investigating that
case," Morris told him immediately. "We're interested."[2]

From the SPLC website:

> In 1988, Tom and John Metzger sent their best White Aryan
> Resistance (WAR) recruiter to organize a Portland skinhead
> gang. After being trained in WAR's methods, the gang killed
> an Ethiopian student. Tom Metzger praised the skinheads
> for doing their "civic duty." Southern Poverty Law Center at-
> torneys filed a civil suit, *Berhanu v. Metzger*, asserting the
> Metzgers and WAR were as responsible for the killing as
> were the Portland skinheads. In October 1990, a jury agreed
> and awarded $12.5 million in damages to the family of the
> victim, Mulugeta Seraw.

After he lost the trial, Metzger was infamously quoted as saying, "The movement will not be stopped in the puny town of Portland. We're too deep. We're embedded now. Don't you understand? We're in your colleges. We're in your armies. We're in your police forces. We're in your technical areas. Where do you think a lot of the skinheads disappeared to? They grew their hair out, went to college. . . . I just did my little bit along the way, like your great salmon. I got up there and laid the eggs and now, if I die, no problem."[3]

The trial spelled the ruin of WAR, which did not recover from the financial devastation of the judgment. Many local activists felt that the trial of Metzger reinforced the false belief that "the Portland nazi problem" was caused by Metzger and his outside agitator minions and that the courtroom defeat of Metzger created a false impression that the nazi problem had been solved.

Some Coalition for Human Dignity activists felt that the SPLC co-opted the Seraw trial to advance their own agenda of targeting and destroying high-profile white nationalists. The SPLC did not stick around to loan its considerable resources and influence to support the continued local fight against embedded white nationalism. They moved on to other fish. And while Metzger was economically compromised, he spouted his racist garbage until the day he died.

The principal beneficiary of the award—which in the end was far less than the mandated $12.5 million—was Mulugeta's son, Henock Seraw. Though one of the most well-known events related to the struggle against neonazis in Portland, the trial elicits conflicting feelings from many activists of that time.

JONATHAN MOZZOCHI
Coalition for Human Dignity

The Metzger trial was really hard to be around. It was not really central to any of our work, and has taken up far too much space.

When I understand American justice, I think of this quote from James Baldwin: "I do not claim that everyone in prison here is innocent, but I do claim that the law as it operates is guilty, and that the prisoners, therefore, are all unjustly imprisoned."

The point of that is that we cannot fight the right by using the justice system. The justice system is a flawed system. It's deeply racist and it's deeply classist. We cannot fight them with cops; that does not work. It will never work.

The Metzger trial was stage-managed American justice. Metzger basically fell on his own sword. He didn't even hire an attorney; he represented himself. Elinor Langer has one take on the trial, but there are quite a few others. Back then, the efforts of the Southern Poverty Law Center to essentially sue the Klan or to sue the far right out of existence were the least important part of the kind of work that they did. The Southern Poverty Law Center had a great deal of programs that were not narrowly focused on fighting the far right, and still do, like their work fighting the death penalty and helping unions organize in the South.

When the Metzger trial came about, there was a great deal of media around it. But fundamental to it is part of Elinor Langer's critique, which was that the trial was theater and it really stretched the judicial principles and whatnot. I think that's correct, but we didn't really care. For the first time in a while, at least, the court system was bending towards fighting racists. I could care less that he had resources taken away, and I'm glad that they went from him to the family of Mulugeta Seraw. The Metzger trial was not a big part of what we were doing and what we organized around. And to defend the Metzger trial as a principled opposition to the far right is problematic—I don't agree with that.

MICHAEL CLARK
SHARP

The Metzger trial was insane. I will say, to the best of my knowledge, every antiracist crew in Portland participated in that. Everybody wore masks. My personal belief is that in that world, there is a real threat, and that if people figure out who you are, there's a very real chance that you could end up dead. That's the price of political activism at that level.

There's a reason that people wear masks, and it isn't because they're thugs. It isn't because they don't want you to know their belief system. It is purely a safety-type deal. People say, "If you need to wear a mask, you shouldn't do it." That doesn't make sense, because if nobody's doing it, we're totally screwed. I mean everyone cares, but maybe your political donations and your vote aren't enough. So I just wanted to put that plug in there.

We all wore masks. There were lots of fights. There were people here from both sides. WAR—White Aryan Resistance—had a lot of nazis out of California that were up here. There were riots down on Broadway, down by the courthouse. I always enjoyed smashing racists and setting people in their place. It was probably a moment where I really became proud that we were doing something that really was facilitating change, and for Metzger to be held accountable for the hate speech.

And here's an irony, right? Like, everybody's on Facebook debating—is this hate speech? Metzger had to pay $10 million for saying the stuff that some other people are saying regularly, all over the news and Facebook and Twitter on a regular basis. Inciting violence.

Appendix D:
THE PRODUCERS

The producers of the podcast *It Did Happen Here* were interviewed about this process by Enrique Rivera of the Multnomah County Library on March 11, 2021.

Enrique Rivera: How did y'all meet? How did this project get started? Why were you interested in working on this podcast? And what were your roles?

Mic Crenshaw: I was involved in being a founder of Anti Racist Action through a street organization called the Minneapolis Baldies, who were an antiracist skinhead crew in Minneapolis in the '80s and '90s. We assisted in not only fighting neonazis in the Midwest, but we actually had some ties with some of the organizing and resistance that was going on here. Since then, I've done a lot of different things. But in recent years, I was looking at interviewing some of the people that I fought nazis with, primarily Black skinheads, for a project called Black Skinhead. I've been living in Portland since I moved here from Minneapolis. Eventually, I worked at KBOO, where I met Erin. We became friends. Erin knew what I was up to, with the Black skinhead stories, and she helped facilitate getting some material resources. That was the beginning of us working together. Celina I also met through work at KBOO, and the rest is history from my perspective.

Erin Yanke: So Mic is working on the larger story of Black skinheads. I had always wanted to tell the story of the murder of Mulugeta Seraw and the cross-cultural organizing that happened around his murder. The Proud Boys and the Patriot Prayer and all of those protests were happening, and there was street activism fighting the alt-right, the new nazis. But there wasn't cross-cultural organizing to support them. Portland as a community was basically letting the kids take it on by themselves. This was a moment where it would be really healthy for us to actually know our history, the lessons, things that we could do that were similar and also things that we can learn from, the mistakes or missteps.

Celina Flores: I had been a volunteer at KBOO. And had for a long time wanted to do some sort of podcast or interviewing or something like that. Erin put out a call for people to do interviews. I was like, "Oh, I want to apply for that." So I did, and I got it. Then it kind of grew from there.

Erin: I was working a full-time job, so I asked Celina if she could step into the project as a producer, along with Mic and me.

How did you find the interview subjects for this podcast?

Mic: I interviewed probably about six or seven people I knew from Chicago and Minneapolis, people that I actually grew up with and organized and fought nazis with.

Erin: Celina focused on the CHD. I focused more on the local ARA and initial SHARP folks. I knew some people from the scene, who knew my work and trusted me. If I didn't know them, I would say, "I'm doing this podcast project with Mic Crenshaw," and that was basically enough for people to trust us. After the interview, they would be like, "Oh, I had a really good experience. I will tell my friends they can trust you." So it was a very word-of-mouth, organic way to get the interviews. People were mostly into it. It wasn't as hard to track them down as it was the CHD folks.

Mic: For the people who were more involved in different antiracist skinhead crews and that aspect of Anti Racist Action, a lot of those people got inspired by hearing the early episodes and actually started to reach out.

Celina: And for my part, finding Abby Layton, I just searched her on Facebook, and she responded, and then we started communicating via email. That's when she gave me a lot of people's email addresses.

All right, thank you. So this next question seems kind of personal, it's about your personal experience with the fight against white nationalism in this time period. Would you want to talk about that?

Erin: I lived in Northern California in the mid-'80s and was in the punk scene, going to shows, but I wasn't really an organizer yet. I was definitely a participant and trying to figure it out. There were some shows in the small town that I lived in, but mostly we went to Sacramento or the Bay Area to see shows. Those places had pretty bad nazi skinhead problems.

I was not ever really a fighter. I had some physical altercations and it was definitely like, this is a problem. How do we get together to fight this? My friends and I talked about it a lot and thought about it a lot. Then in 1988, I moved back to Humboldt and got more involved and more politically active with groups of people and the punk scene. That's where I found my people to stand with.

In November of 1988, Mulugeta Seraw was murdered. At a certain point, I heard about Anti Racist Action through *Maximum Rocknroll*, and then started to see them in action on my trips to the Bay Area. I was like, "This is incredible. This is amazing. This is how we can win." It just felt so empowering and freeing.

I was visiting Portland throughout those years and seeing nazi skinheads, but when I moved here in 1994, it wasn't a visible problem

264 | It Did Happen Here

anymore. At the time, it felt like a victory. I didn't think about them going underground. When I say that "we won," it was from the perspective of that time—we have the streets back, we have our public space back, we can now do other things—because we're not constantly dealing with this in-your-face harassment and violence.

Later I met Mic, and eventually found out that he was one of the founders of ARA and it was, like, amazing.

Mic: I was born in Chicago. I lived there for the early part of my childhood and wound up moving to St. Paul in about '82. Then I wound up going to high school in Minneapolis. By the time I was in high school, I was having some social issues, you know, trying to fit in, struggles around identity. I wound up hanging out in the hardcore punk scene and finding a home there.

Shortly after, a crew of us became really good friends, multiracial young men and women, and we decided that we wanted to become skinheads. We took interest in that particular subcultural expression that was part of the broader punk and hardcore movement. We were becoming skinheads because a couple of older people we looked up to were skinheads.

I personally had a very subjective interest in hanging out with people who were not using drugs and alcohol that were part of the scene because of some issues that I had already had with drugs and alcohol, and I was trying to be a sober teenager. It turned out a handful of these guys were not doing drugs and alcohol. Shortly after, we got together and started to learn about the skinhead subculture—that it started in England actually, in the late '60s. I understood that part of what made the skinhead culture manifest was mixing between Black, West Indian, immigrant youth and working-class white kids in England, and the music they enjoyed was reggae. The scene kind of changed and went deeper underground for a while. When it came back in the '70s and '80s, it was more closely aligned with punk rock.

That was when there was a split in the movement and some of the white kids got militant and became racist in their militancy. There's a lot of complex reasons for that, and that history is a really fascinating history. When I established these relationships with my new friends, we're hanging out, we're wearing the same clothes and listening to the same music, and there's a lot of camaraderie. Right around that time, neonazi skinheads started to get a lot of publicity in *Newsweek*, *Time* magazine, the sensational news talk shows, right? On daytime TV—*Donahue, Geraldo, Sally Jessy Raphael, Oprah*. Show after show there were these neonazi boneheads coming on and getting in fights on live television and talking about being white power. Often they would appear with a panel of guests that were in the Ku Klux Klan or the National Socialist Workers Party, and so forth. So me and my friends are watching that. As we're watching it on TV, we're like, "That's not the true roots of this culture. That's actually a shameful abomination."

For me, even more personally, being a Black kid growing up in United States, I'm identifying the threat of racial terror that is integral to the history of this country from the Klan, and lynching, and so forth. So almost immediately after the explosion of daytime TV that sensationalized white power skinheads, there was a local Klansman who was part of the punk scene who organized the White Knights, a neonazi skinhead gang in Minneapolis. My friends and I decided that we absolutely had to confront that gang, and we did.

Through the process of confronting them, we had to organize ourselves for survival, and it actually became a violent struggle. That was the birth of the militancy that politicized me and my friends and caused us to reach out to other communities, people, individuals, organizations, to form alliances. And that was the birth of Anti Racist Action.

Celina: I remember being a kid and seeing *Donahue* and *Sally Jessy* and all those shows where they were having all the white supremacists on, knowing it was wrong, not really understanding. I didn't come to this work until much later on. I'm about ten years younger than Mic and Erin.

So the next question, what are the similarities or the differences that you see with the neonazi movement of the '80s and the early '90s with today's protests and counterprotests, groups like Patriot Prayer and Antifa?

Mic: Being somebody that has been on the streets and to a lesser degree on the front line now, I've seen firsthand what the violence looks like. That's what people respond to when they see something on social media or on the news—it's often the violence that makes them aware that there's even an issue, that makes them aware of the presence of Antifa and the Proud Boys and some of these other groups.

When we started organizing and resisting and fighting against nazis in the '80s and '90s, it wasn't as sensational in terms of the planned brawls. Now what you'll have is thousands of Trump supporters who plan to come to Portland or other cities to piss people off, to try to offend people and try to start violence. They'll come with shields and blunt-force objects and guns and knives. You know—we've all seen it. So what we see today is the right wing, the alt-right, the ultra-right, the fascist, neonazis all banding together, coming to create violence. They have their reasons, but the outcome is that they're coming to fight in the streets.

What we have on the opposing side and the side that is resisting is people who get identified as Antifa, which is really broad. Anybody could be antifascists if you don't agree with the tenets of fascism, right? But Antifa has been painted in a very kind of narrow frame, basically young white people and black bloc—young white people wearing black head to toe who conceal their identities and go out and vandalize things. That's how it has been characterized.

The reality behind the scenes is that the history that led to what we see today goes back decades and decades. In my time, the way that we participated in our resistance was to find out where the racists were and go to them and execute direct action—fight them where they stood. Eventually, we had to organize outside of our immediate social groups for safety, and because we took the political nature of the work we were doing seriously, we understood we needed to build a mass movement against fascism. So it started in the Midwest.

Minneapolis connected with Chicago; Milwaukee; Indianapolis; Madison, Wisconsin; Lawrence, Kansas. I might be forgetting one or two, but those are the initial cities. They came to what we called a Syndicate meeting in about '86 or '87. That eventually spread around the United States, and there were different ARA meetings held in different regions. Portland, Oregon, was one of the places where the neonazi problem was so bad that people did not feel safe. They didn't feel safe in public. They didn't feel safe in the hardcore punk scene, going to shows. There was a lot of violence. That is what led to white supremacist organizers targeting this city as a place to organize and recruit for their movement, which is what led to Mulugeta Seraw getting murdered.

Erin: I do think that progressive Portlanders aren't really into the idea that Antifa is the broader antifascist "all of us." They are hand-wringing about the violence or window breaking or something—but these were and are the people who put their bodies on the line for this city, for all of us, to make a physical stance against the new right, who are just here to bait us into violence for their right-wing propaganda. The main thing for me is that we—those of us with white privilege, those of us with resources, those of us who are alive—need to see ourselves as antifascists, need to see ourselves as Antifa, instead of letting other people define what Antifa is. We all need to proudly be Antifa.

Mic: You know, we talk about things like intersectionality. We have to understand that even though the terms that we use might have recently made it into our consciousness or awareness, these issues have been going on. I'm hoping a lot of us have seen *Judas and the Black Messiah*, the movie that tells the story of Fred Hampton. It's a precursor. The work we do as antifascists are part of a continuum. You can take a lot of the language that you hear us using in the podcast, and at this event, and you're going to hear Fred Hampton, and you're going to hear the Black Panther Party for Self-Defense using the same language. It's been an ongoing struggle.

In the interviews for this project, people like China—and China specifically as an individual, being a Black woman in a predominantly white subcultural scene in one of the most racist cities in the United States with a racial terror problem—was holding her ground as a young person. Standing up for her right to exist against people whose ideological framework is based on her extermination. So it is what it is. That's a powerful person. I'm glad I know her. I'm glad she contributed. So to hear from her and her words, what she survived, is powerful.

We talked about the methods that were used in that era, and one of the presenters said that nowadays you have to take a different approach. What would you say that approach would be in today's world?

Mic: There's a notorious and famous phrase—the fourteen words, it's a favorite amongst white supremacists worldwide: "We must secure the existence of our people and a future for white children." Even though they're talking about a very patriarchal, racist, genocidal concept, they're also centering heteronormativity as a standard for sustaining the white race, which is really at the basis of white supremacy. When you talk to an educated militant white supremacist, it's about numbers, it's about population, and it's about white people not wanting to be disenfranchised by their minority status, and by being disproportionately violent, to maintain their place of power. You see this reinforced on all levels of society and all institutions. That's what we're facing.

So it's twofold. We do have to think about education. We do have to think about people who have been miseducated to identify with white entitlement as something that places them higher on the spectrum of a biology and human hierarchy. We have to challenge all the ideas that are part of violent white supremacist world domination, which is so ingrained in the history of colonial imperial capitalism's extractive patriarchal processes that have really defined the modern world that we live in. We have to be able to challenge that through consciousness and awareness raising, and critical thinking, and critical analysis.

At the same time, there is going to come a time where people have to put their bodies on the line, and a good amount of those people that are willing to do that need to be other white folks that are willing to actively engage against the consequence that centuries of this colonial imperial, patriarchal capitalist, extractive genocidal project has been ravaging the earth through. So I'm not going to say that we can only think about hearts and minds. When they're coming to commit acts of racial terror, they need to understand in their bodies and in their minds that it's not safe for them to operate. Sometimes it takes force to make that clear.

Erin: People talk a lot about a diversity of tactics, and I think that this is a crucial time for it. There needs to be all kinds of people doing this work, and white people need to be doing the work on ourselves to recognize the white supremacist world that we live in and all of the white entitlement that we have. Some people are going to be way better at winning hearts and minds, and some people are going to be great with education, and some people are going to be really patient, and some people are gonna want to punch the fuck out of boneheads. And we need all, we need every single person. You will find your place if you start looking, and there are a lot of us here to help you find your place, because we have to win. It took us a long time to get here, and there are a lot of people who really just want to stay comfortably white in their comfortably white worlds. Fuck them. Diversity of tactics for real.

Were there any parts of producing the podcast that you wish to share today?

Mic: The whole is greater than the sum of its parts, you know what I'm talking about? We're able to do something together that none of us could have done alone. It's a real testament to the power of a community, and lived history being recognized and respected, and a desire in the community to want to understand what the stories that are parts of people's lived experience can teach us. It's such a powerful resource in a world where we're so encouraged to seek external resources, you know, to see commodities and to buy things to make us more whole. The fact that we have a living history that's not part of the dominant narrative, I feel like it's an opportunity for us to pivot and to gain ground and to continue in the process of redirecting things towards a more just world.

Thank you. I just got one more question for y'all before we open it up to questions from the audience. What would you like listeners to take away from the podcast?

Mic: I'm hoping that people find ways to get involved that they feel is really where they need to be. I don't want people to be encouraged to do things that feel out of their . . . it's tough, you know, because there's not a lot of language. I don't want to use the term "comfort zone," because we're not trying to maintain a comfort zone. I want people to feel empowered and encouraged and inspired to challenge what's happening in a way that's right for them.

Erin: There's a lot of people who weren't here in Portland at the time. I think it's really important to know the stories about where you live. Now because of the thirtieth anniversary commemoration all around the neighborhood where Mulugeta was murdered, there's actually memorials on top of the street signs. So there's a signal to people. Now they can get curious and look Mulugeta up, which I think is awesome.

Celina: For me, to piggyback off what Mic and Erin have said, the idea of community and organizing, in a broad sense. In the podcast, we hear about different groups that came and worked together. I think that that is so important, and is applicable to today.

Mic: While we were doing that work, we got wind—not only through commercial media, but through underground networks and communication like *Maximum Rocknroll*—okay, they had scene reports where they would talk about different punk scenes in different cities. We got word that other cities were also facing nazi problems. So we reached out to the closest cities in our region. Me being from Chicago, originally I was going back and forth between Minneapolis and Chicago, so I established relationships very intentionally with Black skinheads and antiracist skinheads and a crew called Skinheads of Chicago. That first meeting we had in '86, '87—it's so hard for me to pinpoint the year—but we had over a hundred antiracist skinhead crews primarily from the Midwest, and that was the impetus. That was the catalyst. From there it went on, and people would travel and start chapters, or people would find out through word of mouth or through some print literature and they would start chapters in their own city.

We got another question: What has this work taught you about yourself? Any insights you've encountered as you engage in these conversations?

Erin: This is the largest project that I've ever been involved in. The tentacles reached out to more and more places. I've learned a lot just about organization and how you actually pull something like this off.

Most of the podcasts you hear, at the end of it, they're like—thanks to our eight editors, and our four producers, and our seventeen reporters, blah, blah, blah. There were *six* of us doing this work. And with regards to the contents, it's definitely made me much more vocal that there is a place for everybody in this fight and that we have to be really engaged in it.

Celina: For me, it taught me that I love this work. I hadn't ever done anything like this before that was so collaborative and also so engaging with other people. Well, I guess that's not entirely true, because I take photos with people, but in a different way. The synergy of all the elements coming together to create something, as Mic said, greater than the sum of its parts. Some of the insights that I've gained are about finding my place in this struggle or battle. I've questioned that a lot. I feel like I'm a little closer to having that insight into myself.

Mic: Living this life has forced me to acknowledge that I have a lot of PTSD. There's aspects of that that I wish I didn't have to face. It's not like something that sits in the neatly arranged package that you pull out when you choose to, it's something that comes up when it decides to come up. That's the shadow side, I think, internally. The light side of that education is that I became situationally aware. That leads into the concern about, you know, how safe do you feel? Being involved in what I was involved in taught me how to feel safe wherever I go, even in danger. It's almost as if I feel when I'm forced to stand my ground, I feel more at home in that situation than people who haven't been through some of these things. The challenge with all of that is that I exist in a Black body. Black bodies have always been vulnerable to racial terror, and hypercriminalization, and stereotypes and tropes that actually get us killed. And so me standing my ground is different. It's easier for me to lose my life standing my ground than it is for some other people.

How has learning about this history impacted how safe you feel in Portland?

Mic: Safety is such a moving target. I've lived next to a racist neighbor who terrorized my family and threatened to blow my head off. There are people in this audience tonight who came and did house defense for me—thank you. Seriously, people who sat in their cars and drank coffee. Because this man had been shooting his gun inside of his house and threatening to blow my head off. At the time, I had my daughter, four years old, and my ninety-two-year-old grandma living in my home. I didn't want to call the police, right? For a lot of reasons. But I understood that something had to be done.

Some neighbors overheard this man threaten to blow my head off, and they called the police. So one night, I went out and talked to the police as they were in front of the house, taking notes. And I said, "Hey, this man has threatened to shoot me. He fired his gun at my home. My family heard the shot. The neighbors heard the shot." They said, "Yeah, we know. We heard all about it."

So turns out this man has a history of mental health issues and is racist. All I wanted to know was, what am I within my rights to do to protect myself? At the time, I had a felony status that would prevent me from legally owning a firearm. So I didn't want to tell the police that, but I wanted to know whether he was legally within his rights to shoot a firearm, after threatening to end my life. The police told me, they said, "Well, you cannot do anything unless he comes onto your property." I said, "Well, if he comes onto my property, it's too late." So safety is a matter of perspective.

But because of the life I've lived, I've never felt safe, so to speak. What I do feel, I feel like I'm aware of the level of danger that people like me face. I'm in community with people who've also had to confront that level of danger as just part of existing in this society. So safety will be a measure of situational awareness and preparedness at all times.

How can folks show solidarity?

Mic: I understand that some of us don't feel comfortable going down to be in the midst of confrontation, for so many reasons, right? There's damage from tear gas and nonlethal munitions. There's vigilantes who drive cars into protesters—this, that, the other—but what I will say is, like, even if you don't want to be in the line of fire, those places are good places to meet people who have been driven to get out of their house and do something. You can bet the majority of people who've been driven into the street in an effort to do something are going to be thinking critically. They might be open—if you're willing—to spend some time being in relationship, examining those questions: "What can we do together?"

The best way to go about this work is to see it as a marathon, building community. One of the things that made the work effective was because we were kids who loved each other; we were all in love with each other. That was part of the youth, the experience of youth. We weren't our jobs, and our families and our obligations hadn't defined our lives yet. So love was at the core of it. That said, I encourage people to interrupt, but think about it before you do it. Don't rush headlong into danger. But if you do see something happening right in front of you, and there are others around, before you get in the middle of it, check out who else has a problem with what's happening. And see if it's a safer way to interrupt if you build with those people.

Erin: The Institute for Education and Research on Human Rights released Trapper, the antibigotry app, as a way to report hate crimes. You can find antibigotry groups, signs, and symbols of bigotry, so you can learn about the work and help document stuff, stay anonymous as you're learning how to do this work.

Celina: Trapper allows you to report racist things that you see around. They [the Institute for Education and Research on Human Rights] use that to document and find out where these movements are happening. So that's the research piece that you can help with.

Mic: Study history. None of this stuff is new. Having perspective that can inform critical thinking and analysis is helpful. Train your body, train your mind, and train with others. Train with firearms, martial arts, cardio, whatever, but be ready. And then get together with people that you love and figure out how to do things together. Study together. You know, even if it's virtual, agree to what you're reading and get together and discuss it and ask questions. Super simple.

CREDITS AND THANKS

Interviews conducted by: Celina Flores, Erin Yanke, Mic Crenshaw, Annette Newell, Barbara Bernstein, Claire Rischiotto, Ender Black, and Yugen Rashaad

Deep gratitude to everyone who agreed to be interviewed: Abby Layton, Becky, Cecil Prescod, China, Christien Storm, David Jeffries, Devin Burghart, Eric Ward, Gillian, Iran Johnson, Jabari, Jackson, Jason, Jay Nevilles, Jonathan Mozzochi, Jon Bair, Jorin, Kate Boyd, Kelly Halliburton, Krista Olson, Leonard Zeskind, Lorraine, Malki, Martin Sprouse, Marty, Mic Crenshaw, Michael Clark, Mobonix, M. Trelor, Nissa, Pan Nesbitt, Patrick Mazza, Peter Little, Ron Herndon, Scot Nakagawa, Steven Gardiner, Steven Wasserstrom, and Tom T.

This book would have been much poorer without the work of these documentarians and photographers: Becky, Bette Lee, Celina Flores, Coyote Amrich, Dean Guernsey, Elinor Langer, Janice Morlan, John Klicker, Jonathan Mozzochi, Jon Bair, Julie Keefe, Kelly Halliburton, Pan Nesbitt, Rhonda Schaffer, the staff and freelance photographers of *The Oregonian*, *The Skanner*, *Portland Observer*, *Willamette Week*, and *Just Out*, and all of the unknown and uncredited photographers whose works found their way to us.

Special thanks to those who generously gave us time, assistance, and background research: Abby Layton, Anna Stitt, Becky, Brian Layng, Cait Olds, Chanel, China, Chris Dodge, Colin Casserd, David Jeffries, Eliza Canty-Jones, Engedaw Berhanu, Enrique Rivera, Eric Ward, Gregory Nipper, Honna Veerkamp, Jenna Yokoyama, Jodi Darby, Joey Paxman, Jonathan Mozzochi, Jon Bair, Josh MacPhee, Kaylene Beaujolais, Kate Orazem, KBOO Community Radio, Lara Messersmith-Glavin, Lisa Loving, Lyndsey Runyan, Marat Cackley-Hughes, Marti Clemmons, Matt Stefanik, *Maximum Rocknroll*, M. Trelor, Multnomah County Library, Oregon Historical Society, *The Oregonian*, Pan Nesbitt, Patricia McGuire, Patrick Mazza, Pete Deegan, Portland Urban League, Portland State University Special Collections & University Archives, PM Press, Rachel Pfeffer, Robert Fisher, Rural Organizing Project, Ryan Fernandez, Scot Nakagawa, Scott Daniels, Seeding Justice, Sole, Taz Coffey, Tom T., Trillium Shannon, University of Oregon Special Collections and University Archives, Walidah Imarisha, Western States Center, Wade Ostrowski, the Wing Luke Museum, and *Working Class History*

Thank you: 1312 Press, Aaron Elliott, Agnostic Front and Roger Miret, AK Thompson, Alicia Dominguez, Alisa Dix, Amanda Kelly, Ana Helena DeCastro, Ariel Gore, August Alston, Ayun Halliday, Becky Meiers, Ben Popp, Billie Delaney, Blair Allen, Brian Bagdonas, Bob B and the Newsroom, Bruce Poinsette, Cait Olds, Callie Danger, Carson Ellis, Catie Bursch, Catherine Novak, Chloe Eudaly, Chris Dodge, Chumbawamba, Celeste Beck-Goodell, Cindy Milstein, Cissie Scurlock, Claude Marks, Colin Sanders, Cookie Hagendorf, Crackerbash, Damaris Webb, Daniel Lawrence, Devon Riley, Doug Rogers, Ed Edmo, Eden Reinstein, Elaine St. Martin, Elinor Langer, Elma Burnham,

Eliza Canty-Jones, Eric Isaacson, Eric Lipsky, Erica Dawn, Fred Landeen, George Wilson, Grand Style Orchestra, Greg Harvester, Greg Kotis, haya bashir, Igor Vamos, *It's Going Down* podcast, Jackie Davis, Jacob Singleton, Jacqueline Peigare and Family, Jamie Vandenberg, Jason Traeger, Jason Vasquez, Jay Martin, Jen Maynard, Jen Shumway, Jerry A., Jesse Singleton, Jessica Schleif, Jim DeStaebler, John Frentress, Judith Arcana, Kate McCourt, Katie Burkart, Katie Swrenc, Kristian Williams, Laura LoForti, Last of a Dying Breed, Lara Phillips, Lauren Jacobs, Le Guin family, Lydia Crumbley, Mack McFarland, Madball, Mark Bray, Marissa Seiler, Martin Sorrondeguy, Matt Henderson, Matthew Singer, Melanie Brown, Michael Reis, Mike Antipathy, Mike Lastra, Mobonix, Molly Gray, Multnomah County Library, Mulvaney Family, Naomi Kohn, Natasha Lennard, Nili Yosha, Nineteenth Street, The Observers, Olivier Matthon, Outside the Frame, Pam Kunes, Paul Curran and Family, Peter DeStaebler, Poison Idea, Randy Ransone and Family, Ramsey Kanaan, Rebecca Gilbert, Rema Young, Resist, Rose Solomon, Ruby Banaitis, Sara Sandberg, Sarah Schulman, Scott Moore, Shane Burley, Sid Cooper, Sita Walker, Stephen Duncombe, Tim Martin, Toody Cole, Vanessa Renwick, and Vanport Mosaic

Funding support from:
Adam Nee
Institute for Anarchist Studies
Jody Anderson
Marla Davis Fund
Multnomah County Cultural Coalition
Oregon Cultural Trust
Regional Arts and Culture Council

 Regional Arts & Culture Council

NOTES

1 Gus Van Sant, dir., *Ken Death Gets Out of Jail*, 1987, 2 mins.

2 Oprah has long acknowledged that she erred by giving skinheads the space to speak; following this episode, racist skinheads were briefly media sensations on several daytime talk shows—one of them even broke host Geraldo Rivera's nose. For antiracist skinheads and activists, the appearances marked a dangerous rise in status for the young men espousing hate.

3 For a deeper look at the murder and the people involved in it, Elinor Langer's book *A Hundred Little Hitlers: The Death of a Black Man, the Trial of a White Racist, and the Rise of the Neo-Nazi Movement in America* (New York: Picador, 2004) covers the events on the day of the murder, offers portraits of the killers, provides background on Mr. Seraw and his community, and examines the ensuing trial of *Berhanu v. Metzger*.

4 The Posse Comitatus was a group of loosely organized anti-Semitic, anti-Catholic racists in the rural West. Started by a retired Portland businessman and known fascist anti-Semite, they claimed to be present in sixteen of Oregon's thirty-six counties. They were active as the Posse from 1970 to around 1985.

5 Originally launched in 1963 and hosted in Addis Ababa, Africa Liberation Day (now called Africa Day) continues to be celebrated around the world every May.

6 The Youth International Party, or Yippies, were a new left countercultural political group founded in 1967. Stew Albert was a coconspirator of the Chicago 7 and maintained ties with the Weather Underground and the Black Panther Party through the 1970s.

7 Susan Wheeler's second husband was a founding member of the Alabama Black Liberation Front; the ABLF modeled themselves after the Black Panther Party for Self Defense. On September 15, 1970, an informant told the sheriff that the ABLF planned an ambush to prevent a home eviction; the sheriff and seventeen other cops, armed with tear gas, guns, rifles, shotguns, and regular side arms, kicked the door in to find ABLF core members holding shotguns. Miraculously, no one was murdered. All members were arrested; the Alabama Black Liberation Fund met its end, like so many groups, in legal defense fees and prison support. Williams served eight months in jail, during which time he met Susan Wheeler.

8 Christian Identity is a religious sect that in the 1980s commanded wide influence within the white supremacist movement in the United States. It emerged in its modern form in the 1960s. Beliefs center on a variation of British-Israelism, which teaches that people of European ancestry are the chosen people of God.

9 The John Brown Anti-Klan Committee, 1977–1992, emerged from a group of new-left radicals to organize white people to fight white nationalism. Connecting with the radical Black nationalist and anticolonial struggles of the time, the John Brown members created a network of antiracist coalitions around the US. They were deeply

abolitionist—opposed to police, prisons, and US colonial history. The Sojourner Truth Organization, 1969–1985, was a revolutionary group based largely in Chicago concerned with supporting workplace organizing, anti-imperialism, liberation struggles, and fighting white nationalism.

10   Four skinheads firebombed the basement apartment of a house with Molotov cocktails in nearby Salem, Oregon, while eight people slept inside. Six escaped; twenty-nine-year-old Black lesbian Hattie Mae Cohens and forty-five-year-old white gay man Brian Mock perished in the resulting fire. The skinheads were thought to be retaliating for an incident earlier in the day, when four of Ms. Cohen's friends, all of whom were Black, kicked in the door to an apartment in response to hearing a racial slur shouted throughout the building.

11   Founded in England in 1976, Rock Against Racism organized multiracial rock, reggae, soul, jazz, and punk shows to promote the fight against the racist National Front. Their largest event involved a march and a show in London with over a hundred thousand attendees in 1978, with sets by the Clash, Steel Pulse, X-Ray Spex, and others. To learn more, see Rubika Shah's 2019 documentary film *White Riot*.

12   Take Back the Night is a solidarity concept that arose in the 1960s. Women in cities in Belgium and England held nighttime events protesting attacks against women on the street at night. Protests and marches where women hold candles and walk through the streets at night have used that title since then. In successive decades, Take Back the Night marches have spread around the world, especially across college campuses; there is now an official foundation by that name whose mission is to end sexual assault, domestic violence, dating violence, sexual abuse, and all forms of sexual violence.

13   Jim Redden, "Young Nazis: Portland's New Breed of Racists," *Willamette Week*, May 12, 1988, 1.

14   Founded in 1914 to support conscientious resistance to war and military conscription, the Fellowship of Reconciliation has a membership from diverse religious backgrounds who practice conflict resolution through nonviolence. They work in broad coalition and are globally respected.

15   On Sunday, October 7, 1990, the eve of the Metzger trial, between one to two thousand people participated in a march and rally organized by the October 7th Committee. Several CHD activists sat on the broad-coalition committee.

16   The Oregon Mandatory Sentences for Listed Felonies Act, also known as Measure 11, was approved in November 1994. The "tough on crime" act established mandatory minimum sentencing for listed felonies; barred early release, leave, or reduced sentences; and applied to individuals starting at fifteen years old. Jon Bair is correct about the ten-year minimum sentence.

17   In 1998, Victoria Keenan, lost on Idaho back roads, turned around in the driveway at the Aryan Nations compound in Hayden. Her car backfired; she and her son were then chased and shot at by a compound security guard. With the help of Morris Dees and the SPLC—who also successfully sued Tom Metzger—Keenan sued Aryan Nations leader Richard Butler, who filed for bankruptcy a month later. The compound itself was then handed over to Keenan and the Southern Poverty Law Center as part of the settlement. They burned it to the ground.

18   The Proud Boys hate group organized an "End Domestic Terrorism" rally in Portland, Oregon, on August 17, 2019, to encourage the public to brand Antifa as domestic terrorists. The three hundred or so self-described "western chauvinists" were greatly outnumbered by the estimated one thousand Portlanders who turned up to shout them down.

APPENDIX A

1   Gillian explained, "We had a lot of ideas to develop under the name the Homophobic Violence Documentation Project." The Homophobic Violence Reporting Line ended up being the only one the group developed, and thus the names became interchangeable.

2   *Just Out* was a free LGBTQ publication and directory, founded by Jay Brown and Renee LaChance, published in Portland from 1983 to 2013.

3   Holly Danks, "Hot Line Tracks Anti-Homosexual Incidents," *The Oregonian*, March 20, 1992.

APPENDIX B

1   *Denial* is a 2016 film directed by Mick Jackson that is based on the memoir *History on Trial: My Day in Court with a Holocaust Denier*, by Deborah Lipstadt (New York: HarperCollins, 2005).

2   Phil Stanford was a metro columnist for the newspaper *The Oregonian*, which is published in Portland with statewide distribution. He wrote several columns that defended Irving's right to speak and gave legitimacy to his theories.

APPENDIX C

1   Elinor Langer, *A Hundred Little Hitlers: The Death of a Black Man, the Trial of a White Racist, and the Rise of the Neo-Nazi Movement in America* (New York: Picador, 2004), 279.

2   Langer, *A Hundred Little Hitlers*, 279.

3   Langer, *A Hundred Little Hitlers*, 350.

Coalition for Human Dignity sticker, 1991. Courtesy of Kelly Halliburton.

INDEX

Page numbers in *italic* refer to illustrations. "Passim" (literally "scattered") indicates intermittent discussion of a topic over a cluster of pages.

Christian Identity, 58, 61, 206, 258, 274n8
civil rights movement: Portland, *9*
Clark, Michel, 168, 180, *181*, 196, 230–32, 261
Coalition for Human Dignity (CHD), 49–75 passim, 108–17 passim, 122–26 passim, 131–63 passim, 204–21 passim, 236, 241–46 passim; benefit events, *163*; intelligence gathering, 134–39 passim, 143, 160, 162, 207–8; *Oregon Witness*, 67; Peter Little and, 228, 230, 238; posters, *48*, *154*; publications, *158–59*; Shop, 132, 138–39, *138*; Turn It Down Campaign, 211; We Are Not Afraid rally, 156
Cohens, Hattie Mae, 67, 275n10
Communities Against Hate, 65, 73, 148
community self-defense, 140–41
Cook, Megan, 85
Cooley, Azalea, 152
Copp, Patty, 30
Corvallis, Oregon, 25
Crenshaw, Mic, 81–85 passim, *81*, *92*, *105*, 262–71 passim
Cromwell, Vince, 96

Dead Kennedys, 177
Death, Ken, 12, 24, 30, 34
Dees, Morris, 258, 259, 276n17
Democratic Party, 64, 66
Deprived, 110, *111*, 224, *227*
Dignity Report, 54, *158*, *159*
doxing, 125–27 passim, 207, 240
drinking. *See* alcohol and drugs
Duke, David, 216

Eastern Oregon Correctional Institution, 171–72, *200*
East Side Fists, 17
East Side White Pride (ESWP), 15–16, 17, 18, 72, 177–78; Seraw murder, 29–30, 34
Ethiopian immigrants. *See* Berhanu, Engedaw; Seraw, Mulugeta

Eugene, Oregon, x, 72–73, 148; Communities Against Hate, *65*

FBI, 144, 155
Fellowship of Reconciliation, 136, 275n14
Flores, Celina, 262–71 passim
Fugazi, 72–73

Gardiner, Steve, 59–61, 134, 160, 162, 214–16
Garl, Scott, 139
gay-bashing. *See* homophobia
gentrification, 1, 11, 69, 223
Germany, 211
Goldschmidt, Neil, 66
graffiti, *80*, 96, 254; neonazi, 72, 125, 133, 135, 155

Halliburton, Kelly, 110, 227–28, *227*
Hammerquist, Don, 54–55
Hampton, Fred, 266
Hassan, Abdi, 60, *60*
hate crimes, 35, 107–8, 235; legislation, 50; Metropolitan Human Relations Commission log, *51*; Trapper, 271. *See also* Homophobic Violence Reporting Line; Seraw, Mulugeta
Heick, Bob, 152
Herndon, Ron, *38*, 39–40
Hollis, Paul, 78, 85
Holocaust, Jewish. *See* Jewish Holocaust
homophobia, 22, 122, *219*; hate crime hotline, 152, 252–55; Measure 9 (1992), 67, 69, *153*, 252; posters, *154*
Homophobic Violence Reporting Line, 152, 252–55
Hotel Lenox, *6*

Idaho, 49, 52, 209–10, 276n17
immigrants and immigration, 60, 214, 216, 218. *See also* Berhanu, Engedaw; Seraw, Mulugeta

About the Editors

Moe Bowstern is an alum of Chicago's long-gone @-zone, a writer, laborer, Fisher Poet, and DIY social practice artist. Moe is the long-time editor of many publications, including the commercial fishing zine *Xtra Tuf*. She was a writer on the podcast version of *It Did Happen Here*.

Mic Crenshaw was born and raised in Chicago and Minneapolis and currently resides in Portland, Oregon. Crenshaw is an independent hip-hop artist, respected emcee, poet, educator, and activist. Crenshaw is the lead US organizer for the Afrikan Hiphop Caravan and uses cultural activism as a means to develop international solidarity related to human rights and justice through hip-hop and popular education. Crenshaw was a founding member of the Minneapolis Baldies and Anti Racist Action and a coproducer and narrator of the podcast version of *It Did Happen Here*.

Alec Dunn is a printmaker, illustrator, and a nurse. He is a member of the Justseeds Artists' Cooperative and coedits *Signal: A Journal of International Political Graphics & Culture*. He was a writer and an audio editor on the podcast version of *It Did Happen Here*.

Celina Flores is an independent and multidisciplinary photographer and audio producer. She has volunteered as a sound engineer and producer at KBOO Community Radio in Portland, Oregon. She was a coproducer and narrator of the podcast version of *It Did Happen Here*.

Julie Perini makes experimental and documentary films and teaches at Portland State University. Julie was a researcher and archivist on the podcast version of *It Did Happen Here*.

Erin Yanke is a self-taught multimedia artist, radical documentarian, and a lifer. She is operations manager at Outside the Frame and was executive producer of the podcast version of *It Did Happen Here*.

PM Press is an independent, radical publisher of books and media to educate, entertain, and inspire. Founded in 2007 by a small group of people with decades of publishing, media, and organizing experience, PM Press amplifies the voices of radical authors, artists, and activists. Our aim is to deliver bold political ideas and vital stories to all walks of life and arm the dreamers to demand the impossible. We have sold millions of copies of our books, most often one at a time, face to face. We're old enough to know what we're doing and young enough to know what's at stake. Join us to create a better world.

PM PRESS
PO Box 23912
Oakland CA 94623
510-658-3906
www.pmpress.org

PM Press in Europe
europe@pmpress.org
www.pmpress.org.uk

Working Class History is an international collective of worker-activists focused on the research and promotion of people's history through our podcast, books and social media channels.

We want to uncover stories of our collective history of fighting for better world and tell them in a straightforward and engaging way to help educate and inspire new generations of activists.

Through our social media outlets with over one million followers, we reach an audience of over 20 million per month. So if you're on social media, you can connect with us in the following ways:

- **Instagram:** @workingclasshistory
- **Facebook:** facebook.com/workingclasshistory
- **Twitter:** @wrkclasshistory
- **YouTube:** youtube.com/workingclasshistory
- **Mastodon:** mastodon.social/@workingclasshistory
- **Tumblr:** workingclasshistory.tumblr.com

We receive no funding from any political party, academic institution, corporation or government. All of our work is funded entirely by our readers and listeners on Patreon. So if you appreciate what we do, consider joining us, supporting our work and getting access to exclusive content and benefits at patreon.com/workingclasshistory.

Friends of PM Press

These are indisputably momentous times—the
financial system is melting down globally and
the Empire is stumbling. Now more than ever
there is a vital need for radical ideas.

In the years since its founding—and on a
mere shoestring—PM Press has risen to the formidable challenge
of publishing and distributing knowledge and entertainment for the
struggles ahead. With over 450 releases to date, we have published
an impressive and stimulating array of literature, art, music, politics, and culture. Using every available medium, we've succeeded in
connecting those hungry for ideas and information to those putting
them into practice.

Friends of PM allows you to directly help impact, amplify, and revi-
talize the discourse and actions of radical writers, filmmakers, and
artists. It provides us with a stable foundation from which we can
build upon our early successes and provides a much-needed subsi-
dy for the materials that can't necessarily pay their own way. You
can help make that happen—and receive every new title automati-
cally delivered to your door once a month—by joining as a *Friend of
PM Press*. And, we'll throw in a free T-shirt when you sign up.

Here are your options:

· **$30 a month** Get all books and pamphlets plus 50% discount on
all webstore purchases
· **$40 a month** Get all PM Press releases (including CDs and DVDs)
plus 50% discount on all webstore purchases
· **$100 a month** Superstar—Everything plus PM merchandise, free
downloads, and 50% discount on all webstore purchases

For those who can't afford $30 or more a month, we have **Sustain-
er Rates** at $15, $10, and $5. Sustainers get a 50% discount on all
purchases from our website.

Your Visa or Mastercard will be billed once a month, until you tell
us to stop. Or until our efforts succeed in bringing the revolution
around. Or the financial meltdown of Capital makes plastic redun-
dant. Whichever comes first.

We Go Where They Go: The Story of Anti-Racist Action

Shannon Clay, Lady, Kristin Schwartz, and Michael Staudenmaier
With a Foreword by Gord Hill

ISBN: 9781629639727
$24.95   320 Pages

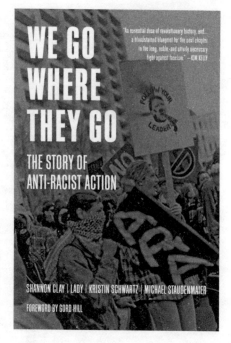

Based on extensive interviews with dozens of Anti-Racist Action (ARA) participants, *We Go Where They Go* tells ARA's story from within, giving voice to those who risked their safety in their own defense and in solidarity with others. In reproducing the posters, zines, propaganda, and photos of the movement itself, this essential work of radical history illustrates how cultural scenes can become powerful forces for change. Here at last is the story of an organic yet highly organized movement, exploring both its triumphs and failures, and offering valuable lessons for today's generation of activists and rabble-rousers. *We Go Where They Go* is a page-turning history of grassroots anti-racism.

"I was a big supporter, and it was an honor to work with the Anti-Racist Action movement. Their unapologetic and uncompromising opposition to racism and fascism in the streets, in the government, and in the mosh pit continues to be inspiring to this day."
—Tom Morello, Rage Against the Machine and Audioslave

"Antifa became a household word with Trump attempting and failing to designate it a domestic terrorist group, but Antifa's roots date back to the late 1980s when little attention was being paid to violent fascist groups that were flourishing under Reaganism, and Anti-Racist Action was singular and effective in its brilliant offensive. This book tells the story of ARA in breathtaking prose accompanied by stunning photographs and images."
—Roxanne Dunbar-Ortiz, author of *An Indigenous Peoples' History of the United States*

Working Class History: Everyday Acts of Resistance & Rebellion

Edited by Working Class History
With a Foreword by Noam Chomsky

ISBN: 9781629638232
$20.00   352 Pages

History is not made by kings, politicians, or a few rich individuals—it is made by all of us. From the temples of ancient Egypt to spacecraft orbiting Earth, workers and ordinary people everywhere have walked out, sat down, risen up, and fought back against exploitation, discrimination, colonization, and oppression.

Working Class History presents a distinct selection of people's history through hundreds of "on this day in history" anniversaries that are as diverse and international as the working class itself. Women, young people, people of color, workers, migrants, Indigenous people, LGBT+ people, disabled people, older people, the unemployed, home workers, and every other part of the working class have taken action that has shaped our world, and improvements in living and working conditions have been won only by years of violent conflict and sacrifice.

This handbook of grassroots movements, curated by the popular Working Class History project, features many hidden histories and untold stories, reinforced with inspiring images, further reading, and a foreword from legendary author and dissident Noam Chomsky.

"The WCH project has hit upon a novel way to communicate our shared history to a new generation of budding radicals and working class revolutionaries and, with this book, has laid out centuries of solidarity and rebellion into an easily digestible (and endlessly engrossing) catalogue of dissent. They make it clear that today's victories build upon yesterday's struggles and that, in order to push forward into the liberated, equitable future we want, we must remember how far we've come—and reckon with how much further there is to go."

—Kim Kelly, author of *Fight Like Hell: The Untold History of American Labor*

Surviving the Future: Abolitionist Queer Strategies

Edited by Scott Branson,
Raven Hudson, and Bry Reed
With a Foreword by Mimi Thi
Nguyen

ISBN: 9781629639710
$19.95   224 Pages

Surviving the Future is a collection of the most current ideas in radical queer movement work and revolutionary queer theory. These essays propose a militant strategy of queer survival in an ever-precarious future. Starting from a position of abolition—of prisons, police, the State, identity, and racist cisheteronormative society—this collection refuses the bribes of inclusion in a system built on our expendability. The writers in this book imagine collective visions of liberation that tell different stories, build alternate worlds, and refuse the legacies of racial capitalism, anti–Blackness, and settler colonialism. The work curated in this book spans Black queer life in the time of COVID-19 and uprising, assimilation and pinkwashing settler colonial projects, subversive and deviant forms of representation, building anarchist trans/queer infrastructures, and more. Contributors include Che Gossett, Yasmin Nair, Mattilda Bernstein Sycamore, Adrian Shanker, Kitty Stryker, Toshio Meronek, and more.

"*Surviving the Future* is a testament that otherwise worlds are not only possible, our people are making them right now—and they are queering how we get there through organizing and intellectual work. Now is the perfect time to interrogate how we are with each other and the land we inhabit. This collection gives us ample room to do just that in a moment of mass uprisings led by everyday people demanding safety without policing, prisons, and other forms of punishment."
—Charlene A. Carruthers, author of *Unapologetic: A Black, Queer, and Feminist Mandate for Radical Movements*

Abolish the Police
Abolish Prisons
Abolish the State
Abolish Identity
Abolish the Family
Abolish Racial Capitalism
Abolish Settler Colonialism
Abolish Society

Surviving the Future

Abolitionist Queer Strategies

Edited by Scott Branson, Raven Hudson, and Bry Reed
Foreword by Mimi Thi Nguyen

The Fascist Groove Thing: A History of Thatcher's Britain in 21 Mixtapes

By Hugh Hodges with a Preface by Dick Lucas and a Foreword by Boff Whalley

ISBN 9781629638843
$22.95 384 Pages

THE FASCIST GROOVE THING

A HISTORY OF THATCHER'S
BRITAIN IN 21 MIXTAPES

HUGH HODGES

This is the late 1970s and '80s as explained through the urgent and still-relevant songs of the Clash, the Specials, the Au Pairs, the Style Council, the Pet Shop Boys, and nearly four hundred other bands and solo artists. Each chapter presents a mixtape (or playlist) of songs related to an alarming feature of Thatcher's Britain, followed by an analysis of the dialogue these artists created with the Thatcherite vision of British society. "Tell us the truth," Sham 69 demanded, and pop music, however improbably, did. It's a furious and sardonic account of dark times when pop music raised a dissenting fist against Thatcher's fascist groove thing and made a glorious, boredom-smashing noise. Bookended with contributions by Dick Lucas and Boff Whalley as well as an annotated discography, *The Fascist Groove Thing* presents an original and polemical account of the era.

"It's not often that reading history books works best with a soundtrack playing simultaneously, but Hugh Hodges has succeeded in evoking both the noises and the feel of a tumultuous 1980s. Proving that pop music is the historian's friend, he has here recovered those who help us best make sense of a scary, precarious, and exciting world."
—Matthew Worley, author of *No Future: Punk, Politics and British Youth Culture, 1976–1984*

"Those who think the 1980s were camp and fun clearly didn't live them. The Thatcher/Reagan era was grim as fuck. This tells the real story from the underground."
—Ian Brennan, author of *Muse-Sick* and *Silenced by Sound*